Bernard Taylor divides his time between writing and acting. He has written a number of novels of suspense and the supernatural (including *The Godsend*, *Sweetheart*, *Sweetheart*, and *Madeleine*) as well as plays and short stories. His factual book *Cruelly Murdered* told the story of the Constance Kent murder case of 1860, one of the most famous crimes in British criminological history, and was described by Colin Wilson as 'a classic of that kind of careful and imaginative reconstruction that can transport the reader, like a time machine, back into the past'.

He collaborated on *Perfect Murder* with the late Stephen Knight, bestselling author of *Jack the Ripper: The Final Solution*, *The Brotherhood: The Secret World of the Freemasons*, *The Killing of Justice Godfrey* and the novel *Requiem at Rogano*. Stephen Knight died of cancer in July 1985.

Other works by Bernard Taylor

Non-fiction

*Cruelly Murdered: Constance Kent and the Killing at
Road Hill House*

Novels

The Godsend
Sweetheart, Sweetheart
The Reaping
The Moorstone Sickness
The Kindness of Strangers
Madeleine

Other works by Stephen Knight

Non-fiction

Jack the Ripper: The Final Solution
The Brotherhood: The Secret World of the Freemasons
The Killing of Justice Godfrey

Novel

Requiem at Rogano

BERNARD TAYLOR
and STEPHEN KNIGHT

Perfect Murder

A Century of Unsolved Homicides

GRAFTON BOOKS

A Division of the Collins Publishing Group

LONDON GLASGOW
TORONTO SYDNEY AUCKLAND

Grafton Books
A Division of the Collins Publishing Group
8 Grafton Street, London W1X 3LA

Published by Grafton Books 1988

First published in Great Britain by
Grafton Books 1987

ISBN 0-586-05587-8

Printed and bound in Great Britain by
Collins, Glasgow

Set in Times

Contents

For
Nanouska

Foreword

by Colin Wilson

Dozens of volumes about true murder cases appear every year, and most of them are marked by a certain brisk, factual approach, which derives from True Detective magazines. It was not always so. Half a century ago, writers like William Roughead, F. Tennyson Jesse, Edmund Pearson, loved to dwell on a murder case as if it was an exercise in re-creating the past. To understand the essence of a case – particularly an unsolved case – it is not enough simply to know the gruesome details of the crime and of the police investigation. That produces merely the impression of the drama, and real life is always more subtle and complex than mere drama. We also need to know the details of the lives of those involved, of the inquest, the police interrogations, and – if the case is solved – of the trial itself. This is what Stephen Knight did in his study of the murder of Sir Edmund Berry Godfrey, and what Bernard Taylor did in *Cruelly Murdered*, a classic of that kind of careful and imaginative reconstruction that can transport the reader, like a time machine, back into the past.

This, as might be expected, is also true of the present book. Each one of these seven cases has its own peculiar atmosphere. I thought I was familiar with most of them, but soon discovered how little I actually knew. In the case of the murder of the child Georgina Moore, for example, I had always accepted H. L. Adam's conclusion in his article in *The Fifty Most Amazing Crimes of the Last Hundred Years*, which I read when I was about ten years old. Taylor's careful presentation of the case has completely changed my opinion. In the case of the 'witch-craft murder' of Charles Walton, I had always taken it for granted that the death was connected with Walton's disagreeable habit of blackmailing local people into a yearly renewal of 'good luck charms', with the implication that if they failed to do so, he would guarantee a year's bad luck. Stephen Knight has come up with what I am convinced is the true solution, and it has nothing to do with witchcraft – even though the chief investigator, Bob Fabian 'of the Yard', saw the mysterious black dog that is reputed to haunt the area.

I am also delighted that the true solution of the Tony Mancini case has at last been put on record. Stephen Knight's presentation of the 'ordeal' of Tony Mancini is sympathetic, no doubt because he interviewed him and liked him, while Bernard Taylor records the nastier side of Mancini's character. Stephen Knight's long interview with Mancini is an important and unique piece of crime reporting, in which we catch a glimpse of the sleazy and oddly futile world of a small-time crook between the wars.

For those who like their mystery to have an Agatha Christie flavour, Bernard Taylor's long account of the Luard case – the 'summerhouse mystery' – will be the high point of the book; here, I think, the author's method of careful investigation is most completely justified.

Whether or not readers agree with all the solutions of the mysteries presented in this book, *Perfect Murder* is nevertheless a piece of crime writing of which Roughead or Pearson would have been proud.

Introduction

It is often said that perfect murders are those of which the perpetrators remain undetected – or at least unconvicted. Some say that truly perfect murders are those in which police and public alike are completely unaware that any crime has taken place. And there must be many such cases; all over the world murder victims lie in their graves while all but the murderers believe the deaths to be due to natural causes. In yet other cases murder victims lie in unmarked graves while even the knowledge of their deaths is known only to their murderers. These, truly, must be the perfect murders, but as by their definition we shall never learn about them, then for the purposes of this book the term must apply to those cases where murder is known to have taken place.

Yet still the reader may argue that the murders written of here can hardly be termed perfect, in that in some cases the murderer's escape has been due more to luck than judgement. Nevertheless, in every case the killer has escaped justice, and such a feat must be worthy of some recognition.

But why, anyway, write of murder at all – perfect or imperfect?

The answer, of course, is that murder is a fascinating subject. Furthermore, our fascination with such a crime is a healthy one. Murder, the ultimate act, is the greatest of crimes, and that a man or woman can be driven – by greed, jealousy, revenge, or whatever – to take another's life must be of ultimate interest to us. For evidence of the latter we have only to turn to our daily newspapers. The headlines that sell the papers do not proclaim some individual's happiness but are as likely as not to scream at us of some unfortunate individual's murder – and the more brutal and bizarre the killing then the greater the news value.

And in reading of a murder, it seems to me that one's greatest fascination eventually becomes focused on the murderer and his motive. Man is always more interesting when acting at the height of some emotion, and that arising out of conflict is likely to be the most dynamic. Witness the fact that a couple at a party having a flaming row will always take one's attention from the most interesting conversation; one may not wish to get involved in the altercation, but that does not prevent one's fascination with it. Likewise, no act is more dynamic than the act of murder.

Given, then, the fascination of murder, an *unsolved* murder is in turn more fascinating than one in which there is no mystery; a puzzle unsolved is *always* of more interest than a solved one.

Hence the subject of this book.

My friend, the late Stephen Knight, and I long ago discussed the idea of collaborating on a book, and eventually decided that one on unsolved murders would be the ideal subject. Sadly, in July 1985, shortly after we had begun work on the project, Stephen Knight died. Later, after a period when the book lay fallow, my editor and I agreed that I should complete it alone.

I have consequently written the greater part of the book – giving accounts of five cases to Stephen's two, and in addition adding a little linking material to one of his chapters.

The seven murder mysteries in this book are cases that, in one way or another, stretched the minds of British detectives to the utmost – one case continuing to do so in the present day. In most of the cases the murderers, due to the passage of time, are long since dead, though in at least one case the killer is almost certainly alive and well.

The motives for the seven murders are various, including greed, revenge and passionate anger; among the victims are a child, a prostitute, and an actor.

In our researches into the various cases both Stephen Knight and I studied whatever contemporary documentation and newspaper reports were available, and wherever and whenever possible visited the scenes of the crimes and spoke with individuals concerned.

In addition, in each case we tried to shed light on the enduring mystery and to come up with some answers. As a result, it is hoped that the enigmas are less inaccessible than they once were.

For assistance in various forms given to Stephen Knight and me during our inquiries into the murders, and subsequent work on the book, I would like to thank Paul Bolitho, Detective Chief Inspector Douglas Campbell of Scotland Yard, PC Barnes of the Sevenoaks Constabulary, Kate Clarke, Tony Dale, Bernard Edwards, Karen de Groot, Chief Superintendent James Dewhurst of the Thames Valley Police, Michael Duggan, J. H. H. Gaute, Peter Giles, Frank Hart, Sue Lampey, Tony Mancini, Donald McCormick, David McGrath of the British Library, F. C. Moffatt, Robin Odell, Roy Purkess, David Simeon, Susan Staples, B. G. Thomas, and Richard Whittington-Egan. I am grateful also to Mrs Nel Cantle for permission to study the papers of her late husband, Ivor Cantle, and to Denbry Repros for their as-ever efficient and excellent work with some of the photographs.

I would also like to thank the *Bucks Free Press*, High Wycombe, and the *News of the World* for permission to quote from the articles by Anne Edwards and Peter Game on Helen Davidson. I am indebted also to the various individuals and bodies who supplied some of the illustrations in the book; acknowledgements will be found accompanying the relevant illustrations. With regard to the text the copyright rests either with myself or with the executors of the estate of the late Stephen Knight.

To any individual who gave help but has not been named here I offer my thanks now.

Bernard Taylor
December 1986

Death of a Quiet Man

The Murder of William Saunders

BY BERNARD TAYLOR

When I approached local historians in the area of Penge to ask about a particular past 'neighbourhood murder' it was usually inferred that the case I was researching was a different one from the actual subject of my inquiries. It was generally assumed that I was looking into the murder of Harriet Staunton who died in the same year, 1877.

The mistaken assumption is understandable. The Staunton murder is famous in the annals of criminology, and much has been written on it. On the other hand, the case of William Saunders, who was killed only eighteen days earlier, is very little known. It has, however, its own very special fascination.

In a secluded part of the parish of Beckenham, Kent at about eleven o'clock on the morning of Sunday, 25 March 1877, two young boys, ten-year-old George Bacon and his friend Alfred Overall, nine, were walking from Lower Sydenham to Penge by way of a footpath through the fields. As they reached a pond adjoining the Penge cricket field they saw something lying in the water and on closer inspection realized that it was the partly submerged body of a man.

While George Bacon remained to keep watch, the younger boy, Overall, ran back to his home to give the alarm. At once Overall's brother went to the local police station and informed Sergeant Philpott who, accompanied by three constables, hurried to the scene.

The body was lying in about two feet of water, and close to the bank, the head embedded in the mud so firmly that when an attempt was made to lift it the hat stuck fast in the soil. When the body had been dragged out – the clenched hands full of mud – it was judged to be that of a working man. He had, it was assumed, committed suicide.

The body was taken to the Park Tavern public house, in Penge Park, which also served as the local coroner's courthouse, and a Penge doctor, Dr Dean Longrigg,[1] was sent for. Arriving at the Park Tavern the doctor examined the body and formally pronounced the man dead. He noted that the man had suffered severe injuries: the nose and jaw were broken, there was a deep wound on the right temple and blood was oozing from a wound above the left eye. It was clearly evident that the man had suffered great violence shortly before his death.

After the doctor's initial examination a local man, Thomas Fitzgerald, who happened to be nearby, was called in to look at the body and, it was hoped, to identify it. After viewing the body Fitzgerald said he was sure that it was that of William Saunders, one of his workmates at the Crystal Palace Gas Company, Sydenham.

William Saunders, aged thirty-four, and employed as a labourer at the gas works, was well-known in the area. Two years earlier he had married a widow, a Mrs Sarah Inman, who was eleven years his senior. She had no children by Saunders, but had been left with six children by her late husband, three sons and three daughters, the eldest of whom, a daughter, was twenty years of age. Only a few hours before his death Saunders, his wife and some of his stepchildren had come to live at 4, Hillmore Grove, Lower Sydenham, moving there from their previous home in Laurel Grove, just a couple of streets away.

Upper Sydenham in south-east London was regarded

---

[1] He was also to be involved in the Staunton murder case.

as one of the more select suburbs of the capital a hundred years ago. Close to the Crystal Palace, it attracted some little wealth, to which a number of rather fine villas still testify. Lower Syndenham, however, was, and remains, the poorer section of the area, a section in which Hillmore Grove was one of its poorer streets.

Thomas Fitzgerald, having left the Park Tavern, now made his way to Hillmore Grove, and knocking at the door of number 4, found the door opened to him by Jane, William Saunders's eldest stepdaughter. Sure of what the answer would be to his question, Fitzgerald at once asked her, 'Is Mr Saunders at home?' The girl responded by turning and calling up the stairs to her mother, whereupon Mrs Saunders opened the front bedroom window and asked the visitor what he wanted. Fitzgerald asked her in turn, 'Is Bill at home?'

'No,' she replied.

'Then I'm afraid,' Fitzgerald said, 'that I have bad news to tell you.'

'What is it?' Mrs Saunders asked. 'Has he drowned himself?'

'I don't know whether he's drowned himself,' Fitzgerald said, 'or whether anybody else has done it for him.'

As he turned towards the front door Fitzgerald saw that two young men had appeared in the doorway and were standing there talking. One he recognized as nineteen-year-old Alfred Inman, Saunders's eldest stepson; the other was James Dempsey, a young man in his early twenties who had recently gone to lodge with Saunders and his family. After telling Dempsey that the dead man was lying in the Park Tavern, Fitzgerald went on his way.

Later that day the body was officially identified by Mrs Saunders as that of her husband, William.

* * *

Soon after identification of the dead man the wheels of officialdom were well in motion. Following Dr Longrigg's examination, the coroner, Carttar, was informed and he at once directed Longrigg to carry out a *post mortem*. The inquest on the death was set for Tuesday, 27 March. That done, Inspector Relf of the Metropolitan Police, assisted by two detectives, prepared to begin investigations into the happening.

As stated, on the finding of Saunders's body in the pond it had at first been assumed that he had drowned himself, and rumour to this effect had swiftly spread through the vicinity. With the discovery of the many marks of violence upon the body, however, the possibility of suicide had quickly vanished from the minds of the police officers and when they set out on their investigations it was with the conviction that they were dealing with a case of murder.

Their belief was further strengthened when, near the scene of the man's discovery, they found that part of a hedge had been broken and trampled upon – signs, they were sure, that the body had been dragged through it.

One of the first interviews took place at 4, Hillmore Grove, where they talked to the dead man's widow. There she told them that her husband had been a very quiet man, and that he had been on the best of terms with herself and his stepchildren. Her first husband's name was Inman, she said. Apart from the four of her children who were living with her, she added, there was another young man, a lodger, James Dempsey, who was engaged to be married to her eldest daughter Jane. He had been living with the family for about two months.

She went on to say that on the previous day, Saturday, they had moved from their previous home in nearby Laurel Grove, Paxton Park. After the removal was complete her husband had given her his wages of nine shillings and threepence. Afterwards, she said, he left the house to visit their neighbour, one of his fellow labourers at the gas works, returning home at about nine o'clock, at which time she had given him a shilling and told him to go out and enjoy himself while she finished putting the house in order. And that, she added, was the last time she had seen him alive.

With regard to the rest of the family's movements on that Saturday, Mrs Saunders said she would swear that not one of them, nor either the lodger, Dempsey, was out of the house after five o'clock. When James Dempsey was interviewed he corroborated Mrs Saunders's evidence as to his not leaving the house after five, as also, in turn, did the eldest son, the nineteen-year-old Alfred Inman.

Next door, the investigating officers called on John Quittenden – later described by Inspector Relf in his report as 'a very respectable man, and one thoroughly to be relied on'. On being questioned, Quittenden said that Saunders, his workmate, had come to his house that Saturday evening and that they had sat together drinking beer. He had left around nine o'clock, he added. Speaking further of the dead man, Quittenden said that Saunders was a quiet, sober man who had often complained of being very unhappy in his home life. 'He told me,' said Quittenden, 'that he had a hell of a life of it at home.'

In the course of further inquiries on the Monday Inspector Relf and Sergeant Philpott interviewed a young girl, Ann Winn, who told them that she had seen William Saunders at about 10.30 that Saturday night. He had been in the company of 'one or two other men', she said, one of whom, she was quite sure, was James Dempsey. She had, she added, seen Dempsey alone some minutes later close to the same spot.

Returning at once to 4, Hillmore Grove, the two officers questioned Dempsey again as to his movements

on the night in question. In response he now swore to
them that he had not left the house after *six* o'clock,
which Mrs Saunders substantiated. A few minutes afterwards, however, when Relf and Philpott had left the
house, Dempsey came running after them as they made
their way along the street. On catching them up he said
he had come to tell them that he had just remembered
that he *did* go out after six o'clock on the Saturday night.
'At what time?' Relf asked him, to which Dempsey
replied that it had not been after eight o'clock. Inspector
Relf then informed Dempsey that he could produce a
witness who saw him out at about 10.30 and again at
eleven o'clock. Dempsey, in reply, said it was not possible. 'You can't bring a witness to say such a thing,' he
said, 'as I wasn't out.'

By the time Tuesday evening came, the time of the
inquest, the investigating officers had lined up a number
of witnesses. It was with the appearance of the seventeen-
year-old Ann Winn, however, that they hoped to produce
evidence that would lead to a conviction. They were sure
by now who was the guilty one.

The inquest was to be held at the Park Tavern public
house, and that evening the interior was packed with a
throng of curious people, including fellow workmen of
the dead man, all eager to hear the statements of the
various witnesses.

The first witness called was Saunders's widow, Sarah.

Early in the evening of the previous Saturday, Mrs
Saunders said, her husband went next door to their
neighbour, Quittenden, with whom he was on friendly
terms. He came back indoors at about nine o'clock, at
which time she gave him a shilling and told him to go out
while she got the place in readiness after the move from

Laurel Grove, Paxton Park. He then left the house, she stated, after which time she never saw him alive again.

In answer to further questions she replied that she did not feel uneasy about his absence until about one o'clock on Sunday morning as she believed he had returned to the house of their neighbour, Quittenden. At that time, she went on, she sent her youngest son next door to make inquiries, but he had found that the Quittendens had retired to bed. When the boy had awakened them he was told by Mrs Quittenden that Saunders 'had left about half-an-hour previous'. In answer to further questions she said that her husband was a steady man, but there were times when 'he took a drop too much and became irritable'. On the night in question he had been sober when he left home. Asked whether he had ever hinted at a wish to take his own life, she said that about two and a half years earlier she had heard him say that he would destroy himself, but she had never heard him say so since. They had been married for two years, she added, and did not quarrel. Neither her eldest son nor Dempsey the lodger were in work, she stated, adding, 'My husband had them all to keep.' Even so, she said, her husband had been on the best of terms with all in the household, and there had been no row at home that night.

The coroner then questioned the widow with regard to her original statement to the police that no one had left the house after five o'clock that Saturday. The police having since found evidence to the contrary, the coroner wanted to know why she had made such a statement when it was now known that James Dempsey, the lodger, had been seen out at a later hour that night. Eventually Mrs Saunders replied that Dempsey *had* gone out for some things later in the evening, but that she had forgotten it. When she had earlier told the police that no one apart from her husband had left the house after five o'clock it had been untrue, she added. 'I'm sorry I told the police what wasn't true,' she said, 'but I was confused.'

The next witness was John Quittenden, the neighbour, who stated that Saunders had been at his home drinking beer with him until about nine or ten o'clock, at which time he had left. He remembered Mrs Saunders's son coming to the house at about one o'clock the following morning to inquire after his stepfather, he said, but his wife had *not* said that Saunders had left 'half-an-hour previous'. On the contrary, he said, he had clearly heard his wife say that Saunders had left '*at about ten o'clock*'. In reply to the coroner, he stated that he had worked with the deceased for some time, and believed him to be a very steady man and not likely to commit suicide. He had heard him say on several occasions, he went on, that he would leave his wife, as his home was 'a hell upon earth'. Asked whether he had heard any sounds of a quarrel or other disturbance that night, he said he had not, adding that he had gone to bed and slept.

James Dempsey, who was called next, deposed that he had last seen the deceased at about nine o'clock on the Saturday night. He had heard Mrs Saunders tell her husband to go out for a little time whilst she put the beds straight, they having just removed from Paxton Park. He and the deceased, he said, had earlier brought the last lot of things to their new home.

Dempsey then reiterated his last statement to the police, saying that he did not leave the house after eight o'clock that evening, but after a good deal of cross-examination he eventually admitted that he had gone out later, adding that he had gone out for some whisky and biscuits at about ten o'clock. He did not, though, he said, see anything of Saunders.

The coroner then asked Dempsey why it was, when Saunders did not return, he did not go out and make inquiries for him. Dempsey replied, 'I don't know. The first thing I heard of his death was from a man who called at twelve o'clock on Sunday morning. On hearing the news Mrs Saunders fainted, and I had to attend to her for nearly four hours.'

Inspector Relf came forward then and related how he and Sergeant Philpott had called at Mrs Saunders's house on Monday to make inquiries and that the witness Dempsey had sworn that he did not go out after six o'clock, which statement Mrs Saunders had substantiated. Afterwards, Relf said, when he and the sergeant had left the house Dempsey had run after them in the street to tell them that he had forgotten, but that he *had* gone out later on that Saturday night – but not after eight o'clock. Inspector Relf added that he had then informed Dempsey that he could produce a witness who had seen him out at about 10.30 and again at eleven o'clock on Saturday night. To this Dempsey had replied that no such witness could be brought as he wasn't out.

Inspector Relf then asked permission for the witness to be called. The coroner agreed, adding that in all fairness to Dempsey he should be present whilst the witness was giving evidence.

Ann Winn, of nearby Watlington Grove, was then called.

She stated that she knew both James Dempsey and William Saunders by sight well, though was not personally acquainted with either. On Saturday night at ten o'clock, she said, she left her home and proceeded to Paxton Park, from where she accompanied her sister to a butcher's shop in central Sydenham. Afterwards they returned, the complete journey taking about half-an-hour. After leaving her sister in Paxton Park she came to the corner of Kent House Road and there waited for her young man. Whilst standing in the Kent House Road, she said, she saw Saunders accompanied by a man dressed in a light suit standing between the barber's and the grocer's shops, and as she passed by she heard Saunders say, 'That's a bloody lie.' She did not, she said, notice the face of the man who was with him.

She further stated that she then went home and in ten minutes returned to the Kent House Road, at which time she saw James Dempsey leaving a nearby grocer's shop; he was dressed in a light suit. Saunders, she said, was nowhere in sight. On being questioned further, she said she couldn't swear that it had been Dempsey she had first seen with Saunders, as she did not see the man's face, but she was quite certain that it was he who came out of the shop at 10.45; she had pointed him out to her young man who was with her at the time. Knowing Dempsey well, she said, she could not be mistaken in the man.

At this the coroner turned to Dempsey, who was wearing the light-coloured suit which he usually wore, and ordered him to put on his hat and turn his back to the witness.

'Is that like the man you saw?' the coroner asked Ann Winn, to which she replied: 'It's like him, but I won't swear it was him.'

Sergeant Philpott, who had been growing increasingly disappointed, then asked the girl, 'Didn't you tell me, when I was making inquiries, that you could *swear* that Dempsey was the man who was in company with Saunders?'

'I might have said so,' came Ann Winn's unsatisfactory answer, 'but I meant that it was Dempsey who came out of the shop.'

Dempsey, further questioned by the coroner, *now* admitted that he had gone out at about half-past ten. He had forgotten all about it, he said, adding that he had gone out to buy some whisky. 'But I wasn't gone ten minutes,' he said. 'I ran all the way.'

Dr Longrigg was called next. While the police officers had been busy with their investigations the doctor had conducted the *post mortem*. In the course of it he found that apart from the nose and jaw being broken, Saunders's collarbone and three ribs had also been broken. Also one of the man's teeth had been broken off and the inside of the mouth was lacerated. Longrigg was certain that Saunders's body had been thrown into the pond after death. In addition, judging by the position in which it was found, and with the head sticking fast in the mud, the body had been pitched into the water in the roughest manner possible. He stated that in his opinion 'death was the result of violence, inflicted by other parties, and not from drowning', adding, 'It would be difficult for a man to throw himself into a pond after suffering such injuries.'

Following Dr Longrigg's statement it was decided to adjourn the inquest for just over a week, until Wednesday, 4 April.

One thing that became apparent during that first day of the inquest was the poor impression that certain individuals had made as witnesses. Echoing the feelings of other journalists and the investigating officers, the reporter for the *South London Press* wrote:

The statements made by the widow of the deceased, and some members of the family, including a man who was shortly to marry one of deceased's daughters, were not at all of a satisfactory character. They differed very materially from the statements they at first made to the police who questioned them on the matter, and in answer to the interrogations of the coroner they admitted that in the first instance they had told the constable many falsehoods.

Giving a note of hope, however, the *Sydenham, Forest Hill, and Penge Gazette* followed their account of the inquest with the following:

We understand that the police are in possession of private information leading to the supposition that the deceased was kicked to death, and then carried to the pond and thrown in. For obvious reasons particulars are not divulged, but it is most probable that before these lines are perused by our subscribers two, if not three persons will be apprehended on suspicion of being connected with the crime.

Whatever that private information was – if indeed it existed – we do not know, but as the time passed the police had become even more convinced that their first suspicions were on the right track. Their chief suspect was the lodger, James Dempsey, and it was also suspected that Saunders's eldest stepson, Alfred Inman, was very much involved in the killing. Finding sufficient evidence that would lead to any conviction, however, was not proving to be an easy matter.

Following the first day of the inquest Chief Inspector Palmer of the Criminal Investigation Department of Scotland Yard was brought into the case, and in conjunction with Inspector Relf continued the search for evidence that would lead to a charge and subsequent conviction.

In a report on his investigations Palmer wrote that on the night of the killing, Saturday, the 24th, there had been a good deal of rain. This, he wrote, 'no doubt destroyed traces which might have led to the murderer or murderers'. However he did find something. His report continues: 'On making examination near the pond and also along the lane which leads towards the deceased's house, I found blood on three gates in the lane through which the body must have been carried.' Furthermore, with regard to William Saunders's movements that night after leaving Hillmore Grove, Palmer found that the ill-fated man had gone to the Prince Alfred public house.

Palmer was also convinced that the lodger, Dempsey,

was responsible for William Saunders's death. The great difficulty, however, was finding evidence to support the belief.

On Wednesay, 4 April the inquest was resumed, the first witness being Alfred Inman, Mrs Saunders's eldest son.

When the young man's mother had initially been questioned she had been adamant that no one from the house, apart from Saunders himself, had gone out after five o'clock on that Saturday. She had soon had to change her story, however, for it had swiftly been proved that Dempsey had been out that night after ten o'clock. Now with Alfred Inman's appearance it was revealed to the curious spectators that he too had left his home for a time that evening.

When questioned by the coroner, Inman eventually admitted that he had gone to The Dolphin, a public house in Sydenham Road. He went alone, he said, and whilst there sat in the taproom playing shove-ha'penny with three other customers. When he left he had been sober, he went on, adding, 'We only had a pot of four ale amongst the lot of us.' He and one of the other three had paid for the ale, he said. 'I should think I left about half-past-ten or eleven,' he replied in answer to questions, going on to say that he walked home alone. When asked whether he had stopped at the Prince Alfred pub on the way he said he had not, neither had he seen or spoken to anyone on his way back to Hillmore Grove.

Inman went on with his deposition:

'When I got home I found my mother, my sister, my brother Harry, and Dempsey, and my youngest sister there – I think all in one room. I had a bit of bread and meat and went to bed; that was about eleven o'clock. I went to bed at the same time as Dempsey. I heard nothing more of my father that night. I first heard that he had not returned in the morning when my sister told me that he had not been home. I heard it as soon as I got up; they were all talking about his not having come home.' Asked whether he had been asked to go out and look for Saunders, he said, 'My mother never asked me to go out and look for him; she asked me to put up the bed. Then later my sister came and said, "Bill has been found drowned in the pond."' He then said that his two younger brothers had gone to the Park Tavern and had come back saying that it was indeed their stepfather. 'Did you go out then?' he was asked. 'No,' he replied, 'I stopped at home doing up the bedstead, and afterwards mending my trousers which were torn.' He did not, he stated, go to see Saunders 'until the Tuesday afterwards'.

Hearing that Inman had waited three days before going to see Saunders's body, the coroner then asked – as well he might: 'Upon what terms were you with Saunders?'

'I was always good friends with him,' Inman replied. 'I used to go out walks with him. We all lived happy together.'

'How is it,' asked the coroner, 'that you did not go to see whether it was him after he had been found dead?'

Inman: 'Because my clothes were so ragged.'

Following further questioning it was soon revealed to the spectators in the courtroom that on the Monday night following the killing – before going to see the body of his stepfather – Inman had gone with James Dempsey on a very particular errand. And those who had perhaps wondered why Ann Winn had changed her mind as to her absolute certainty of seeing Dempsey with Saunders on the Saturday night might well now have thought that the reason for that change of mind was becoming clear. For suddenly it was revealed to the court that Dempsey and Inman had been to the girl's home.

'Why,' the coroner asked Inman, 'did you go to see her?'

'To ask if she had seen Dempsey on Saturday night,' Inman replied.

Asked what had been said to the girl, Inman replied:

'Dempsey said to her, "Can you swear that you saw me talking to Saunders on Saturday night?" and she answered that she thought she saw him.'

'Did Dempsey threaten the girl?' the coroner asked.

'I don't know.'

'Did *you* speak to the girl on Monday night?'

'Yes, I told her to tell the truth.'

'Did you threaten her?'

'No.'

'Did you tell her it was a hard thing to swear just by light dress?'

'I forget.'

'Did you,' the coroner said, 'also go to see her on the Tuesday?'

'Yes.'

'What did you go for?'

'Dempsey wanted to ask her something, and I went for the walk.'

When asked what Dempsey had wanted to ask the girl Inman said he didn't know.

'Do you mean to say that you don't know what he went to speak about?'

'No, I don't know.'

'He did not go to ask her whether she was going to the inquest?'

'I don't know, sir; I don't know what he said to the girl.'

That line of questioning ending, Inman was asked by a juryman when his mother first came to the tavern to see

Saunders's body. He answered that she had done so on the Sunday.

The next witness called was Albert Inman, fourteen, who deposed that on the Saturday night he had left his place of work nearby at about midnight. When he reached home, he said, Dempsey opened the door to him. Before breakfast on the Sunday morning he learned that his stepfather had not been home all night, and his mother sent him and his brother Harry, sixteen, to try to find out what had happened to him. When he returned to the house, he said, his mother was crying and she told him, 'Bill has been drowned.'

Thomas Fitzgerald was the next witness and he told how he had gone to Saunders's house to break the news to Mrs Saunders, and how, before he had done so, Mrs Saunders had said, 'Has he drowned himself?'

Dr Longrigg, who was called next, repeated much of his previous evidence regarding the injuries to the body, stating again that he was certain that the deceased was dead before he had been thrown into the pond. He was quite sure, he said, that the man did not inflict the injuries upon himself. He added also that he believed that the blows to the victim had come from different directions.

After the doctor had stepped down the coroner addressed the jury after which, without retiring, they returned a verdict of: 'Wilful murder by some person or persons unknown.'

After the verdict had been given the coroner asked for the concurrence of the jury in petitioning the Home Office to offer a suitable reward for information leading to the apprehension of the murderer or murderers.

The inquest over, the Home Office was contacted and soon afterwards posters were going up in the area offering £100 reward for information leading to a conviction, and a pardon 'to any accomplice (not being the person who actually committed the Murder) who shall give such evidence as shall lead to a like result'.

Unfortunately it brought no results.

So the case of William Saunders remains officially unsolved in Scotland Yard's files. And it will remain so.

Whilst no charge was ever made, however, it is certain that the investigators believed that James Dempsey was guilty of the murder – and possibly that Alfred Inman was guilty also.

And it is difficult to see that there is any reasonable cause to doubt their convictions. Unfortunately for justice and the investigators of the time, however, no direct evidence was discovered that could conclusively prove Dempsey's guilt, or even his involvement.

Now, looking back – granted, with the benefit of hindsight – the investigations do seem to have been somewhat inadequate for the purpose. Several points came to mind which might have been raised, one feels, and several questions which should have been asked and answered.

Chief Inspector Palmer, in his report of 11 June, said that he had examined the house of the deceased, and also the clothes of James Dempsey and Alfred Inman, but had found no traces of blood. We do not know, however, when this examination took place. Palmer's first Metropolitan Police report is dated 5 April, and as the murder took place on the night of 24 March, it is reasonable to assume that several days had gone by before the house or the suspects' clothes were examined. By which time, of course there would have been ample time to get rid of any incriminating evidence.

Alfred Inman, in his evidence before the coroner's court, said he did not go out to look for his stepfather nor go to see the body, because for one thing his trousers were badly torn and had to be mended. No one seems to have picked up on this. His clothes were obviously fit to go out in the day before, but now, suddenly, just a few hours later, they are in need of repair. How did they come to be so badly torn? Perhaps in a struggle?

It must have been obvious to everyone at the inquest that not only Dempsey, but also Alfred Inman and his mother were doing what they could to hide the truth. The investigating officers and many of the newspapers commented upon the 'unsatisfactory manner' in which the evidence was given by the two young men and Mrs Saunders.

In the course of the inquiries they were often found to have been lying. Both Dempsey and Inman at first denied having left the house that night, and were both subsequently found to have lied; likewise Mrs Saunders lied as regards the two young men having left the house that evening. Each one of them had to change his story in the face of evidence to the contrary. It is an interesting point to note that Dempsey said at first that he had not left the house after five o'clock on the Saturday. Later, under questioning, he changed this time to six o'clock; then eight o'clock, then ten o'clock, then 10.30.

There is a great deal in the evidence of the two young men that does not bear close examination. The motives behind some of the discrepancies may be perfectly innocuous, but even so it does seem that there might have been further investigation along certain lines – with perhaps more fruitful results than had so far been achieved.

For example, when Dempsey was questioned as to why he did not go to the Park Tavern when he heard from Fitzgerald that Saunders had been taken there after being found dead in the pond, he replied that he had had to attend to Mrs Saunders, who had fainted on hearing the news. 'I had to attend her for four hours,' he said. Yet in the house at that time was Jane, Mrs Saunders's eldest daughter; also her eldest son, Alfred. Were *they* not capable of attending to their mother? Why should she require the attendance of the lodger?

When Alfred Inman was asked why *he* did not go to the Park Tavern to see his stepfather he gave the excuse that he 'stopped at home doing up the bedstead' and mending his trousers which were torn.

Taking both Dempsey and Inman's statements in conjunction one is led to believe that Dempsey spent four hours attending to Mrs Saunders while her son, Alfred, was so little concerned with her condition that he spent the time erecting a bedstead and mending his torn trousers. The two stories are just not compatible. Further, in his evidence Alfred Inman said he was 'always good friends' with his stepfather, adding, 'I used to go out walks with him.' And yet, when came the terrible news that 'Bill', his stepfather, friend and companion, had been dragged out of a pond, dead, Inman did not go to see his body until the following Tuesday, the day of the inquest. Obviously Dempsey was similarly touched, and one is left with the inescapable conclusion that the Park Tavern was the very last place the two young men wanted to visit. Why? The two younger Inman boys, Harry and Albert, went quite willingly to look for Saunders, and neither did they waste any time in going to see his body as soon as they had learned of his death.

Alfred Inman, in his evidence, said that he and Dempsey went to bed at eleven o'clock on the Saturday night, but the fourteen-year-old Albert stated that when he got home from work after midnight it was Dempsey who opened the door to him.

Assuming that Dempsey was guilty of Saunders's murder, was Alfred Inman also involved? And if so, was Inman involved in the actual killing, or did he merely lie in order to protect Dempsey? There is no doubt that he and Dempsey were close; several times in the course of his evidence Inman referred to Dempsey as his brother.

As has been shown, both Dempsey and Inman, in spite of earlier lies to the contrary, were eventually forced to admit that they were out of the house on that wet Saturday night. According to their own accounts they did not meet, but it is established that they were geographically close, certainly in the region of the junction of Sydenham Road and Kent House Road where Dempsey was seen by Ann Winn. As Palmer says in his report: 'At the time the deceased was having angry words in the Kent House Road with the man supposed to be Dempsey, the stepson Alfred Inman was within a few yards from the spot, and doubtless Dempsey was there too, but I am unable to find any witness who can bring them together.'

That was one of Palmer's great problems, that he could find no witness who recalled having seen Dempsey and Inman together. Another insurmountable problem was the fact that Ann Winn would no longer swear that Dempsey was the man involved in angry words with Saunders, though when first questioned on the matter she had assured Sergeant Philpott that she was certain that Dempsey had been the man.

It must be almost certain that Ann Winn saw Dempsey with Saunders that Saturday night. And it is equally certain that Dempsey must have been aware that she had seen the two of them together, or why, otherwise, would he and Inman have visited her? Sergeant Philpott told Dempsey on the Monday that he could produce a witness who saw him out at 10.30 and again at eleven on the Saturday night, and soon afterwards Dempsey went to talk to Ann Winn. And he went again – and once more in the company of Alfred Inman – on the following day.

Dempsey probably wanted to find out *how much* she

had seen and heard, and exactly what she had said to the investigating officers – also, whether she had been called to the inquest and, if so, what she was going to say. It is obvious that he was very much afraid. And did he during one of his visits make any kind of veiled threat to her if she testified to having seen him in the company of Saunders? Whatever was said, it is reasonable to infer from what transpired that she was intimidated by his visits, for afterwards she told Philpott that she would no longer swear to having seen Saunders in Dempsey's company.

It is surprising that after Inman had revealed to the coroner's court the two visits to Ann Winn, Dempsey was not recalled and questioned as to his reasons for making them. He was not, though, and strangely it appears that the coroner was content to accept Inman's account of the visits. Neither was Ann Winn recalled. It must be obvious to anyone that if Dempsey had had nothing to hide he would have had no reason whatever to go and see Ann Winn and question her as to what or who she saw or thought she saw. Also, there is no record of Dempsey ever having been asked whether he had tried to intimidate the girl. It is astonishing that such questions were never asked, that such a possibly crucial factor in the case should not have been followed up but was allowed to be forgotten.

And what of Mrs Saunders, the widow who, according to her statements, had lived in such harmony with her second husband during the two years of their marriage? It cannot be supposed that she was in any way involved in the killing, but it certainly appears that she did all she could to cover up the guilt of the guilty party or parties. When Fitzgerald came to tell her the bad news she said to him, before he had even told her what had happened: 'Has he drowned himself?' A very curious thing for a woman to say in the circumstances. Also, as has been shown, she continually lied as regards the movements of her son and the lodger on that Saturday night.

It is odd too, how at pains she, her family and Dempsey seemed to be to impress upon everyone that they and Saunders had all lived happily together. Yes, Saunders had talked of suicide before their marriage, she said, but never afterwards – suggesting that marriage to her had ended all his unhappiness.

How different from the story told by the 'respectable and reliable' witness John Quittenden, who said that Saunders had sometimes said that he would leave his wife; that he had 'a hell of a life of it at home', that his life with his wife and stepchildren was 'a hell upon earth'. And Quittenden had no reason to lie.

One has only to look at Saunders's situation to see the truth in Quittenden's words. Saunders was said by all to be a hardworking, very quiet, sober, steady man, not given to quarrelling. At thirty-two years of age he marries a woman eleven years his senior and from then on shares his home with her and four of her children, the number soon to be added to by the eldest daughter's young man who comes to reside as a non-paying lodger. And not only does Saunders have to work to keep himself and his wife but also her eldest son and the lodger, neither of whom was in work. When he got to the house that Saturday after leaving work he gave his wife his pay for the week, nine shillings and threepence, out of which she gave him a shilling for himself. There is no doubt either but that she gave some of the remainder to her son and the lodger, for they both had money to buy liquor that evening.

It seems clear that Saunders's presence in the house was not welcomed by his family. He comes over always as the outsider – albeit the meal-ticket too; obviously what feelings of happiness and harmony might once have been there had long since gone.

Assuming still, then, that Dempsey was the actual killer of William Saunders, what, then, was the probable motive for the killing, and how did it happen? Without further evidence one can only speculate.

When the moving-in was finished for the day Saunders drank some beer with his friend and neighbour, John Quittenden, after which he returned to his home where he was given a shilling by his wife and told to go out again while she finished getting the house in order. There was apparently no mention of anyone else being asked to leave. Nevertheless, probably sometime between nine and ten o'clock Saunders left the house – and was perhaps happy to do so, in spite of the fact that it was a wet March night.

He never returned again to his home, to the family where he had been living so 'happily'.

It would appear that after having a drink at the nearby Prince Alfred pub he met Dempsey. How did they meet? Was it by chance? Had there perhaps been some falling out, some high words before Saunders had left his home, and had Dempsey gone after him? There was some disagreement, anyway. Perhaps over money. Perhaps there was some resentment on Saunders's side. Resentment is always felt by the person who is invariably the giver. Likewise, the debtor usually eventually feels guilt – which almost invariably turns to hostility.

That Saturday night, one can imagine, Ann Winn passed by just as Saunders and Dempsey were having angry words together. Inman was standing watching. 'That's a bloody lie,' she heard Saunders say. Returning five or ten minutes later she saw Dempsey coming out of a shop; of Saunders at this time there was no sign.

What happened then? After Ann Winn saw Dempsey

coming from the shop did he and William Saunders meet again? And was Alfred Inman also present? Possibly. Probably. Whatever, it seems likely that at that meeting anger flared and that in a rage Saunders was brutally attacked and killed.

Did it happen in a quiet street, unseen and unheard by any passerby? It was likely there were fewer people than usual out that night, owing to the wet weather. Did Dempsey strike Saunders to the ground and then, perhaps with the help of Inman, kick the man to death? Afterwards, on discovering that Saunders was dead, the desperate decision would have been made to try to cover up the fact of murder, to try to make it look like suicide. So the body was dragged to the pond and pitched into the water . . .

For all the certainty of the police that Dempsey at least was guilty, no charges were ever brought. Likewise the offered reward of £100 brought no further evidence and the killer – or killers – went free.

As mentioned earlier, the death of William Saunders was followed by another murder in Penge, and it is quite possible that Saunders's killer was aided to some degree in his escape from justice by this factor. The death of Mrs Harriet Staunton occurred only a week after the closing of the inquest into Saunders's murder and before the reward notices were even posted. Mrs Staunton's death was at first supposed to have been due to natural causes, and arrangements were going ahead for the funeral when the Penge police received information that led to the funeral being stopped and the coroner being contacted. A subsequent *post mortem* and inquest were to result in charges of murder being brought and the victim's husband and three others standing accused in the dock. It was a sensational case, and it is possible that the demands it created took over to some degree the interest and commitment of the police, and that as a result the Saunders murder was more or less pushed into the background.

. . . And there it remained till eventually it faded from memory and even the remotest hope of catching whoever was guilty was gone.

A Long and Winding Road to Death

The Strange Case of Georgina Moore

BY BERNARD TAYLOR

The first intimation to the general public of the Georgina Moore mystery came with the appearance in the illustrated papers of a sketch of a little girl, and the information that she was missing. It was the weekend of Saturday, 28 January 1882. Beneath the drawing was the offer of a £40 reward. Said the notice:

MISSING

From 7, Westmoreland Street, Pimlico, since noon, 20th ult., GEORGINA MOORE, aged 7½ years, tall for her age, complexion very fair, with bright colour, hair golden with fringe on forehead, eyes (full) blue; dress, dark blue serge frock, dark ulster with two rows of black buttons, white straw hat trimmed with black velvet, dark blue knitted stockings, button boots.

A Reward of £10 will be paid by the Secretary of State for the Home Department, and £5 by Mr Moore, 105, Winchester Street, Pimlico, and £25 by Mr Ingram, Auctioneer, 34, Sussex Street, SW, for such information as shall lead to the discovery of the child.

After breakfast on the morning of Tuesday, 20 December 1881, Mrs Mary Moore and her two children, Harry and Georgina, had left their home at 105, Winchester Street to walk the short distance to the home of the Laing family at 7, Westmoreland Street. Mrs Moore and Mrs Laing were close friends, and Mrs Laing's daughter, Lily, was about Georgina's age. Soon after their arrival the children left for their school which was situated in the same street.

Soon after twelve noon the children returned to 7, Westmoreland Street where Mrs Moore and Mrs Laing served midday dinner. Georgina did not eat much of the meat and potatoes put before her, though she ate some of the currant pudding that followed. The school gates were usually opened again at ten minutes to two, and about half-an-hour before that time Georgina was anxious to get off again so that she could play for a while before it was time to go in to class. So, with a halfpenny from Mrs Laing to spend at the sweetshop, she said goodbye and left.

Georgina was expected back at her home in Winchester Street soon after school ended at four o'clock, and when she had not returned by 4.30 her mother went out in search of her. To her great dismay, however, she found no sign of her. Later that evening she asked Simeon Laing, Mrs Laing's husband, to take a message to her husband, Stephen, at the building site where he was working, telling him that Georgina had not returned home. On being informed, Stephen Moore came at once and, along with several friends from the neighbourhood, began a search for his daughter, during the course of which he reported her disappearance to the local police. Said Mrs Moore later of her husband's efforts to find the child: 'He was in and out all night for that purpose.'

All efforts were to no avail, however. But then the next day Mrs Moore learned from a little boy that he had seen Georgina during the dinner hour of the previous day talking to a tall woman in a light ulster. The description at once brought to mind the landlady of their previous home at 51, Westmoreland Street, Mrs Esther Pay, who frequently wore such a coat, and Mary Moore immediately went to make inquiries. On Esther Pay opening the door to her, Mary Moore asked her whether she had seen anything of Georgie. She had come to her, she said, as she had learned that Georgie had been seen talking to a woman in a light ulster, and because Georgie knew Mrs

Pay and would go anywhere with her. Esther Pay responded by saying coldly that she had not seen the child and then closing the door.

The days went by and still there was no sign of the missing child. About a week after her disappearance Inspector Henry Marshall of Scotland Yard's Criminal Investigation Department was charged with pursuing the matter. As a result of his inquiries and of listening to local gossip his efforts eventually took him to see Esther Pay at 51, Westmoreland Street. This was on 5 January. Mrs Pay's husband, William, was not at home, but she was there. Accompanying the inspector was Stephen Moore, Georgina's father. Asked if she knew where the child was, Mrs Pay said she knew nothing about it, and asked, 'Why have you called upon me?' 'Because the rumours are that you have taken the child away,' the inspector replied. At this Mrs Pay turned to Moore, saying, 'You know where I was on the 20th; I was with Carrie Rutter.'

The inspector called again the following day and talked to her alone in the front parlour. 'I've come to see you again, Mrs Pay,' Marshall said. 'I thought perhaps seeing you alone would be better.' 'Really, Mr Marshall,' she replied, 'I know nothing of it. I don't know how it is that people suspect me.' At that a man's voice called inquiringly from another room, and Mrs Pay called back that it was somebody there asking about little Georgie. She then said to the inspector, 'That's my husband. He's in bed – drunk.'

On 15 January a child's white straw hat, trimmed with black velvet, was found hanging on a willow bough hanging over the River Medway near the railway station of Yalding, a village near Sevenoaks in Kent. The hat was dry but it had obviously been in the water. It was found by James Humphreys, Esther Pay's uncle, who lived very nearby. He saw no significance in the discovery.

In the meantime Inspector Marshall continued his inquiries, added to which the reward notice was placed in the illustrated papers. Then, just two days after the notice's appearance, the search for little Georgina Ann Moore came to an end.

The discovery took place on the afternoon of Monday, 30 January, when a barge was travelling on the Medway close to where the hat had been found, near Yalding Station. The bargee, Alfred Pinhorn, was using the boom when he found that a hook on it had caught in something near the bank. Moments later he discovered to his horror that he had drawn to the surface the body of a child.

Quickly Pinhorn called to his mate on the towpath, Joseph Swain, who lifted the body on to the bank and then ran for a policeman. Soon afterwards PC James Hall of Yalding was hurrying back with him to the river bank on which lay the body of the dead child. Lifting the body, which was much decomposed, the constable found that it was attached to a length of wire, part of which was still in the water. On pulling it out he found fixed to it a firebrick into which was stamped the word TYNE. The wire was wound several times around the child's body, which was covered with clay from the river bed. The hands of the child were clenched and the knees bent and drawn up to the chest. It was clear that this must be a case of murder.

When the Criminal Investigation Department in London had been informed of the discovery, Inspector Marshall became even more suspicious of Esther Pay as the spot where the body had been found was said to be very close to the home of her parents. Accompanied by his assistant, Sergeant Cussens, and having informed Stephen Moore that he would be required to see if he could identify the body, the inspector set off at once for Yalding.

Arriving in Yalding, Inspector Marshall found that the

river passed only about three-quarters of a mile from the back of Esther Pay's parents' house in the next village of Nettlestead, and that anyone wishing to reach the river from the house had merely to take a footpath that started beside the garden and then follow it across two fields – the second a hop field – to the railway line. On the other side of the line lay the river.

Very early the next morning Stephen Moore arrived in Yalding and in the company of the inspector he was taken to the outhouse of The Railway Inn wherein lay the child's body. Without hesitation he identified it as that of his missing daughter.

Inspector Marshall had earlier learned that Esther Pay was at that moment staying at the home of her parents, and as soon as Moore's identification was complete, the inspector and the sergeant set off for the house. On their arrival, just after nine o'clock, Esther Pay's mother, Mrs Humphreys, invited the two officers inside and showed them to a bedroom in which they found Mrs Pay. She was a tall woman, dark-haired, thirty-five years of age.

'Well, Mrs Pay,' said Marshall, 'I've come to see you again.'

'How did you know I was here?' Esther Pay asked indignantly.

Ignoring her question, Marshall said, 'It's about the child Moore again.'

'I know nothing of it,' she said.

'But have you not heard,' he said, 'that yesterday a child was found in the Medway, at the back of your house?'

Surprisingly she replied, 'No.'

'Well, such is the case,' said Marshall, 'and I must detain you – certainly on suspicion of stealing it – and you *may* be charged with causing its death, inasmuch as its body has been discovered near your house.'

'Well,' Esther Pay replied, 'you must prove it.'

Esther Pay, née Humphreys, was born in 1846. One of eight daughters and a son, she had lived most of her young life at the house near Yalding, until in her twenties she had gone to London where she had met a wheelwright, William Pay, and in August 1869, married him. It was not a happy marriage. Later she and her husband had gone to stay in the house of his sister and brother-in-law, Caroline and James Rutter, at 51, Westmoreland Street, Pimlico. It was there that Esther Pay first met the Moores.

Neither were the Moores – Stephen and his wife Mary – a particularly happily married couple, mainly because of Moore's immoral character. He and his wife – she came from Whimple, Exeter – had married in 1873 in Bristol, after the birth of their son Harry, afterwards going to live in Bath where their daughter Georgina was born. It was there that Moore became involved with a Mrs Emma Irwin, a widow who kept a grocer's shop, introducing himself to her as a bachelor, by name Harry Williams. During the first two years of his intimate association with Mrs Irwin she bore him a child, naming it Harry Williams, after the father. The baby lived only three days. About this time, it appears, Moore felt it was perhaps a little wiser to let her know that he was married. Shortly afterwards he left his family in Bath and moved to London where he took lodgings, about three months later learning from his wife that she had gone back home to her parents in Exeter, taking the two children, Harry and Georgina, with her.

For a while living a bachelor's life in London, Moore continued to carry on his association with Emma Irwin in Bath, and also began an affair with her sister, Alice Day, who lived in Nunhead. A little later, however, in 1877, there was a reconciliation with his wife, following which she came to London to join him, at which time they took rooms in Pimlico at 51, Westmoreland Street with Mrs Rutter as the landlady. Still, however, with his wife back at his side, he continued with his extra-marital associations, seeing Emma Irwin when he could, and also, about once a fortnight over a long period, travelling to Nunhead to see Alice Day. Then in 1879 Alice Day arrived at the house and informed him that she was pregnant and that he was responsible. Moore denied it and, according to his later testimony, never saw her again. Furthermore, with Emma Irwin learning of his association with her sister, it seems that she decided that enough was enough and ended her relationship with him.

Moore didn't mind. He was now focusing his attention closer to home. In 1877 the Rutters had moved out, passing on the tenancy of 51, Westmoreland Street to Mrs Rutter's brother, William Pay, who had been living at the house for nine months with his wife, Esther. Very soon Stephen Moore and Esther Pay were involved in an affair.

The affair between Moore and Mrs Pay seems to have continued without a hitch until Mrs Pay's husband discovered it. Then, following a scene, the Moores were given notice to leave. They didn't go far, only to Winchester Street, a short distance away. Neither did the move finish Moore's association with Mrs Pay; he took advantage of her husband's job – Pay was employed by a firm of furniture dealers and removers and had to leave the house early each morning – and visited her in the man's absence.

And so the situation continued until, in the summer of 1881, Pay discovered that the affair between Moore and his wife was still going on. There was a furious quarrel, during which Pay subjected his wife to considerable violence.

It was following this final scene, it appears, that Moore

made up his mind to sever his association with Esther
Pay, and, telling her that he was doing it solely for her
own good, he ended the relationship. In truth he probably
felt that the pleasure wasn't worth the aggravation, particularly when there was no shortage of like pleasures
available without the accompanying bother.

And he didn't remain lonely for long. Very soon
afterwards, and much to Esther Pay's growing distress, he
became involved in relationships with two other women,
a young servant, a Miss Carroll, and another woman, a
Mrs Maidment, who lived near Regent's Park.

According to Moore, as he later testified, he last saw
Esther Pay in the July of 1881, not seeing her again until
the Friday following the day that his daughter went
missing. On this occasion, he said, he was near Drummond's Bank where he was working with the building
company that employed him when Esther Pay came to
him. He could not explain how she knew he was there, he
said. He had recently shaved off his beard and whiskers
and she remarked upon the difference it made to his
appearance. She hardly knew him at first, she told him.
As they talked together the subject moved on to that of
his missing child.

He next saw her, he said, in the company of Inspector
Marshall at her home, and then on the evening of Friday,
27 January. On this latter occasion they met at about
8.15, at her request, in Sloane Square, walked across
Hyde Park and then stopped at a pub for some refresh-
ment. He then returned with her to a house in Lower
Sloane Street where she had just taken lodgings in the
name of Mrs Black; she had left her husband, she had
told him. In her room she told Moore that the following
day, Saturday, she planned to go to her parents at
Yalding, and that after she had had a short holiday with

them she intended to find a situation as a servant in a gentleman's family.

Moore met her again the following day at Charing Cross Station, after which they walked down the Strand and had a glass of wine together. He bought her some flowers, they had some tea, and then back at the station she gave him some money for him to buy her train ticket to Yalding. There also he bought for her a copy of *The Penny Illustrated Paper* which contained a portrait of his daughter. At no time, he said later, did he have any suspicion that she might be responsible for the loss of his child.

In Yalding, Moore, having identified his daughter's body, was taken to the spot where it was found. He was not completely unfamiliar with the area, some two years earlier having accompanied Esther Pay on a visit to her parents there.

While Moore was going to view the place where his daughter's body had been found, Inspector Marshall was facing Esther Pay in her bedroom in her father's house. She, having told Marshall that he would have to prove her guilt in the fate of the dead child, went on to say that she had brought nothing with her from London but 'a birdcage, a bag, and a small parcel'. Then she added, 'When I came down on Saturday night I overshot my mark by two stations – Marden and Staplehurst – which caused my arrival here late. If you go to the station-master at Staplehurst and make inquiry I dare say he will remember me, or a lady, as having made a mistake.'

Marshall, however, not really concerned with what she had brought with her on this present occasion, helped Cussens search the room (and subsequently the whole house). In a small reticule belonging to Esther Pay was the copy of *The Penny Illustrated Paper* bearing the portrait of Moore's daughter, and a rent book for the woman's new lodgings in Lower Sloane Street, London. Marshall also found a letter, undated and unsigned. As he began to read it Esther Pay said, 'You know who that is to; it's to Moore, the father of the child.' The letter read as follows:

Nettlestead,

Darling,

I arrived home quite safely later than I expected. My brother met me quite safely at the station. Found all well except my mother. Dear, write me a few lines; I think so much of you in your trouble. I seem so far from you now. If you hear any tidings let me know at once. Poor little darling! I hope you will find her. I do not think I can stay so long as I intended here. There are lots of snowdrops and daisies in bloom. Tell me, dear, all the news you can, and take care of yourself, although I know it is no use asking you to do that for my sake now. Mother and I think of going into Maidstone for a few hours tomorrow. Oh! darling, it is so dull here. I'm afraid I cannot stay long. I will see you if you want me.

Moore had received one letter from Esther Pay that very morning before leaving London; obviously the letter the inspector had found in her room had also been written very recently.

When Marshall had finished reading the letter Esther Pay asked several questions about Moore, and Marshall told her, 'He's down here.' She then asked if she could see him, but Marshall refused. 'Has Georgina been found?' she asked. 'Yes,' he said. 'Have you seen my husband?' she asked then. He replied, 'Yes, on several occasions, and he's told many people that you are implicated in the child's disappearance.' 'Don't you believe him,' the woman retorted.

Later, at about ten o'clock, Esther Pay was taken to Yalding Station where the inspector left her ensconced in the waiting room in the charge of Sergeant Cussens while he went away again to resume his investigations. While the inspector was gone Esther Pay asked the sergeant:

'Whereabouts did they find Georgie, then?'

He replied: 'Just below the footpath which crosses the line leading to your house.'

'Well,' she said, 'that's strange that she should be found down here, and so near my home. I'm sure no one knows my address here except Mr and Mrs Moore and my husband. And it's very strange to me if Moore doesn't know something about it. He's so artful. You'd better look after him, for I shouldn't be surprised if he's not missing very shortly; I know he's not on very good terms with his wife, and now he's got rid of Georgie you'd better look very sharp after him, for if he once gets away you'll never catch him.' A little silence went by and then suddenly she burst out, 'Do you think it's likely, if I did such a thing as this, I should bring her down so close to my home?' Sergeant Cussens replied that he didn't know. Mrs Pay went on:

'Whoever did it knew perfectly well that my home is down here, and no doubt it was done to plant it on me.' Later, Sergeant Cussens testified that she repeated this assertion several times.

Returning to Yalding Station about three o'clock that afternoon, the inspector found Moore standing on the platform, waiting for the 3.17 train. A few minutes later when Esther Pay was brought from the waiting room she saw Moore and asked if she might speak to him. 'No,' Marshall replied.

'Will he ride in the carriage with us?' she then asked.

'No, I have reasons for not allowing him to do so.'

'Well,' she said, 'don't be surprised if he bolts, and then you'll find the most guilty party is gone.' A little later she added, rather cryptically, 'You'd better stop any tele-grams to Bristol.'

Afterwards, on board the London-bound train, Esther Pay said that she believed the child had been killed out of spite for Moore. 'He has served women very badly,' she said, ' – some that I know worse than me – and he has served *me* bad enough. Why don't you discover *them*, then you might get on the right track. One can only die once, and I shall not die a coward.'

Later that evening Esther Pay was escorted to the Westminster Police Court and placed in the dock. Apart from the various police officers, from both the Kent and the Westminster constabularies, Stephen Moore was pres-ent. There Acting-Superintendent Hamblin said to him:

'You had better state the identical words you said to me just now.'

Moore then said, directing his words to the woman in the dock: 'All along I have considered you innocent in this matter, but now that the body has been found so near your home I am of a different opinion. I think you must be implicated.'

'How can you say so?' Esther Pay retorted. 'Mind this isn't the means of your own character being investigated – which may bring out something you may not like.' She stared at him, but Moore made no answer, not looking her in the face.

Following this the prisoner was charged with the murder of the child.

The following morning Esther Pay was brought up before the magistrate, Mr Partridge, at which time Inspector Marshall told how he had gone to the cottage of the prisoner's parents near Yalding and arrested her. When he had related to the magistrate how Pay had said that the child had been killed out of spite as Moore had 'served women very badly' – not least herself, the magistrate asked whether the inspector had said anything to give rise to her words. 'No, your worship,' Marshall replied. 'She was very talkative, and we couldn't stop her. It all arose owing to her not being allowed to see Moore. She seemed much annoyed at this and at him. I didn't lead up to the conversation at all.'

Describing his examination of the body, Marshall said, 'I saw the body yesterday and helped to strip it. It had four or five thicknesses of wire bound round the chest. There was a brick attached to the body, on which are impressed the letters TYNE. As a matter of fact, Moore identified both the body and the clothing.'

Esther Pay was then asked whether she would like to say anything, and she turned to the inspector and asked:

'Do you remember me asking Moore at Yalding Station: "Do you think I did this?" and he replied, "No"?'

'I heard you call out something indistinctly to him, which I didn't catch,' Marshall said. 'And the reply I didn't hear at all.'

'He said "No",' Esther Pay said, 'and his opinion has been altered since.' Then she went on, 'Did you hear me say, "Are they poor little Georgie's things?" and he saying, "Yes."?'

'I don't remember such a question,' Marshall said; then to the magistrate: 'I must say I had considerable difficulty in keeping Moore and her apart. They wanted to get together.'

Said Pay: 'Did you not begin the conversation in the carriage about Moore?'

'No,' said Marshall. 'You began it by complaining of Moore's not being allowed to ride in the carriage.' To the magistrate: 'I told her, as I have said, that I had reasons for not allowing it.'

Esther Pay: 'I said, "I'm sure neither Mr nor Mrs Moore would think I could hurt Georgie."'

Marshall: 'You didn't say anything of the kind.'

Esther Pay: 'Don't you remember me saying, "Moore must be very two-faced."?'

'No, I don't remember any such words.'

Esther Pay: 'I'm afraid you don't remember a great deal.'

'That is untrue – like a good many things you have said.'

Following this exchange the prisoner was remanded for a further week.

That same Wednesday afternoon at Yalding the inquest into the child's death was due to begin at two o'clock at The Railway Inn. Stephen Moore, who was due to be present, missed his train. Immediately following the opening, therefore, and after the child's body had been viewed by the jury, the inquest was adjourned till the following Friday. Further, it was decreed by the coroner that it would be resumed at The George Inn, which would allow the proceedings a little more room.

Following the adjournment of the inquest two doctors, Dr Bond of London and Dr Wood of Yalding, carried out a *post mortem* examination of the body. In the meantime the police continued with their inquiries, intensifying their search for anyone who had seen the child on the afternoon of 20 December.

After the *post mortem* permission was given for Georgina's burial. The funeral was set for Saturday, 4 February, at Brompton Cemetery, and a remarkable scene ensued. Over the preceding days the sexual intrigues and exploits of Stephen Moore had become the subject of common gossip, leading to great disapproval of him, if not the belief of many that he was somehow involved in his daughter's sad and cruel death. *The Kent and Sussex Courier* wrote of the funeral:

The coffin was placed in an open car, and a crowd of more than two thousand people assembled in the neighbourhood of the residence of the parents in Winchester Street. On the father being seen to enter one of the mourning coaches he was groaned and hissed at, and a large force of police under two inspectors had great difficulty in protecting him from personal violence at the hands of the mob. A strong cordon of constables was obliged to be formed round the vehicle, and they accompanied the cortège in this manner to the place of interment, Brompton Cemetery, the crowd augmenting along the line of route, and continuing their demonstrations of disfavour at his conduct. The scene within the cemetery was shocking and scandalous in the extreme, and so threatening and violent was the attitude of the rough crowd, that the police took the responsibility of locking Mr Moore in the mortuary chapel, and he was unable to go to the grave or return to the other mourners. He was not released to return home until after dark, when the crowd had dispersed.

In contrast to the antagonism shown towards Stephen Moore, a great deal of public sympathy was shown towards his wife, Mary.

While Esther Pay was held in custody in London, the inquest at The George Inn, Yalding and the summary hearing at the Westminster Police Court ran over several weeks, in tandem, with witnesses going back and forth between the two places.

The inquest was completed first, bringing a verdict of 'Wilful murder against Esther Pay', whereupon the coroner committed her for trial at the next assizes.

At Westminster, however, the hearing before the magistrates was continuing. One of the first witnesses had been Mrs Moore who testified to the prisoner's fondness for the deceased child, saying that Georgina would 'go with her anywhere'. Later, telling how Georgina had not returned from school that afternoon, and that she 'never saw her alive again', she broke down and sobbed bitterly.

She was followed by various individuals from both London and Kent, including several who testified to seeing a child in the company of a woman en route to Yalding during the afternoon and evening of 20 December. One of the witnesses was PC Hill of Pimlico who testified to seeing Georgina Moore in the company of a female walking in the direction of Ebury Bridge. After he had described his view of the woman the prisoner was requested to turn around in the witness box so that PC Hill might have a sight of her back. Reported *The Illustrated Police News*: 'This she did promptly, smiling pleasantly at the same time, and taking the opportunity to exchange a nod of recognition with someone behind.'

Throughout the hearing, apparently, she remained outwardly quite calm and composed.

One witness who caused a particular stir was Stephen Moore who, in an effort to establish a motive for the crime, was questioned at length about his rather dissolute past, including his affair with the prisoner. Following these shocking revelations, a man living near the river at Yalding testified to having heard a child cry out at some time around 20 December.

In the courtroom then was produced a woollen scarf which had been fished out of the river the day after the body had been found, and from near the same spot. Witnesses were produced who testified that the prisoner had knitted and owned a scarf of similar colour, design and stitch, and the prosecution attempted to prove that the scarf now produced was that same scarf. Whether it was, however, could not be demonstrated as there was so much confusion among the witnesses as to the shade of the wool of Esther Pay's scarf – was it blue, or mauve, or black; was the decorative chain stitch large or small?

The business of the scarf then gave way to the medical evidence. Dr Thomas Bond, who along with Dr Wood had carried out the *post mortem*, said that there was a dark mark on the front of the neck extending from the root of the tongue to the breastbone. There were no abrasions or marks at the back of the neck, nor was there any indication of the pressure of a cord. The lungs contained no water. The stomach was full of undigested food. In the witness's opinion the child had been dead from a month to two months. He believed strangulation from pressure over the larynx was the cause of death. There was no evidence to show that death was the result of drowning.

Cross-examined, Dr Bond said:

'I first saw the body on the 1st February about two o'clock in the afternoon, and at that time there was no wire around the body. I found currants and a white pulp, resembling bread or rice, in the stomach. I did not find any meat. There might have been potatoes, for the white pulp might have been rice starch, meal starch, or potato starch.'

In answer to a further question Dr Bond said that he and Dr Wood of Yalding were quite in agreement and had issued their reports jointly. Questioned by Mr Duerdin Dutton on behalf of the prisoner, he said that it was possible there was meat in the stomach but that he had not noticed any trace of it.

Eventually the hearing came to an end and Esther Pay was remanded on a charge of murder to take her trial at the next assizes.

During the time the inquiries had been proceeding there had been great dissatisfaction shown by the Kent magistrates who objected strongly to the case being taken out of their jurisdiction. The local justices argued that, both the woman Pay and the body of the child having been found in Kent, it was an improper proceeding to examine witnesses from Kent in the metropolis, and that the case, sooner or later, should be brought before the justices of the county. The Public Prosecutor, on the other hand, contended that the course adopted in hearing the whole case at Westminster was quite within the law. The Kent magistrates were not impressed, and the *Daily Telegraph* duly reported on 12 April:

At the Kent General Sessions at Maidstone yesterday it was decided that a memorial should be presented to the local Government Board, drawing attention to the inconvenience likely to arise from a repetition of the course pursued by the Metropolitan Police in the Yalding murder case, in arresting the prisoner charged with the crime, which was committed in Kent, conveying her to London, and there conducting the case against her. An opinion was very generally expressed that the adoption of such a course was not only inconvenient but unfair to the prisoner.

The same newspaper went on to say that 'a soldier named Reuben had given himself up to the police at Kildare, in Ireland, confessing that he was with Esther Pay when the child, Georgina Moore, was murdered'. The confession, as expected, was subsequently found to be valueless and nothing came of it.

Esther Pay's trial came up at the Lewes Assizes, Sussex, opening on Thursday, 27 April, when she was brought before Baron Pollock. Little interest was manifested at the opening of the court, but before long the courtroom was full and the ushers were having to turn people away.

Mr Poland was prosecuting, assisted by Mr Biron and Mr Eyre Lloyd. Esther Pay was defended by Mr Edward Clarke, QC, MP, and Mr Safford.

Said *The Daily Chronicle*, 'The accused, a fine-looking, well-dressed woman, appeared perfectly self-composed, and, upon the charge being read to her, answered in a firm voice, "Not guilty." She was allowed to be seated during the hearing of the case.'

Mr Poland, in opening the case for the Crown, told how, in September 1878, Esther Pay and her husband had gone to live at 51, Westmoreland Street, where were living Stephen and Mary Moore and their two children, Harry and Georgina. 'In that way the prisoner became on intimate terms with the Moores, and no doubt was very kind to this little child, whom she used occasionally to take out with her, having no children of her own.' After a time Moore and the prisoner 'became on terms of improper intimacy'. Then in March or April of 1881 the Moore family left Westmoreland Street to live at 105, Winchester Street, a little way off, but the intimacy between Moore and Esther Pay continued until about June. That autumn Moore went to live with a woman (Mrs Maidment) at 6, Berkeley Road, Regent's Park, remaining with her until 23 January; she going under the name of Mrs Moore. During this time Moore's lawful wife and children continued to reside at 105, Winchester Street, and Moore maintained them and went to see them from time to time. While cohabiting with the other woman at Berkeley Road, Moore had intended to have his little girl to stay with him during the Christmas week. Said Mr Poland at this point in the proceedings:

'It might be convenient at once to tell the jury that it was alleged on the part of the prosecution that this murder was committed by the prisoner at the bar in order to revenge herself upon the father of the child, with whom she had had these improper relations, which existed up to June last year.'

Mr Poland went on to say that on the morning of 20 December, Moore left his mistress at Berkeley Road early in the morning and went to his own house in Winchester

Street where he saw his wife, after which he left for his job with the building company, its site at that time being Drummond's Bank. That same Tuesday morning, about nine o'clock, Mrs Moore and the two children went to the house of a friend, Mrs Laing, at 7, Westmoreland Street, after which the children went off to school, returning for midday dinner at twelve noon.

'About a quarter-past-one,' said Mr Poland, 'the child Georgina, having dined at No. 7, left for the purpose of returning to school, the gates of which were opened some ten minutes or so before two. A neighbour had given her a halfpenny to buy some cakes, and the child went away perfectly well and happy. She was a nice little thing, and was dressed in the ordinary way for school by her mother, who never after saw her alive. It was clear she was not at school in the afternoon, and nothing was known as to what had become of her until her body was found in the River Medway, at Yalding, on Monday, January 30th, at a spot eight hundred and fifty yards from the house where the prisoner's mother and father lived.'

Continuing his speech, Mr Poland went on to say that the prisoner was not seen in London after 12.45 that Monday afternoon, and that when inquiries were made later that day at her house it was found that she had gone out and had still not returned by eleven o'clock that night. The prosecution were alleging, he said, that the prisoner had taken the child from London to Paddock Wood, and from Paddock Wood to Yalding, and that there she took the life of the child and threw the body into the river.

Another matter for the jury's consideration, he said, was this: that the deceased was a timid child and was not likely to go with any person she did not well know. And the jury should remember, he added, that it was broad daylight, and it was next to impossible that a strange woman could have taken the child against her will through the streets of London and nearly forty miles by railway without attracting attention. 'One's common sense,' he said, 'suggests that it must have been a person in whom the child placed implicit confidence, and with whom she would willingly go; and there is overwhelming evidence, from the kindness of the prisoner to this child, that the latter would have gone anywhere with her. I might state that there are two or three ways of getting to Yalding, the most direct being by South-Eastern Railway to Paddock Wood. It is suggested by the prosecution that she went that way; but that instead of continuing the journey by train from Paddock Wood she got out at that station and took the child along an indirect road for the purpose of avoiding persons who might happen to know her.'

Mr Poland then referred to several witnesses who had seen a woman and child on the longer road from Paddock Wood to Yalding, and also to a man near Yalding Station who, that evening, had heard what seemed to be the cry of a child. 'The theory of the prosecution,' he said, 'is that the child was killed by strangulation, and that after death the prisoner attached a firebrick to the body by means of some wire – with both of which articles she had previously provided herself – and that she then threw the body into the River Medway. Seven, eight, or nine feet of wire was fastened round the body, and great precaution seemed to have been used to make the brick secure. It is further suggested that she did not return to London that night, but stayed at the house of her father and mother.' With regard to the latter point he went on to say that he would produce witnesses who saw the prisoner at Yalding Station the following day. It was alleged by the prisoner, Mr Poland continued, that on Tuesday afternoon, 20 December, she was in company with a Mrs Emma Harris and her own sister-in-law, Mrs Rutter, and that she went to the Aquarium; but evidence would be called to show that the statement was untrue.

Then, after asking the jury to give the evidence their best and closest attention, he called the first witness.

This was Alfred Pinhorn, the bargee, who testified to finding the body of the child on the afternoon of 30 January. When opposite Yalding Station, he said, the pole he was using became entangled in something, and on pulling it up he found it was the body of a female child. There was wire tied to the body, and a brick hung by the wire.

Cross-examined by Mr Clarke, he said the water was about four feet below the top of the bank, and that the body, when he found it, was about eight feet from the edge of the water. The river was about fifty-one or fifty-two feet wide at that point. The barge, he added, had run slightly aground, but he had got it off before pulling up the body.

After Alfred Pinhorn came Pinhorn's mate, Joseph Swain, who said he had pulled the body ashore with a boat-hook.

Next came PC James Hall who testified to having been summoned to the spot on the towpath on the discovery of the body. There was wire wrapped twice around the body, outside the clothes, he said. The brick was in the water. There was 8′ 4″ of wire from the body to the brick. The body was doubled up. The brick and wire were produced at this, and then on a diagram the spot was pointed out by him where the body had been taken from the water, which was said to be about fifteen or sixteen yards from the spot where the footpath left the towing-path and went on to lead past the house of the prisoner's parents.

The next two witnesses were Albert Large – who testified to finding the scarf in the water – and PC Preedeth who washed it, showed it to Mr Moore, the father of the child, and then handed it to Inspector Marshall.

James Humphreys (prisoner's uncle) was called next and, examined by Mr Poland, said that on 15 January he had found a child's hat on the opposite side of the river from where the body was found. The water had gone down since 20 December, he said. The hat was about three hundred yards from where the body was found and could have drifted there. He heard of the body being found afterwards, he said, and then had given up the hat. Cross-examined, he stated that the hat was six or seven feet above the water when he found it. There was no other high flood during January after he found the hat. The water was at its highest on 19 December. When the water was very high all the towing-path was under water. Asked whether he knew Laddingford and the road to The New Inn, he said that he did. There were very few houses there, he said, and it was a very lonely road. There were woods and ditches on either side.

Police Sergeant Vennell, who was called next, said that he knew the cottage where the prisoner's parents lived. There was a path leading to the spot where the body was found, which spot was seven hundred yards from the house. There was about six or seven feet of water where the body was found. The towing-path must have been under water just below where the body was found. On 19 December he should think the water would not have covered the path nearest where the body was found. Cross-examined by Mr Clarke, he said, 'There is a rise in the path on the Yalding side commencing about seven yards from where the body was found. I have seen the flood when the towing-path could not be got at at all, but I should not think it was so on December 19th.'

The next witness was Stephen Moore – whose appearance must greatly have pleased the sensation-seekers who were hoping for further shocking revelations. They wouldn't be disappointed.

He told first how, about five years earlier, he and his wife and son and daughter had gone to live at 51, Westmoreland Street, Pimlico, after which time the land-lord and landlady, Mr and Mrs Rutter, had left, their places being taken by Mr William Pay – brother to Mrs Rutter – and his wife, Esther – the prisoner.

While resident in the house, the witness said, he became 'immorally connected' with Mrs Pay, and even though he and his wife and family left in the March or April to move to Winchester Street, his intimacy with Mrs Pay continued. Furthermore, he added, he gave Mrs Pay a latch-key to his new home at Winchester Street.

The intimacy with the prisoner continued, Moore added, for about six weeks after his departure from 51, Westmoreland Street, and then came to an end. Said Moore:

'The intimacy was broken off because I was seen talking to her by her husband. It caused some unpleasantness and I avoided talking to her again.' The prisoner had no children of her own, he continued, adding, 'She was very kind to my daughter, and my daughter appeared to be very fond of her.'

Moore went on to say that in the previous October he had gone to live with a married woman in Berkeley Road, Regent's Park, who had then called herself Mrs Moore. During this time, he said, he continued to support his wife and children in Winchester Street where he sometimes called in the mornings before going to his work. His daughter, he said, had never visited the house in Berkeley Road, and he did not believe that the woman there had ever seen his daughter, though he had shown her a photograph of his daughter.

On the night of 19 December, he continued, he stayed

at Berkeley Road, early in the morning, at about a quarter-to six, going to his home at Winchester Street. After remaining with his wife for about twenty minutes, he left for work at Drummond's Bank near Charing Cross. He did not go home to dinner that day, he said, but worked overtime. He continued:

'At about half-past eight that night a neighbour, Simeon Laing, came to me and told me that my daughter was missing. I went home at once. After going to Berkeley Road to fetch a photograph of my daughter I went to the police and gave a description of her, to aid in the search.'

He went to work the next day, Wednesday, he said, and on the following day wrote a letter to the prisoner, asking her to meet him. He had heard that Mrs Pay knew where the child was. The letter (which was now read out in court) he gave to his wife to take to Mrs Pay on the Thursday night. He went on:

'In consequence of the letter the prisoner came to see me in Spring Gardens on the following day at twelve o'clock. I said, "I want to see you about Georgie. When did you last see her?" She said, "About a fortnight ago. You don't think *I* know anything of her, do you?" I said, "No, but the report is going about that you know." She seemed very sorry that my child was lost, and said she hoped we should soon find her. I asked her then if she remembered what she had once said concerning Georgie, and she said, "Yes, I thought of it as soon as I heard she was lost." On a previous occasion when we had had some words she said if we had not been good friends again she would have taken Georgie away. When she was reminded of her words she said to me, "I only said that in a joke".'

Moore went on to say that the prisoner had then told him that she had been with Mrs Rutter, her sister-in-law, all the afternoon and evening of Tuesday, looking at the shops. 'On the following Monday or Tuesday,' he continued, 'she called at Winchester Street and saw me. My wife was present. She asked me whether we had heard anything of Georgie. I told her we had not. Afterwards she made several inquiries about the child. I saw some notes she sent to my wife with the same object. She continued to make these inquiries up to the time she left London.'

At this point one of the notes Esther Pay had sent to Mrs Moore was read out in court. In it she asked Mrs Moore to tell her husband to meet her, the prisoner, the following day, Friday, in the King's Road. Moore told the court that he went to meet her, continuing: 'She asked me whether I had any tidings, and told me she was going away. I arranged to meet her on the following day at Charing Cross Station to see her off. At Charing Cross I got her a ticket to Yalding and went with her as far as London Bridge. She had a parcel and birdcage with her, and I bought her a *Penny Illustrated Paper* containing the portrait of my daughter. Before I left her I asked if she would mind me letting Inspector Marshall know where she had gone, and she said she did not. On the Tuesday night following I received a letter from her.' The letter, beginning, 'My Darling' and written in very affectionate terms, was here read in court.

After Moore had told the court that he had visited the cottage of Mrs Pay's father some time previously, he was questioned about his visit to Yalding following the discovery of his child's body.

'On January 31st,' he said, 'I went to Yalding and in an outhouse there I saw the body of my child. On that day Mrs Pay was taken into custody. I saw her come out of the waiting room at the station when she was in custody and she said, "You don't think I've done this?" and I said, "No." I saw her again at the Westminster Police Station when she was being charged. She asked me why I had changed my mind, and I told her it was owing to the child being found so near her home; I thought she must be implicated in it.'

Cross-examined by Mr Clarke, Moore said that he had taken Mrs Maidment, with whom he had been living in Berkeley Road, to see the body of his daughter at Winchester Street. 'My wife didn't see Mrs Maidment,' he said. 'She was in another room.' Further cross-examined, he seemed unable to remember when he had married his wife – 'I'm not sure whether it was 1872 or 1873,' he said – or exactly when his daughter was born – 'either in 1874 or 1875'.

Then came a question that must have brought a few thrills to some of the eager spectators: 'How many times have you been married?' asked Mr Clarke.

'Once.'

'Only once?'

'My answer is once.'

'Only once?'

'I say I have been married once.'

'Have you been through the marriage ceremony more than once?'

'I can only say that Mrs Moore is my lawful wife and the only one I have.'

The judge intervened here: 'That is no answer. A person may have been married four times and give that answer with perfect truth.'

Moore: 'I can give no other answer.'

The judge: 'You must answer the question.'

Moore: 'Am I bound to say anything which will criminate myself?'

The judge: 'That is a different thing if you say so. You may say that you can't answer for fear of incriminating yourself.'

'That, then, my Lord, is my answer.'

Moore was then asked further personal questions and with his answers more details of his private life came out into the open. After saying that he and his wife had married after the birth of their son Harry, who was born in 1873, he was questioned about his relationship with his various mistresses, including Mrs Irwin at Bath and her sister Alice Day at Nunhead. Mrs Irwin had named her son Harry Williams, he said, which was the name by which he himself had first been known to her. The boy had only lived three days. He had seen Mrs Irwin yesterday and the day before yesterday and on a day in the previous August. With regard to Alice Day, Mrs Irwin's sister, he said that he had not seen her since she had come to him telling him that she was pregnant and claiming that he was responsible.

Mr Clarke then asked whether he knew a person by the name of Carroll.

Said Moore: 'I decline to answer.'

Mr Clarke: 'You must answer. Do you know a young woman by the name of Carroll?'

Reluctantly, and with a little prodding from the judge, Moore was forced to admit to yet another liaison. Up till the April or May, he told the court, he had been working as a carpenter at a house in Kensington Gardens and had made the acquaintance of a young woman by the name of Carroll who was a servant there. He went out with her several times and continued to walk out with her right up to the previous December. He had seen her as recently as yesterday, he said, but declined to tell where. Then, when the judge insisted that he answer, he said that he had seen her at Palace Street, Westminster. In answer to further questions, he said that he had seen her between December last and the previous day, adding that their association had continued right up to the present time.

Asked about his affair with Mrs Maidment in Berkeley

Road, he said his wife had not known that he was sleeping with Mrs Maidment and had never asked him. His association with Mrs Maidment had really only lasted till the time his daughter was lost, he said. After that time he had not visited her so often. He believed now that she was living with her husband once more. Asked from where had come the photograph of Georgina which his wife had had in her possession, he said be believed it had come from Mrs Pay, who afterwards had the photograph back.

He was then questioned about his own movements on the day of 20 December and said that he worked with a man named Heppel till eleven o'clock and with two others, Beaumont and Nightingale, till half-past eight. A man named Johnson kept the time-sheets, he said, and a dozen men had seen him at work.

Mrs Pay, he said in answer to questions, always appeared to show a real interest in the child. In the conversation six months previously she had said, 'I shall steal the child and bring it up myself.' When he saw her off to Yalding, he said, he went to London Bridge with her 'to make sure she had quitted London, as other people suspected her'. He had no object in getting her out of London, he said. He had had no ill-feeling against her during his improper intimacy with her.

After copies of the birth certificates of his children had been produced – including that of his child by Mrs Irwin – he was asked where Mrs Irwin was on 20 December. He said he did not know. Nor did he know the whereabouts of Alice Day. Neither of them, he said, as far as he knew, had any connection with Yalding. He was still on friendly terms with Mrs Maidment, and as far as he knew, Miss Carroll was two hundred miles away from London when his daughter disappeared. Miss Carroll had never seen his daughter, he added, neither had Mrs Irwin, nor her sister, Miss Day.

With this, Stephen Moore's evidence ended, evidence which had dragged through the mud the reputations of several now-sadder-but-wiser women, and which might also have served as a warning to any others, married or otherwise, who had possibly experienced feelings of attraction towards him. By the time his evidence ended there must have been humiliation in several breasts, apart from that suffered by his already long-suffering wife.

Dr Bond of London was called next, and he deposed to having assisted at the *post mortem* examination of the child's body on 1 February. The body was in a very decomposed state, he said, and must have been dead over a month, possibly two months. The death in his judgement was caused by strangulation. On the neck were signs of pressure, and internally there was extravasation of blood, indicating that great pressure had been used during life. There were no signs of death by drowning. There was undigested food in the stomach, showing that the child had partaken of a meal shortly before death – he would say within two hours. Cross-examined on the last point, he said: 'I should say the food had been partaken of less than three hours before death.'

Dr Bond was followed by Dr Wood of Yalding who supported Dr Bond's evidence. After this, Mrs Moore was called.

The Daily Chronicle said she 'appeared in a very weak condition, and was accommodated with a seat'. In answer to questions she said that the prisoner had been very kind to her daughter and used to take her out and buy her sweets and toys. The child was a very timid child, she said. She told how she and the children had gone to the house of a friend, Mrs Laing, in the morning and that the children had returned there to dinner after morning school. Mrs Laing gave Georgina a halfpenny after dinner, she added, and the child left at a quarter-past one for the purpose of playing about till school time at two o'clock. Georgina should have returned about a quarter-past four but she did not do so. On Thursday morning, the witness said, she saw the prisoner at her door and told her that she had lost Georgie. Said Mrs Moore: 'Mrs Pay said she knew nothing about her. She seemed very cool and didn't say much.'

She then testified to the fact that her husband had written Mrs Pay a letter, asking her to meet him. The prisoner, she said, after some pressure, agreed to see Mr Moore – but insisted that her husband, William Pay, did not know about it. The prisoner did come, Mrs Moore said, and subsequently sent several letters inquiring about Georgie, and several times used the expression, 'How sad it was.'

Mrs Moore went on to say, in answer to questions, that after the child's body was found in the water she was shown the clothes, which were the same as the child wore on Tuesday, 20 December. A little bow was missing. The black scarf, which was shown to her, and which was found in the water, did not belong to the child, she said.

Cross-examined, she said she knew that her husband was in the habit of going out with Mrs Pay. He was out a good deal previous to the child being lost. She had borrowed a photograph of Georgina from Mrs Pay to give to the police. Bills were printed of the child being missing, and Mrs Pay asked for some of them to forward to a relative of hers who was engaged on the railway. Mrs Pay appeared anxious about the child, she said.

The little boy Arthur Harrington, seven years old, was the next witness. He testified that he went to school in Westmoreland Street and knew Georgina Moore and her brother Harry, and also Lily Laing. On the Tuesday, 20 December, he said, Georgina came to school in the morning and stayed till twelve o'clock. After dinner he

saw Georgina with Lily Laing at a sweet shop near the
school. He saw Mrs Pay with Georgina. He did not know
her before. She had an ulster on, and either a hat or a
bonnet. Mrs Pay spoke to Lily Laing and the latter
answered her. Some time afterwards he was shown some
ladies at the police station and was asked to pick out the
lady he had seen with Georgina on the Tuesday. He
thereupon went and touched Mrs Pay.

Cross-examined, he said he did not remember ever
seeing the lady before. He only remembered the cloak, a
light one; no other lady had a cloak of that shape on. 'The
cloak she had on,' he said, 'was of the same colour as the
one the lady had on when speaking to Georgie.' Inspector
Marshall had told him to look out for a cloak like the one
the woman had on who was talking to Georgie. Questioned by the judge, he said he could not remember when
he first saw the woman.

Schoolteacher Elizabeth Fennell who was called next
said she was there when the boy Arthur Harrington
picked out the prisoner. He walked to and fro, she said,
and then put his finger towards her, the prisoner. Shortly
after Elizabeth Fennell's evidence was given the court was
adjourned till the following day.

The first witness to be called the next day, Friday, was PC
Hill. He stated that he knew the child Georgina Moore
well as she was in the habit of playing with his children,
and that he had known the prisoner by sight for about
two years. Between two o'clock and a quarter-past-two
on the afternoon of Tuesday, 20 December, he said, he
was coming out of a butcher's shop when he saw a woman
and a child walking along Sutherland Street towards
Ebury Bridge. He did not then identify the woman as Mrs
Pay, but described her subsequently as about 5'6" tall,
with a light ulster, dark hair, and a black hat. Later, on 8

February, he was at the police court to identify the woman. There were about a dozen women there, and he walked up and down the line and pointed out the prisoner as the woman. She in every respect resembled the woman he had seen with the child.

Cross-examined, he said he had repeatedly seen her so dressed before and after the day in question. He only caught a momentary sight of the pair and did not see the woman's face. He recognized her at the police court, he said, by the ulster and the hat. He had heard on 21 December of the loss of the child, and on the 22nd had mentioned to his superior officer what he had observed. It was not until 3 February, however, that he had contacted Inspector Marshall of the Criminal Investigation Department.

After PC Hill came a surveyor who gave information on the various distances of particular routes of interest in the case. He was followed by Mr Charles Barton, a fly proprietor of Paddock Wood, whose stables were two hundred and sixteen yards from the railway station. It was his habit, he said, to meet the 4.12 train from London, and some few days before or after Christmas he was at the stables when that train arrived. A woman and a child came to him. He did not know who the woman was, and could not say whether the child was a boy or a girl. Earlier, at the summary hearing, he had revealed that he was extremely short-sighted. There was nothing wrong with his hearing, however, and he went on to tell the packed courtroom that the woman had made inquiries as to the fare from Paddock Wood to Yalding. He told her the fare was four shillings and she expressed surprise, saying, 'So much?' 'Yes,' he told her. 'It's four miles.' She said, 'I thought it was about two.' At this he said to her, 'There'll be a train shortly and you can go for threepence.' 'I don't want to go by train,' she replied. He did not, he added, notice which way the woman and child went after leaving him.

At the hearing at the Westminster Police Court before the magistrate, the witness had said that it struck him as a curious thing that a woman should want to go by cab at a cost of four shillings, a distance she could travel by rail for threepence. He had never had such an application before or since, and afterwards he had spoken of it to his wife. When the woman had walked away, he added, she did not take the child by the hand; the child was running along beside her.

The next witness was nineteen-year-old Charles Cronk, an ostler of Paddock Wood, who had briefly known Esther Pay as Esther Humphreys in years gone by. About a week before Christmas, he said, he was standing before The Kent Arms at about 4.14 when he saw a woman and a little girl go by. They were coming from the station and going in the direction of Judd's Corner. The weather was dull and drizzly, a fine rain falling. The woman was walking at a fair pace. She was rather tall, about 5'8", and was wearing 'an ulster sort of thing' and carrying a bag or parcel. The child was walking a little way behind her. He heard the woman say to the child, 'Come along, my dear.' As the woman passed him he saw her face and thought it seemed familiar to him, that she was 'Esther Humphreys'.

Earlier, following questioning by the police during their inquiries, he had stood in the yard at the police court and, having been asked to pick out the woman he had seen, had failed to do so. Indeed, the only identification had come from Esther Pay, who, standing in the line along with the other women, had said to him, 'How do you do? I know you, you're a Cronk, aren't you?' At this he had said, 'Yes, but I don't know you.' 'Well, *I* know *you*,' she said.

Next came Samuel James. Examined by Mr Biron he

said he was a labourer living at Brenchley. Just before Christmas, he said, he was outside The Elm Tree public house when he saw a woman and child go by towards The New Inn; they were coming from Paddock Wood. The woman was wearing a light ulster, 'with a bit of black stuff' round her hat or bonnet, and carrying a small bag in her hand. She was of fair, medium height and was over thirty years of age – perhaps thirty-six. The child was dressed in dark clothes; he didn't see her face. Later he had been taken to Lewes Prison to see if he could identify the woman. The prisoner was among the women there but he had picked out another person.

Next came William James, who said he was with his father, the previous witness, outside The Elm Tree public house one evening before Christmas when he saw a woman and a child come along the street. The woman, who seemed to be dark-complexioned, was wearing an ulster. The girl had a fringe across the front of her forehead, and was wearing high boots. It was on 20 December, he said; he was quite certain about the date, as that was the day he had worked on a particular farm. Later he was asked if he could pick out the same woman from the dozen or so women standing in a line at the Lewes Prison. Asked whether he had picked out the prisoner, he said, 'I stood in front of the prisoner but didn't pick her out because she looked so bold' – a remark which brought a laugh in the court. As he was leaving, he said, he had picked out a woman other than the prisoner.

After the Jameses came Hannah Pout, wife of Henry Pout who was landlord of The Queen's Head, Queen Street, Brenchley. She said that on Tuesday, 20 December, between four and five o'clock a strange woman came to the house and had half a quartern of gin just inside the door. She was between thirty and forty and of a fair height, with something light on and a black veil over her face. She had a parcel in her hand. Cross-examined, the witness could not say whether the woman had worn a hat or a bonnet. She thought the parcel, she said, was a paper parcel and about the size of a pair of boots. The parcel lay on the woman's arm as she drank the gin. She had been to London to try to identify the woman but had been unable to do so.

Cross-examined, she said she saw no child with the woman. Asked, 'Do you recognize the woman in the dock as being the woman who came to your house?' she replied that she did not.

Mrs Pout was followed into the witness box by Stephen Barton, a labourer from Yalding who recalled being at The Queen's Head on 20 December. He was there with some other men about half-past four, he said, when a woman came in, was supplied with some gin and stayed a few minutes. Later, he said, he had been to London to see if he could recognize the woman and had picked her out from among fourteen or fifteen women. The woman he had picked out was exactly similar to the woman who had come into the public house, he said.

Cross-examined, he said it was beginning to get dark when the woman entered the public house; there were not yet lights in the room and the place where she stood was darker than any other part. He looked out of the window when she was leaving, he said, and saw her walk down the road. She had a child with her.

The next witness was another who had been drinking in The Queen's Head that afternoon of 20 December. He, George Waghorn, said he was in the public house when the woman came in. She was rather tall and wore a heavy fall over her face. He did not notice her clothes. She stood in a dark passage and drank something. Standing in the dark passage as she was he could not see her very well. After she left he went to the window and saw her walking with a child towards Yalding. The child had 'long, lightish' hair hanging down its back. He was unable to recognize the child, he said. He was unable to pick out any particular woman when later asked to do so, he said.

Thomas Judd, erstwhile landlord of The New Inn, on the Yalding road, came into the witness box next, and stated that on the night of 20 December, about six or half-past six, a woman and a child came into his house and went into the front room. Shown a photograph of Georgina Moore, he said that to the best of his belief it was the same child. He thought the little girl was about seven or eight, about the same age as his own daughter. She seemed to be very tired and weary. The woman asked him for twopennyworth of hard biscuits, but he had none of these and she then asked for some soft biscuits and he supplied her with twopennyworth. She gave the child one of the biscuits. He also served the woman with three-pennyworth of whisky. Since that time, he said, at the direction of the police, he had been to look at a number of women and had identified the prisoner as being the woman who had come to his house. When the woman and the child left the premises just after seven, the woman asked the way to Laddingford and he showed her the way. The child when she left seemed weary and drowsy and did not seem to want to go. They went off in the direction of Laddingford. He had never seen either of them before. The only words he heard between the two came from the woman, who said to the child, 'Come dear, eat your cake.' He had, he said, given specimens of the biscuits to Inspector Marshall.

Under cross-examination he said that it was a wet, foggy, drizzling night when the woman and child came to his public house. He had not noticed whether they were dark or fair. The child, he said, had a white, woollen shawl around her.

After further evidence which proved conclusively that the incident had taken place on the night of Tuesday, 20 December, this completed the prosecution's evidence with regard to the journey which they believed had been taken by Esther Pay and the child.

The next witness, a labourer named George Bradley, who lived near The Railway Inn at Yalding, about a hundred and fifty yards from the spot where the child's body had been found, told of hearing a cry on the night of 20 December. He reached home about five in the evening on that day, he said, and after he had had his tea, something between six and nine o'clock he heard a scream from the direction of the hop gardens, which were close to the spot where the body was found. In cross-examination he said he could speak definitely as to it being the 20th of December, though would not swear that it could not have been later than nine o'clock. He heard the scream only for an instant, and went to the door, but hearing nothing more he took no further notice. There were floods at the time, he said, and on the Monday the water was high. In re-examination he said he should think that on the Tuesday evening the towing-path opposite the spot where the body was found would be under water – though not much. The body was found opposite to where the path was higher, he said, and he didn't think the water would have risen more than a foot over the path.

The prosecution then produced witnesses who, they believed, would prove that the prisoner had been with her parents in Yalding on the night of 20 December.

The first witness called with regard to this move was Mrs Susan Kemp, who lived at Lillyhoe Farm, Wateringbury, and who said that she knew Mr and Mrs Humphreys. A few days before Christmas, she continued, on the Wednesday or the Thursday, she went to Yalding Station with her children and her aunt, and there took tickets for the ten o'clock train to Maidstone where she had some business to transact. On the platform, she said, she saw Mrs Humphreys, and a woman with her who was leaning on a fence with her hands to her head. She saw the woman's face, she said, and heard Mrs Humphreys address her as Esther.

Mrs Kemp went on to state that since that time she had seen a number of women brought together and had picked out the prisoner from among them as the woman she had seen that day at Yalding Station. The witness said that a conversation passed between her aunt, Mrs Ashby, and Mrs Humphreys in the other woman's presence, and that she herself, the witness, joined in the conversation. During this conversation, she said, the woman with Mrs Humphreys mentioned that she had been married twelve years and had no children. Mrs Ashby then said to Mrs Humphreys, referring to the woman with her, 'What's the matter with your daughter? Isn't she well?' Mrs Humphreys replied, 'I don't know about that, but she don't like going home because her husband uses her so bad.' After that remark was passed, the witness and her children and Mrs Ashby got into the carriage in the fore part of the train, and the witness noticed Mrs Humphreys and the other woman go to the rear part of the train, but did not observe them enter any carriage.

Under cross-examination, Mrs Kemp said that as far as her knowledge went that was the first time she had seen the woman who was with Mrs Humphreys. The conversation on the platform commenced by Mrs Ashby inquiring about Mrs Humphrey's brother who, in the summer, had committed suicide by shooting himself. She remembered the August Bank Holiday when she was on the platform with her children and Mrs Ashby, and she would swear that she did not see Mrs Humphreys and her daughter Esther on that occasion.

The next witness was Mrs Kemp's aunt, Mrs Susan Ashby. She fixed definitely the day of her being at Yalding Station with her niece as Wednesday, 21 December. While waiting on the platform, she said, she saw Mrs Humphreys, whom she knew, and another woman who was leaning on a rail. She asked the woman, she said, if she did not feel well, but the woman made no reply. She did not take any notice of the woman's complexion or dress, she said, and could not say whether the prisoner was the woman. She confirmed that she had asked Mrs Humphreys what was the matter with the lady, and that Mrs Humphreys had replied that she did not know excepting that she objected to going back to London because of the ill-conduct of her husband. Under further examination Mrs Ashby said that Mrs Humphreys had been wearing a red and black plaid shawl.

Martha Sayers, living at The Blackbird and Thrush Inn, Kent, said that on the August Bank Holiday she had gone to the club feast at Mr Brassey's Park, Aylesford, and had taken a train from Yalding Station. Whilst waiting on the platform, she said, she saw Mrs Kemp and her children, and also Mrs Ashby. She had seen nothing, however, of Mrs Humphreys and her daughter on that day.

The prosecution now turned their attention to trying to destroy the alibi that Esther Pay had set up for herself for the day and night of 20 December.

The first witness in this respect was Mrs Eliza Clarke who had some most interesting things to tell the court. She began by saying that she and her husband had lodged at the house of Mr and Mrs Pay in Westmoreland Street and had been due to leave for other lodgings at Peabody Buildings on 20 December. On that morning, Mrs Clarke said, Mrs Pay told her that she was later going to the Aquarium with Mrs Harris. At about half-past twelve in the afternoon the witness had to leave the house, and asked the prisoner to look after her children briefly while she was gone. At that moment, said Mrs Clarke, Mrs Pay was at her bedroom door, and was wearing her ulster. Mrs Pay agreed and Mrs Clarke left the house. Returning fifteen minutes later, however, Mrs Clarke found the prisoner had gone. Mrs Clarke went on to say that later, that evening, she returned to 51, Westmoreland Street in order to return the keys and pay the rent owing to the prisoner, but found the prisoner's rooms closed and locked up. The next morning between nine and ten o'clock, she said, she returned once more to the house, and knocked twice but got no answer. About twenty minutes past one that same day the prisoner came to Peabody Buildings to see the witness, Mrs Clarke, and said to her: 'Mrs Moore has lost little Georgie,' adding that she was so sorry about it. She then went on to say to the witness, 'I didn't come back until ten o'clock last night, and both I and Mrs Rutter got very wet. I was with Mrs Harris at the Aquarium, and in the evening I went with Mrs Rutter.' At this time the prisoner was wearing an ulster and a brown dress.

The next time they had any conversation, said Mrs Clarke, was on the following Tuesday when Mrs Pay told her that Mrs Moore had still not found Georgina, and added, surprisingly, that her own (Pay's) husband had said to her, 'I believe you know where the child is.' At this, said Mrs Clarke, she had said to Mrs Pay, 'That's the general opinion.'

Later, said Mrs Clarke, Mrs Pay said to her, 'I don't believe Mrs Moore will find the child again; it's been missing so long.' Questioned further, the witness said that possibly a year earlier she had heard Mrs Pay speak of what a bad man Mr Moore was, and that she would 'stick' him or 'shoot' him – she couldn't remember which it was.

On one occasion, the witness continued, Mrs Pay had

told her that Inspector Marshall had been to see Mrs Rutter. 'But she was drunk at the time,' Mrs Pay said, 'so God knows what she said to him. I suppose they'll get me hung between them.' After that, said Mrs Clarke, the prisoner requested that if anything should come out of the matter affecting her, the prisoner, she, the witness, should 'speak up for her'.

After some examination which attempted, unsuccessfully, to connect the scarf found in the water with the prisoner, Mrs Clarke was allowed to step down.

She was followed by her husband who stated that all the time he had been moving in and out of the house at 51, Westmoreland Street during the removal of their belongings on the afternoon and evening of 20 December he had seen no sign whatever of Mrs Pay. Further, he confirmed Mrs Pay's visit to Peabody Buildings the following day at about twenty minutes past one, when, during the 'few minutes' of her stay she had said that she had been 'to the Aquarium with Mrs Harris yesterday', and had also said that Mrs Moore had 'lost little Georgie'.

Mrs Elizabeth Laing of 7, Westmoreland Street was called next, and she stated that on 20 December she went to 51, Westmoreland Street where she had a conversation with Mr Pay. Mrs Pay, she said, was not at home.

She was followed by her husband, Simeon Laing, a nephew of Mrs Pay. He told the court that when he returned home from work on the evening of Tuesday, 20 December, Mrs Moore, who was staying at his house, told him that her daughter was missing, after which he and Mr Moore went out to search for the child. On the 26th or 27th of December, he said, he met the prisoner who said to him, 'Has Mrs Moore heard anything of little Georgie?' 'No,' he replied. Said Mrs Pay at this, 'I'm very sorry for Mrs Moore, but it serves *him* damned right.' She then asked him, the witness, whether he knew anything about it, to which he replied:

'Well, to tell you the truth about it, I believe you know more about it than any breathing soul.' At this she said, 'How can you think I could do such a cruel thing and be such a cannibal as to take the child away? I was always very fond of Georgie.' 'I know that,' Laing said, 'and that's my reason for suspecting that you know more than anybody else.' The prisoner had then gone on, Laing said, to repeat protestations of her love for the child, telling him that she had spent shillings on the child on sweet-stuffs, toys and cakes, and adding that that, no doubt, was the reason people suspected her. She told him that on 20 December she went out and did not return until past midnight; she had been out with Carrie Rutter, her sister-in-law, and they had gone to Fulham and Hammer-smith and other places. When she returned home, she said, her husband had said to her, 'Moore's people have been sending round here about little Georgie who has strayed.' Said Laing, 'She told me she said to her husband, "Well, I'm very sorry for Mrs Moore, but as for Moore, it serves *him* damned right."'

Cross-examined, he said the prisoner suggested that handbills should be circulated all over the country and that the Home Secretary should be contacted in order that a reward might be offered for the discovery of the child, and information be conveyed to foreign countries, as many children had been decoyed away from England.

The next witness was Emma Harris who said she was on friendly terms with the prisoner but that it was not true that they went to the Aquarium together on 20 December. They had not been out together anywhere during the week before Christmas. As far as she could recall, she had not seen the prisoner since the 13th or 15th of

December. She had not been to the Aquarium for years, she added.

She was followed by Caroline Rutter, the sister of the prisoner's husband. She stated that it was not true that she and the prisoner had been out together in Fulham Road looking at the shops on the afternoon of 20 December. She had not seen the prisoner on 20 December. She had seen nothing at all of the prisoner between 17 December and the 23rd. With regard to the 20th, she said, Mrs Pay told her that she had had 'a spree' at home with Mrs Harris, but as she did not wish to get her (Mrs Harris) into trouble she asked the witness to state that they had been out together.

Cross-examined, she said that her brother, William Pay, the prisoner's husband, had since gone away from Westmoreland Street, and that she did not know where he had gone. He was not a sober man, she added, and had a very violent temper.

Mrs Rutter was the last witness called that day, and after the Pays' marriage certificate had been produced, the case was again adjourned.

Friday, 28 April. A good crowd of spectators had gathered on this, the third day of the trial.

The first of the prosecution's witnesses that morning was James Rutter, the husband of the last witness. He testified that on one occasion after Christmas, Esther Pay had told him that Inspector Marshall had been to see her to inquire where she was on the day the Moore child had been lost. She added that she had told the inspector that she had been 'for a walk with Carrie to see the shops in King's Road and Fulham', and asked him to tell his wife to say the same thing if questioned on the point.

Following Rutter, an ironmonger and his assistant testified to having sold a single firebrick to a woman around the time of Christmas – though they had later been unable to identify the prisoner – after which Inspector Marshall was called to the stand. He related how he had twice gone to the home of the prisoner to ask her whether she knew anything of the disappearance of the child. On the first occasion Stephen Moore was present, he said, and the prisoner, after saying, 'I know nothing about the child,' turned to Moore and said, 'You know where I was on the 20th; I was with Carrie Rutter.' On the following day, Marshall said, he called again. This time as he was questioning Mrs Pay he heard a voice calling from the next room. 'That's my husband,' said Mrs Pay. 'He's in bed drunk. And he thinks you're Moore, so you'd better leave.' Obedient, Marshall had left the house.

The Inspector went on to tell how he had gone to view the child's body with Moore in Yalding and later had arrested Mrs Pay at her parents' house. After relating what the prisoner had said on the way to London with regard to her not being allowed to speak to Moore, the inspector gave way on the stand to Sergeant Cussens.

The sergeant repeated the things the prisoner had said to him, and stated that when he and the inspector called at the home of the prisoner's parents on the morning of 31 December there was much excitement. The prisoner's father came to them when they were about to leave and asked his daughter what it all meant, and whether she was guilty or innocent. She threw her arms around his neck and said to him, 'I am innocent.' Mr Humphreys then said to her, 'If you are innocent you can stand up and have no fear of either God or the Devil.'

The next witness was Dr Dupré, an analyst who had been given some of the biscuits such as those the witness Judd had sold to the woman on the evening of 20 December. He said he had also examined the contents of the dead child's stomach, having received a jar of semi-fluid consisting chiefly of starch. All the starch that could be identified was wheat starch, corresponding with that in the biscuits. Any wheat starch would correspond to it. There were particles of the inner skin of the grain. There were also a number of currants intermixed and some particles of corned beef. There were no currants in the biscuits. The starch could not have been in the body longer than two hours before death. In his opinion the child ate well almost up to the point of death. The contents of the jar smelt strongly of pineapple essence, possibly showing that the child had eaten sweets shortly before her death.

The next head of evidence concerned the trains to and from Yalding around the time of the child's disappearance. It was pointed out that a train left Charing Cross Station at 2.52 P.M. and reached Paddock Wood at about 4.10. From Paddock Wood a Maidstone train left at 4.29, reaching Yalding a few minutes later.

With witnesses testifying to the fact that William Pay, husband of the prisoner, had been at work all that day of the child's disappearance, the prosecution's case was brought to a close.

Mr Clarke then opened the case for the defence.

In his address to the jury he said he would produce witnesses who would prove that the prisoner and the prisoner's mother could not have been seen on Yalding Station platform on the morning of Wednesday, 21 December. To this effect the first witness was called. This was William Humphreys, the prisoner's father. On his appearance Esther Pay burst into tears and wept bitterly.

Humphreys, seventy-two, said he worked as bailiff for a local hop-farmer, having been in the man's employ for the past fifty-one years.

In his evidence he stated that before 28 January his

daughter had not been home since the previous August, when she had come down two or three days before the August Bank Holiday. He recalled, he said, that she and his wife had gone off together by train on the August Bank Holiday, returning the following day, Tuesday. His wife was ill with neuralgia from the 15th to the 26th of December, and had had to wear a handkerchief around her head. She was ill for eleven days, during which time she was not able to go out anywhere, although she could walk about. He used to leave her at home and find her there when he came in. He usually went to bed about nine, sometimes at half-past nine, he said, though there were times when he did not return from work till eleven.

This completed the evidence of Mr Humphreys, during which his daughter, Esther, had regained some of her self-control. With the calling of the next witness, however, she again began to weep.

This was Mrs Mary Humphreys, the prisoner's mother. She confirmed her husband's evidence as to her being ill with neuralgia from the 15th to the 26th of December. She was confined to her house the whole of that week, she said, and never went out. Her only son lived near her and had visited her every day, his wife twice a day. On the August Bank Holiday, she went on, she and her daughter had been on Yalding Station platform waiting for the train to Maidstone when they had met Mrs Harris and Mrs Ashby. She spoke to them about her brother's death in the previous June, and while she spoke to them her daughter Esther was standing beside her. As for what she had been wearing, she had been in mourning. She hadn't been wearing a red and black plaid shawl. She had such a shawl, but she had never worn it going to Maidstone. She had not seen her daughter between August and January, she said, adding, 'And on that I would take a solemn, dying oath before God and the Lord Jesus Christ.'

Under cross-examination she said that when unwell in the December she had had no doctor, and that she had used to get up and come downstairs and walk about. Questioned about the shawl, she said she wore it about the neighbourhood, and would wear it to go to Yalding Station. It was a warm, winter shawl which she would not wear in August. Asked whether she had said – as previous witnesses had sworn – that her daughter did not like going back to London as her husband ill-treated her, she said it was untrue that she had said such a thing, and indeed had not been aware of such a fact until the January. It was equally untrue, she said, that the women had asked her whether her daughter was ill. She agreed that she customarily addressed her daughter as 'Esther'.

At this point two letters, dated the 16th and 26th of January from the prisoner to her mother, were read out. Couched in affectionate terms, the letters spoke of the prisoner's trouble through her husband's drinking, and said that she feared she should have to leave him and go into service, and that before doing so she would like to spend a week with her parents. In the second letter were the sentences: 'You are the only one I care for now,' and 'I can tell you about it better when I write.'

The newspapers would report the following day that during the reading of the letters Esther Pay became much affected and cried.

After Mrs Humphreys had stepped down, her son, daughter-in-law and daughter were questioned, at which they gave confirmatory evidence as to Mrs Humphreys being unwell in Christmas week. This concluded the evidence for the defence and Mr Clarke got up to address the jury on behalf of the prisoner.

In his speech, which took up the rest of that day and

part of the following, he reminded the jury that their verdict would determine a question of life or death, in which, above all else – as a mistake would be irrevocable – the proof ought to be such as to exclude all reasonable doubt. The case, he said, was of an extraordinary character.

The case for the prosecution, he stated, was that Moore had had an immoral intimacy with the prisoner and that, because he broke it off – only, as Moore said, for her sake and to spare her difficulties with her husband – she, out of revenge, took his child away in the middle of the day in the open street, took her down to Yalding, and there in the darkness of the night, barbarously and cruelly murdered the poor child; then, with superhuman strength, she had flung the body, loaded with a heavy brick, into the river, close to a path leading to her father's house. Surely such a murder was too barbarous for a woman to commit, he said, even if there were a motive for it.

He then suggested that the murder had not been committed in Yalding at all, but had been committed in *London*, and that the dead body had been brought to Yalding and placed at a spot in the river near to where it had been found, and that if the prisoner had done it then she must have meant to be detected. Whoever had done it had meant to throw suspicion on her. It was no hasty murder, he said, committed after some outburst of ungovernable passion. Obviously it was a deliberate act, and, he believed, the act of a man. For only a man could have fastened the wire so firmly around the brick; and likewise the attaching of the brick to the child's body was performed with practised hands. Further, the length of eight feet of wire between the body and the brick clearly showed that the body was meant to rise – the brick remaining as a weight to anchor the body to the spot – so as to throw suspicion upon the prisoner. Indeed, the

prisoner herself had suggested this theory, observing that
'somebody had done it intending to plant it' upon her.

Mr Clarke then went on to state that he did not believe
it was *possible* that the murder could have been committed at Yalding that night, nor, indeed, as he had said, at
Yalding at all. It was supposed by the prosecution, he
said, that the prisoner had chosen the night of 20 December for the dreadful deed; and if so she must have gone
out into the street at Pimlico with the brick and the wire
in her hands to try to find the child – but at the outset,
and at every step of the case, the theory was obviously
absurd. In truth she had no motive for revenge or
resentment against Moore, and no witness but Mrs
Clarke, her lodger, proved any expression of hers which
could indicate such feelings. There was no evidence of
such feelings in her mind, nor was there cause for them,
for in truth Moore had never deserted or abandoned her,
but had merely discontinued intercourse for her own sake.
Why, then, should the jury, without evidence, presume
the existence of such feelings, and suppose that she was
nourishing and cherishing such deadly feelings of
revenge?

But assuming a motive for such a dreadful deed, he
went on, what a day to choose for it – the day when her
lodgers, the Clarkes, were leaving! – whereas if she had
only waited until the next day they would have been gone.
But, the theory of the prosecution was that she went out
into the street to find the little girl and that, contemplating
such a crime which would entail her absence from the city
all day and night, she had told a witness that she was
going to be with a friend in town. Then the theory was
that she took the child to Paddock Wood by rail, and
then, instead of going by rail to Yalding a few minutes
later, went a roundabout route by road. But if it was
suggested that it was still partly light and that she feared

recognition, why had she not waited for the child after afternoon school? The theory was, though, that she took the child by road to Yalding, walking the whole way from Paddock Wood, and that she returned to London the next morning by train. He urged that the improbabilities of the theory were such as to require evidence of great cogency. Yet though the woman had called, unnecessarily, at various places and had been seen by various persons on the road, hardly any of them had recognized her at all, and none of them satisfactorily.

At this point the case was adjourned, to be resumed the following morning, Saturday, at which time Mr Clarke continued with his address to the jury.

Referring to the prisoner's statement to various persons, the police among them, that she had been out with her sister-in-law Mrs Rutter on the day of the murder, Mr Clarke said the only evidence to the contrary had come from the Rutters – which evidence, he said, was by no means conclusive. He then went on to dismiss the prosecution's theory that the prisoner had been seen at Yalding Station on the morning of Wednesday, 21 December, stating that the prosecution's witnesses were obviously mistaken, confusing that day with a meeting that had taken place in August. From beginning to end, he said, the case rested upon the statements of a series of witnesses called to speak to the identity of a person seen between Paddock Wood and Yalding on 20 December, but the difference in their views as to the kind of person they had seen really amounted to evidence for the defence. Further, the fact of a full, undigested meal being found in the child's stomach was proof that the murder was not committed at Yalding. Dr Bond had said that the meal could not have been taken more than two or three hours before death, and if that were so, it must have been taken on the road. However, the fact that there was no evidence of a meal having been taken between Paddock Wood and Yalding was conclusive proof that the murder must have been committed in London.

After this speech with its rather surprising assertions he then went on to speak of the actual commission of the crime and the disposal of the body.

Owing to the state of the floods on the night of the 20th, he said, which submerged the towing-path, it was impossible to suppose that a woman, in the darkness, would have waded through the water, and then have been able to throw the body of the child and the brick, which together must have weighed 60 or 70 pounds, a distance which must have exceeded eight feet.

He went on to say that the words the prisoner had spoken to Sergeant Cussens were fully consistent with her innocence, and, further, that it was difficult to believe that, were she guilty, she would have gone to stay with her parents near where the body was. He ended by saying that it would be one of the happiest days in the lives of the jury if they were able, nay, bound to say that upon the evidence before them the prisoner was not guilty of the crime, and by doing so restore her to her home and her parents.

As counsel resumed his seat there was a slight attempt at applause which was immediately suppressed. During the resumed speech the prisoner had once again shown much emotion, particularly at the beginning. The more cynical might wonder if perhaps she had learned that the poisoner, Lamson[1], had been executed the previous morning and that as a result she had become more aware of her own mortality.

However, now that the defence counsel had put its case

---

[1] Dr George Lamson was hanged for having murdered his young brother-in-law in Wimbledon in December 1881.

it was the turn of Mr Poland for the prosecution to give his reply. After detailing the evidence of identification, and contending that on the whole it was perfectly reliable and conclusive, he alluded to the alleged interview on the Yalding Station platform on the morning after the murder. He pointed out that both Mrs Ashby and Mrs Kemp were purely independent and disinterested witnesses, whilst on the other hand Mrs Humphreys and the other members of her family were personally interested in the fate of the prisoner, and therefore their evidence must be considered with extreme caution.

There was also the fact, he said, that the prisoner was not seen in London until twenty minutes past one on Wednesday, a period extending from two o'clock the previous afternoon. The prisoner's statements as to her going out with Mrs Rutter and Mrs Harris on the Tuesday afternoon had been proved to be absolutely false. If she was in London on the afternoon of that day, why had not one or more witnesses been called to prove where she was? The conduct of the prisoner and her apparent anxiety with regard to the fate of the child were clearly that which might be expected of a guilty woman, her object being to cast suspicion on other persons whom they now knew to have been unduly familiar with the child's father.

The jury had to bear in mind, Mr Poland went on, that such a crime could only be brought home by circumstantial evidence. There could be no *direct* evidence, for if the person who took the child away had been recognized by any person who knew her, the crime would not have been committed – the risk would have been too great. Therefore the jury could only look at all the available evidence that had been put before them and ask themselves whether on that evidence they were satisfied that the prisoner was guilty of the crime charged in the indictment.

So far as the prosecution were concerned they had placed before the jury all the facts obtainable, and having done that had done their duty. It now remained for the jury to do theirs.

With Mr Poland's address completed, the judge, Mr Baron Pollock, began his summing up, saying in the course of it that this was a case in which the jury could pursue no middle course. It was patent to all that the trial was one of those in which only circumstantial evidence could be adduced, and it was for the jury to determine what parts they could accept and what they could reject. He did not think on the present occasion they would have any great difficulty. If they felt there were any facts on which they could not perfectly rely, they would of course give the benefit of the doubt to the prisoner. The first consideration for the jury was what motive the prisoner could have entertained for contemplating so barbarous a crime.

In reviewing the evidence and tracing the movements of the prisoner and the deceased – as indicated by the evidence for the prosecution – during the afternoon of the day on which the murder took place, he laid great stress upon the evidence deposed by Mr Judd, the landlord of The New Inn, whose house was visited on the day in question by apparently the same woman and child as had been observed at different points of the journey from Paddock Wood. He then said that there was not a single fact that pointed to Moore as being the murderer of his own child. It was not fair to assume that because he was a dissolute and immoral man he would take the life of his child without any special motive. It was a remarkable fact, he then said, that the prisoner, or those acting on her behalf, had not produced any witnesses to prove where she was on the afternoon of the murder.

In closing, he said that in all his experience he knew of

no case in which greater pains had been taken to obtain every possible piece of evidence bearing upon the momentous issue before them. He then begged the jury to apply all the powers of mind they possessed to the case, and to say deliberately and fearlessly whether they found the prisoner guilty or not guilty.

At sixteen minutes past five the jury retired and the prisoner returned to her cell. Hardly twenty minutes had passed, however, before the jury returned to their places, and great excitement was manifested as the prisoner reappeared in the dock and took up a position against the front rail. She seemed quite composed while the names of the jury were being called over, giving no sign of any inward emotion. Then, the Clerk of Arraigns, having asked the foreman of the jury if they were agreed on a verdict, and having received an answer in the affirmative, asked what that verdict was.

'Not guilty,' said the foreman.

There was applause, and while the relatives of Esther Pay wept with relief she herself smilingly bowed to the jury and thanked them. Moments later, even as her relatives were striving to embrace her, she was being conducted from the courtroom, shortly afterwards to leave the courthouse by a rear entrance to avoid the great crowd that had assembled outside the front of the hall.

So Esther Pay's ordeal was over, for which she owed much to her defence counsel, Mr Clarke, though it seems clear that the judge, going by his summing up, was convinced of the woman's guilt. However, Esther Pay was acquitted, and with her acquittal she was freed and the terrible murder of little Georgina Moore fell into the catalogue of unsolved crimes.

Was Esther Pay innocent, or was she guilty?

The only accounts of the case this writer has come

across are by H. L. Adam in the book *The Fifty Most Amazing Crimes of the Last Hundred Years*, and *Killers Unknown* by John Godwin. Both of the brief accounts are very much on the side of Esther Pay, Adam's being subtitled: *The terrible ordeal of an innocent woman brought into the shadow of the gallows by mistaken witnesses*, and Godwin's: *The Martyrdom of Esther Pay*.

H. L. Adam, in his belief that Esther Pay was a woman wrongly accused, pointed an accusing finger at an unnamed man, obviously William Pay, Esther Pay's husband. Adam was quite sure that the motive was revenge, but that the revenge was directed not at Moore, but at Esther Pay herself. His account, however, contains so many errors in the most basic facts that not much credence can be placed in his theory.

In John Godwin's account he appears to have taken his information from Adam's earlier piece and to have further embellished Adam's already fanciful story with fruits of his own fertile imagination. Hence in a chapter full of inaccuracies the thirty-five-year-old, long-married Esther Pay becomes 'a comely, dimple-cheeked young woman' of twenty-five, and the labourer Stephen Moore a 'clerk', a 'gentleman' of 'the lower middle-class' who 'drank tea with his little finger extended'. Suffice to say that Godwin's irritating account – he even invented names for some of the principal characters – has no place in any factual catalogue and can be dismissed by anyone interested in researching the true story.

With regard to the theory of Esther Pay's defence counsel (and later the writers Adam and Godwin) that the killing was carried out by a man, it might be noted that no witnesses ever came forward to testify that they had seen Georgina Moore with a man that day.

Even so, there were some who supported a belief in Esther Pay's innocence. In the editorial column of *The*

Morning Post the following Monday, 1 May, a great deal of space was given to a reflection on the case and the trial, in the course of which was said:

If Pay desired to kill the child it seems almost inconceivable that she should have taken her down to a neighbourhood in which she [Pay] was known, and where she ran such an imminent risk of being recognized. Prima facie, Yalding was the last place to which Pay would take Georgina Moore in order to kill her . . . We fear very much that the murder of this little child will be added to the long category of undiscovered crimes.

On the other hand it is clear that other parties believed that Esther Pay was guilty. *The Penny Illustrated Paper* of 6 May wrote:

                    The Pimlico Mystery
remains a mystery. The trial of Mrs Esther Pay, upon the charge of murdering the little Pimlico girl, Georgina Moore, at Yalding, terminated at Lewes on Saturday, the accused being acquitted. Mrs Pay and her relatives evinced much emotion on hearing the verdict of the jury. Naturally! The accused woman has had as narrow an escape of being sentenced to death as prisoner ever had . . .

So, did she or didn't she? As far as this writer is concerned, Esther Pay was as cold-blooded and calculating a murderess as ever was.

In putting voice to such a belief, however, one should examine the case against her.

First the motive. If Esther Pay did not kill Georgina Moore, then who did? Who else had a motive for such a terrible crime? H. L. Adam maintains that Georgina was killed in an act of revenge against Esther Pay, but this theory does not stand up to examination. As was pointed out to the jury, Stephen Moore might have been dissolute and immoral, but that does not mean that he would have murdered his little daughter simply in order to be revenged on his erstwhile mistress. By all accounts Moore loved Georgina. Besides which, what did he have against Esther Pay? Nothing. Anyway, the speculation here is pointless as he had a completely watertight alibi for all that day of 20 December.

William Pay also had an alibi for that day, so he can also be dismissed as a suspect. Besides which, he had no motive for murdering the child. He knew that Moore and his wife had been lovers, but that affair had ended six months before. He was described as a drunkard and a violent man, granted, but a man who attacks his wife in a rage on finding that she is unfaithful is very unlikely to be the same man who would plot to steal and cold-bloodedly murder an innocent child.

It is interesting to note with regard to William Pay that he was not present at his wife's trial. Going by his earlier comments to Inspector Marshall, he was convinced of his wife's guilt from the very start. His absence from the courtroom when his wife was on trial for her life indicates that he had not changed his mind, otherwise he would surely have been there to offer support in her hour of need, in spite of past differences.

In the matter of motive, however, Esther Pay certainly harboured resentment against Moore. This was revealed in several instances, i.e. when she told Inspector Marshall how Moore had ill-used her; also when she told Mrs Clarke that she would 'stick' or 'shoot' Moore, and her words to Moore himself that if they had not remained friends she would steal Georgina away from him – and this latter threat is hardly a threat from a rational mind. Furthermore, when speaking of the child being missing, she said it 'served Moore damned right'.

The truth of the matter is that Moore probably tired of her and was glad of the excuse to finish the association, besides which he had already begun to see another woman. Just a glance at his career and it becomes evident that he found it impossible to sustain a relationship. Whether the woman were his wife or a mistress, the pattern was the same: each one was soon discarded for a new face.

Esther Pay's defence counsel said that she had no reason to resent Moore as he had not abandoned her, but had simply terminated the relationship 'for her sake'. It is clear, though, that she had remained in love with Moore, or was in some way obsessed by him. The letter she wrote to him from her parents' home at the time of the child's discovery proves that: 'Darling . . . take care of yourself, although I know it is no use asking you to do that for my sake now . . . I will see you if you want me.' And her words also indicate that she still wanted him, and would have gone to him very readily. Her loving him had done her no good, though. He had deserted her and then formed relationships with other women. Clearly then, Esther Pay, unhappy with her husband and seeing her erstwhile lover with other women while she, abandoned by him, still wanted him, found her obsession growing. And, caught fast in her obsession, she determined on revenge for the wrong she felt her lover had done her.

Having established that Esther Pay definitely had a motive for the murder, it is also seen that she had the opportunity. Whereas both her husband and ex-lover had alibis for that day, she had none, for the one she had tried to fashion for herself had very quickly come apart. Both Mrs Rutter and Mrs Harris made it clear that she was not with them at the time she claimed, and though Esther Pay's defence counsel said that there was only the word of those witnesses for such a contention, their word must be believed. For what reason did they have to lie and so try to send an innocent woman to the gallows?

And, of course, Esther Pay's lying as to her whereabouts on that Tuesday afternoon and Wednesday morning begs the questions of *why* she was lying, and where in fact she was at that time. She was not in London, or someone would surely have come forward to make it known, particularly when so much – her life – was at stake.

H. L. Adam contends that she spent the particular time with a lover but that she would not reveal who it was or where they had been together. His contention doesn't stand up to examination. Faced with the possibility of death as she was she would have told the truth. After all, her own marriage was as good as finished, and she had left her husband (or he had ejected her), so what did she have to lose by telling of some secret meeting with a lover? She had nothing to lose and everything to gain.

Her defence counsel said she would not have left home on 20 December to take the child away as her lodgers, the Clarkes, were due to leave on that day and they owed her rent. But Esther Pay had already made her plans for that particular day, and clearly had made them well in advance. Further evidence of her singleness of purpose is the fact that Mrs Clarke asked Esther Pay to look after her children for a few minutes that lunchtime while she slipped out. When Mrs Clarke returned only fifteen minutes later, however, Mrs Pay had gone, leaving the Clarke children unattended. Neither was Esther Pay at the house that evening nor the following morning.

Esther Pay was acquitted almost certainly because of a lack of really satisfactory identification of herself and the child together.

There were two identifications in London, one by the little boy Harrington, and the other by PC Hill, but once the woman and the child got to Kent the sightings of them became regarded as unreliable. And yet those sightings are not as unreliable as might at first appear.

Having arrived at Paddock Wood her first thought was to hire a cab to Yalding. She didn't want to go there by train as she couldn't take the chance of being recognized at Yalding Station in the company of the child. Finding, however, that the price of the cab was far more than she had bargained for, she set off to walk. Later, the cab-driver, Barton, who was extremely short-sighted, was unable to describe her or the child.

From then on the woman and the child were seen at various intervals on the long, roundabout road from Paddock Wood to Yalding, and although only two out of the eight witnesses were later able to pick out Esther Pay from among more than a dozen other women, surely it must be clear that that woman and that child were Esther Pay and little Georgina. The defence counsel, speaking of the series of witnesses called upon to speak to the identity of a person seen between Paddock Wood and Yalding on that evening, said that 'the difference in their views as to the kind of person they had seen really amounted to evidence for the defence'.

This was by no means so. From the testimonies of nearly all the witnesses one gains a very clear picture of Esther Pay's tall figure as, carrying a parcel *and* a bag (she was certainly seen carrying a parcel, and no woman would leave her home to travel for several hours without her bag), and, clad in a light-coloured ulster and wearing a dark hat with a veil around its brim, she strides along the road towards Yalding. It is miserable, drizzling. Running at her side, or sometimes a few steps behind, is little Georgina Moore, wearing a dark ulster, high button boots, and a straw hat, her long fair hair hanging down her back.

Soon after 4.15 they are walking the two hundred and fifty yards from Barton's stables to The Kent Arms where they are seen by Charles Cronk, then a further distance of almost a mile to The Elm Tree public house at Judd's Corner where they are noticed by Samuel James and his son William. Passing on by, the woman and child walk a further mile to The Queen's Head public house, Queen Street, Brenchley. Here, leaving the child outside, Esther Pay drops the veil on her hat and goes inside where she buys some gin and stands drinking it in the dim passage, just inside the door. Her presence here is remembered by the landlady and two of her customers, one of whom later picks her out at an identity parade. On leaving The Queen's Head, the pair are next seen at The New Inn, almost a mile further on, where they both go indoors. Here the woman drinks a little whisky while the child nibbles at a biscuit. When the pair left, said the landlord, Thomas Judd, it was after seven.

The road from The New Inn continues directly to the spot where the child's body was found, some two and three-quarter miles further on.

The shorter, direct road from Paddock Wood to Yalding was given in court as approximately three and three-quarter miles, while the longer, roundabout route as five and a half miles. Little Georgina Moore walked a long and miserable road to her death that night.

A point with regard to the relatively small number of witnesses who later identified Esther Pay as the woman they had seen – five out of a total of twelve: it should not be surprising that there were not more, for most of the sightings were only casual ones – a woman passing by with a child, or having a quiet drink in a shadowy corner of a passage in a public house. The reader has only to ask himself whether he would be able to recognize some shop assistant from a time two months previously in order to realize the difficulties in such a task.

A further point made by defence counsel was that Esther Pay had no need to eschew the train and to walk from Paddock Wood to Yalding to escape being recognized. All she had to do was to snatch the child later in the day, following afternoon school, at which time she would have been protected by the darkness. The answer to this is that Esther Pay intended being back at home in Pimlico that night. She had no intention of staying away all night. It was the price of the cab fare from Paddock Wood to Yalding that so delayed her and changed her plans.

As stated, it was the prosecution's belief that Esther Pay spent the night of the 20th at her parents' home and returned to London the following morning. The witnesses they produced supported their theory although it was denied by Esther Pay's parents. As the prosecution pointed out, however, Mr and Mrs Humphreys had an interest in the case and therefore their statements should be regarded with caution. On the other hand the two women, Mrs Kent (who later picked out Esther Pay on an identification parade) and Mrs Ashby, who claimed to have seen Esther Pay and her mother on the station platform that morning, had no vested interest in the matter, and it can hardly be supposed that they would have lied when such a lie could lead to a woman's execution. Also it is very doubtful that they were mistaken as to the time of the alleged meeting. It is interesting also that Mrs Ashby described Mrs Humphreys as wearing a red and black plaid shawl on that December day. Mrs Humphreys admitted that she owned such a shawl and said that it was a winter shawl and that she would indeed wear it going to Yalding Station.

A further interesting point with regard to the question of Esther Pay's staying or not staying with her parents that night of the 20th was her father's certainty as to the time and duration of his wife's illness, neuralgia. He said she had been ill for eleven days, from the 15th to the 26th

December. One wonders how he could be so certain of the time span and the dates; one has only to look back into one's own past to a time when one suffered from, perhaps, a bad cold, to realize that the date of such an event can remain very elusive.

The prisoner's defence counsel insisted that Esther Pay's behaviour at the time of the loss and subsequent discovery of the child was that of an innocent woman. On the contrary, however, her behaviour was not consistent with that of an innocent person. When Mrs Moore went to inquire of Esther Pay as to Georgina's whereabouts Mrs Pay was very unresponsive ('She seemed very cool and didn't say much.') and soon closed the door. Mrs Moore was so disturbed and unsatisfied with the response that she got her husband to write to Mrs Pay asking her to meet him, which, 'after some pressure', she agreed to do. Further, when told of the disappearance of Georgina, Mrs Pay said that it 'served Moore damned right'. Also, in spite of the fact that Mrs Pay had just been writing what was in effect a love letter to Stephen Moore, as soon as she was told by Inspector Marshall that she was being arrested she tried to put the blame on to Moore. In addition, with regard to her behaviour, she said on that same morning that she had not heard that the child's body had been found the previous day. This is very hard to believe; one imagines that word of such a discovery would spread through the area like wildfire. It would be interesting to know whether Mr and Mrs Humphreys knew that morning of the discovery of the body. Inspector Marshall, however, does not appear to have asked them such a question.

Esther Pay's defence counsel further contended that as a substantial amount of undigested food had been found in the dead child's stomach she must have been killed within two hours of her having eaten her midday dinner on that fatal Tuesday, as there was no witness to the child having stopped to eat a meal at any public house on the road from Paddock Wood to Yalding. The contents of the child's stomach consisted mostly of wheat starch, a number of currants and small traces of corned beef. There was also the strong smell of pineapple essence. The answer is obvious: if Esther Pay did not buy food for the pair of them on the road (apart from the biscuits sold them by Thomas Judd) then she brought food with her – perhaps corned beef sandwiches and cake. Esther Pay left her home just after 12.30 on the Tuesday afternoon and it is likely that the child was murdered sometime after eight o'clock that evening. Esther Pay stopped to buy liquor on two occasions, the first time gin and the second time whisky – on the first occasion leaving the child out in the rain while she stood in the warm drinking her gin. Concerned as she was, then, for her own comfort it is surely not conceivable that she herself would have gone eight hours without a single bite to eat!

In all likelihood she and Georgina ate at The New Inn where Mr Judd sold them the soft biscuits. He said they went into his front room. They were also there alone, obviously, for any other witnesses to their presence would have been sought and brought forward. Further, according to Mr Judd, they were there for over half an hour, and it is very unlikely that he would have remained in the room with them all that time. It was probably at this time, during his absence or his casual coming and going, that they ate whatever food Esther Pay had brought with her in her bag. At one time, Judd said, he heard the woman say to the child, 'Come dear, eat your cake.' Clearly, then, the child was eating cake at some time in Mr Judd's front room.

Another point used in the defence of the prisoner was the fact that the child had been found so near to her parents' home. While the prosecution felt that it was damning evidence, the defence contended that it was an indication of her innocence – the body was *meant* to be found, they said; the length of wire, eight feet, had been quite judiciously used to allow the body to float to the surface while remaining anchored to the spot. It indicated, they said, that someone had deliberately tried to plant the killing on the prisoner, for Esther Pay would not have left the body so close to her parents' home.

But of course the body was *not* meant to be found. If it *had* been, and was meant to have been found near the home of Esther Pay's parents, it would not have been wrapped around with wire, weighted with a firebrick and thrown into the river. It would have been dumped somewhere in the vicinity where it was *certain* to have been discovered. As it was, if the bargee had not gone out of his way on the river, if he had not actually gone slightly aground, the body might not have been discovered for a very long time. The firebrick and the length of wire were there to keep it hidden, and hidden it was intended to have remained.

Incidentally, the defence's contention that the length of wire was judiciously used to allow the body to float to the surface and so be discovered is quite nonsensical. For one thing, if that had been the intention then the killer would have to have been quite sure of the depth of the river at that particular spot!

With regard to the towing-path being flooded at that time, there was considerable doubt that it would have been under water at the spot next to where the body was found – which is further indication that the body was put there by someone who knew well the river and the surrounding area. Quite obviously the body was found at that particular spot in the river *because* the adjacent path was higher at that point and so was above the flood.

Esther Pay chose the river at Yalding because it was handy and because she knew the area well. And she was sure that, once in the river with the weight, the body would never be found.

In further regarding Esther Pay's choosing to dispose of the body near her home it must be remembered that a hundred years ago people travelled very much less than today; it was a time when many people never moved out of the particular villages where they were born. It is hardly surprising, therefore, that she chose a place close to her home. She would have to choose from those places she was familiar with, and it is likely that she could not be sure of the suitability of any other spot. In addition, if, after disposing of the body, she should chance to need a place nearby where she could safely spend the night, then having her parents' home just across the field would have made her chosen venue an ideal place.

One comes then to the actual means Esther Pay used in killing the child and disposing of the body in the river.

In an imagined scenario one can see Esther Pay and Georgina Moore moving along the road beside the canal, crossing over the bridge and then, opposite The Railway Inn, stepping down on to the towing-path that leads beside the swollen river. A hundred and forty yards or so along and the path splits in two, the left fork moving up beside the railway line.

On this particular night of 20 December 1881 Esther Pay continues on the towing-path a few yards beyond where the footpath branches off. And there in the darkness of the night, and in the added shadow of the copse that stretches almost to the water's edge, she comes to a stop and takes the child by the throat. Georgie is able to scream, just once, a scream that is heard by George Bradley in his home beside The Railway Inn. He moves to the door, opens it, but hearing nothing further closes the door again.

On the river bank the child is soon dead, and Esther Pay unwraps the parcel, taking out the firebrick and the wire. Crouching over the body she binds the brick to the chest, and then wraps the wire several times around and then bends the body so that the knees are brought up to the brick. She then binds the whole with the rest of the wire. It remains then only to throw the body into the water, and far enough away from the bank so that it will not be discovered.

Esther Pay's defence counsel, speaking as if she were some frail, weak little woman, said that she could not have thrown the body – weighing sixty or seventy pounds – a distance of some eight feet into the river. But she was a tall, fit woman, and such a task would have presented her with no difficulty. One can imagine how she could do it. Standing at right angles to the river with feet astride, she stoops and lifts the trussed body by its arms. It is easy then. Swinging the body back and forth a couple of times to gain momentum, she pitches it out into the swollen waters of the river.

And it is done.

It was perhaps as the child was thrown from the bank that the weight of the brick caused the wire to unwind to some extent. If not then it unwound later as the body turned and rolled, shifting back and forth in the tidal flow of the river. Whatever happened, however, for the time being the body was well out of sight; the only sign remaining being Georgina's hat which failed to sink and was eventually caught on the willow bough.

The roundabout route from Paddock Wood to Yalding seems long even today, when travelling by car, and to little Georgina Moore all those years ago who had to walk in the rain and dark, the muddy, then-unmade road must have seemed a very long and exhausting one.

Several of the scenes connected with the crime have changed a good deal over the hundred-odd years that have intervened. On the road only The Elm Tree remains of those public houses that figured in the evidence. Likewise The Railway Inn, where the body was laid and where the inquest opened, has also been swept away, although The George Inn at Yalding, where the inquest was resumed, is still going strong.

The scene of the crime, too, has much changed since the murder took place. The sheltering trees that crowded the bank between the river and the railway are still there but the river itself at that point is very different. The tongue of land formed by the loop of the Medway at the point where Georgina Moore was killed has since been made into a little peninsula – the loop itself now a marina – and the far side of the once quiet water is now chock-a-block with cabin-cruisers, house-boats and pleasure barges.

A short distance from the river bank, higher up, the footpath still runs beside the railway line. The stile is still there, too, leading one over the line, up the steep steps on the other side and so over the fields towards the Maidstone road. There, just a few yards along to the north, the Humphreys' house still stands. A large cottage of some dozen rooms, and now divided into two dwellings, it appears little altered from the outside and looks almost as remote as it must have done on the day Inspector Marshall went there – without a warrant – to arrest Esther Pay for the murder of Georgina Moore.

And it was a murder of which she was undoubtedly guilty, and if the prosecution and the investigating officers had been a little sharper she would very likely have been convicted. Certainly the judge appeared to be convinced of her guilt.

Not, of course, that Esther Pay's champions would have it so. In the defence counsel's address to the jury, Mr Clarke said, 'Surely such a murder is too barbarous for a woman, even if there were a motive for it.' This of course is nonsense, as any brief study of criminal history will show; by no means has the male sex maintained a monopoly when it comes to cruelty. Faced with such a comment as that from Mr Clarke there immediately spring to mind such names as Elizabeth Brownrigg, Jeanne Weber, Kate Webster, Mary Ann Cotton, and Constance Kent.[1]

The murders for which Esther Pay and Constance Kent were charged have certain things in common. In both cases the victim was a child, which in each instance was not the subject of personal animosity. The motive, too, was the same.

Of what became of Esther Pay following her trial and acquittal nothing is known. We are left merely with a portrait of the woman as she was at the time of the murder. And a most horrific murder it was. There must be few to equal it for its cold barbarity – taking the little child, Georgina Moore, and embarking with her on a journey of some seven-odd hours for the sole purpose of killing her, while all the time pretending such solicitude – 'Come dear, eat your cake.'

And how can one explain such a crime, except perhaps as resulting from some kind of madness that sometimes grows out of embittered and warped emotions. As Congreve said, 'Heaven has no rage like love to hatred turned, nor Hell a fury, like a woman scorned.'

---

[1] See *Cruelly Murdered* by Bernard Taylor.

Murder in Fish Ponds Wood

The Tragedy of the Luards

BY BERNARD TAYLOR

Tragedy had touched the lives of the Luard family before the summer of 1908. Early in the winter of 1903 they had learned that the younger of their two sons, Eric, twenty-five years old, a lieutenant in the Queen's Own Regiment and the King's African Rifles, had died of fever during a campaign in Garrero, Somaliland.

In common with millions of other bereaved parents, Major-General Luard and his wife survived the tragedy. But they could not rest while their son's body lay on foreign soil. So, almost three years later they had his body brought back to England. In 1906 on 12 July, in the churchyard of the little Kent village of Ightham, Charles and Caroline Luard stood side by side while their son, Eric Dalbiac Luard, was buried. The small, lowstanding headstone his parents erected to his memory bears the inscription: 'Brought home to Ightham . . .'

So, perhaps – as much as parents are ever able to – with their son having been 'brought home', the Luards were at last able to come to terms with his death. They had their other son – albeit he was abroad – and they had one another. In spite of their bereavement they had, in fact, a great deal – material comforts, respect, friends and contentment. In all likelihood they saw nothing ahead of them in their advancing years but a continuation of their quiet lives in their mutual happiness with one another.

The contentment they knew was not to last. Five years after their younger son's death there was another tragedy – one that would bear its own fruit within a matter of days. And where the first tragedy had rocked the foundations of their happiness, this one would completely wipe them out.

The murder of Mrs Luard, on a summer afternoon in 1908, caused a sensation throughout the country.

It took place on 24 August in the county of Kent, 'the garden of England', on the verandah of a summerhouse in a particular spot which must surely be one of the most naturally beautiful in the whole county. The area in which the murder took place is known as Seal Chart, which is situated between the villages of Ightham and Seal, about four and a half miles from Maidstone and about the same distance from Sevenoaks. Today the area of Seal Chart remains relatively unspoilt, but in 1908 it was even more sparsely populated, most of its acreage being in the shape of woodland.

Not every visitor to the spot, however, saw beauty there. A reporter for *The Daily Chronicle*, unimpressed by the scene, wrote shortly after the murder:

A peculiar, forbidding spot, this Seal Chart, consisting of large stretches of fir forest, intermingled with small oaks, birches and other trees. Its woeful appearance is only relieved at this time of the year by the glow of pink heather and the brown of the fading bracken. In the midst of this wooded wilderness is situated the ill-fated summerhouse. Its loneliness is sufficiently apparent without the aid of a dastardly crime to darken its prevailing gloom . . .

The first intimation that any members of the general populace had of the dastardly crime was when Major-General Luard came hurrying into his neighbour's stable yard with the news that his wife was dead. 'Dead! Shot!' he gasped out, and then again: 'Dead! Shot!'

Major-General Charles Edward Luard, fit and active for his sixty-nine years, was a tall, upright man with close-cropped grey hair, balding, and drooping moustache. His wife Caroline had been born of wealthy parents in Gill-foot, Cumberland. Known as Daisy to those close to her, she was tall, fair-haired and attractive, and eleven years younger than her husband. The photograph in the contemporary newspapers shows a face which, for all the fineness of its bones, has strength and determination. Very much liked and respected in the area of Ightham, she devoted much of her time to helping the poor, both in their homes and, prior to its recent closure at that time, at a nearby cottage hospital for children.

The Luards had married in 1875 and had two sons, both of whom, like their father, opted for military careers. At the time of the murder their surviving elder son, Charles, was with the Norfolk Regiment, serving in South Africa.

General Luard's career had been a distinguished one. The son of Major Robert Luard, he had spent his early years in Ightham. A descendant of a Huguenot family who had sought refuge in England about 1685 at the revocation of the Edict of Nantes, Charles Luard received his commission in the Royal Engineers at the age of seventeen. In 1864 he was in command of the 9th Company at Woolwich – the year when a powder magazine at nearby Erith exploded and blew a huge break in the river wall. Under the directions of the young Luard the breach was successfully closed in the time of a single tide, so averting the flooding of the adjacent area. Four years later Luard accompanied a mission to the Sultan of Morocco, and in 1871 devised the scheme for the rearmament of the Fortress of Gibraltar. In 1882 he was promoted lieutenant-colonel and, in command of the Royal Engineers in Natal, spent some years in South Africa, serving in anticipation of a resumption of hostilities with the Boers. In 1886 he was made a colonel, and a year later promoted major-general. Soon afterwards he retired

from the army, at which time he and Mrs Luard went to
live in a large, attractive house known at Ightham Knoll,
situated on the main road between Ightham and Seal, and
from where for the next fourteen years, Major-General
Luard served as a Kent county councillor.

In August 1908, the general and Mrs Luard had been
married for thirty-three years, and, by all accounts, thirty-
three happy years. Living quietly in their country home,
they were often observed by the neighbours as they
walked arm-in-arm along the country lanes, 'just like a
honeymoon couple', as one of those neighbours was later
to describe them.

Among the closest neighbours to the Luards at Ightham
Knoll were a retired stockbroker, Horace Wilkinson, and
his wife, who lived at Frankfield House, a large dwelling
standing in its own spacious grounds, Frankfield Park, of
which the nearest border to the Luards was about half a
mile away to the west. The Luards and the Wilkinsons
were good friends and often spent time in each other's
company, sometimes dining together. Frequently at other
times the two wives would meet to talk and pass some
pleasant, companionable hours. The two women had been
associated in innumerable charitable works, which association, it was said, had brought the couples together. One
result of the relationship between the two families was
that the Luards used the footpaths and by-ways of the
Frankfield Park estate as freely as if the land were their
own.

One particular venue sometimes used by the two
women was an attractive summerhouse that stood within
the Wilkinsons' grounds at its most south-eastern corner.
Referred to usually as 'the Casa', the summerhouse was
situated three hundred yards from the nearest dwelling –
the cottage inhabited by Mr Wilkinson's coachman – and
was set on a high hilltop overlooking Fish Ponds Wood,

the latter so named for the string of five large, rectangular fish ponds situated at the edge of the wood near the Sevenoaks road. The summerhouse, built twelve years earlier for Mrs Wilkinson to replace an older model that had been destroyed by fire, was of a bungalow design. It had a tiled roof, was comprised of several rooms, and had, running the length of its front, a verandah with a cement floor which was enclosed by a wooden balustrade. Partly erected on piles, the building was set on the edge of a glade, two of its sides shadowed by overhanging trees. From its verandah one was afforded a beautiful view of the wooded hillside below.

During the colder months the summerhouse was usually empty and locked, but in the warmer times Mrs Wilkinson would open the place up and sometimes live in it for a week or two. At other times it was used as a sort of picnic venue and, occasionally, it was said, Mrs Wilkinson and Mrs Luard would meet there to chat over a cup of tea. At the time of the murder the Wilkinsons were away from the area, and the summerhouse had been empty and locked for a month.

According to the account of General Luard of the movements of himself and his wife immediately before the tragedy on that Monday, 24 August, the following story emerged:

As the general and his wife planned to go away for a brief holiday at the weekend, the general stated that day his intention of walking to the Wildernesse Golf Club at nearby Godden Green after lunch to fetch his clubs. In a generally wet season it was a pleasant day and Mrs Luard said she would go part of the way with him for a walk; she couldn't stay out long, though, as she was expecting a visitor, a neighbour; a Mrs Stewart from nearby Batswood Cottage, Ightham, had been invited for afternoon tea.

At 2.30, calling to their Irish terrier Scamp, the Luards

set off from Ightham Knoll. They began by walking a
little over half a mile along the main road which ran
towards Sevenoaks, then, near a spot known as Seven
Wents, turned off to the left to take a narrow path which,
leading through Fish Ponds Wood for a third of a mile,
brought them to the summerhouse. The narrow pathway,
winding through the tall bracken, led them right onto the
summerhouse's verandah, which they traversed to the far
end, at which, regaining the path again, they continued
on their way. A further three hundred yards along the
path and they reached a wicket gate leading on to a
narrow lane with, on their left, a bridle path. At this
point, which was close to St Lawrence's School, they
parted, General Luard to continue on to the golf links,
and Mrs Luard to return to Ightham Knoll to prepare for
her visitor. As Mrs Luard turned to begin her return
journey, the general watched her for a few moments until
she was hidden from his view by a bend in the winding
track. Then he went on his way.

Going straight on to the clubhouse at Godden Green,
General Luard picked up his clubs and set off back
towards Ightham Knoll, reaching it – with the help of a
lift in a motorcar – about 4.30. On his return he was
surprised to find that his wife was not in the house but
that the visitor, Mrs Stewart, had arrived and was waiting
in the drawing room. Going in to meet her, the general
apologized for his wife's absence, and then, after waiting
for a few minutes, gave the visitor some tea.

The time went by, and still there was no sign of Mrs
Luard. After a little while Mrs Stewart said she had better
be going as she had to get home to meet a friend coming
from the railway station. The general, by now alarmed at
his wife's continued absence, rose with her, saying that he
would walk part of the way with her and go on to look for

his wife. When he had called Scamp to him once again, he and Mrs Stewart left the house.

Together they set off along the main road – the same route taken earlier by the general and his wife – walking for about fifteen minutes until they got to Seven Wents. There at 5.15 they parted, Mrs Stewart to return home and the general to take the path through the wood, the one he had taken earlier and by which he expected his wife to return to Ightham Knoll.

It was quiet and peaceful that late summer afternoon as the elderly man and his dog made their way along the path that wound through the thick bracken. The only sound was that of the birdsong. The general, though obviously somewhat uneasy at his wife's tardiness, could have had no inkling of the cause of it. Perhaps, in search of some reason, he told himself that she must have met some neighbour and fallen into conversation, uncharacteristically forgetting the time and her appointment – or perhaps there had been some minor crisis in the area and her services had been required. Whatever went through his mind he could not have guessed that there had been a catastrophe of such magnitude that his world would never be the same again.

As he approached the summerhouse the dog ran on before him and was soon out of sight. Then, as the roof of the building came in view he heard the dog whining. A few moments later the verandah of the summerhouse was right before him.

And there, lying on the verandah's cement floor, was the body of his wife, the dog standing beside her.

'I thought at first,' the general was to say later, 'that she was in a fainting fit, but on going closer I saw that there was blood on the floor. Then I thought that possibly she had burst a blood vessel. On going still closer I saw that her face and head were covered with blood, especially her head . . .'

Mrs Luard lay prone on the cement floor of the verandah, her head resting on the right cheek in a pool of blood. The skirt of her dress was torn. Rather unnaturally her arms were stretched upward with the palms uppermost. Beside her body lay one of her gloves, half inside-out, and the general saw that the rings had gone from her left hand. Looking more closely at her head, he saw that she had been shot. Taking her arms, he laid them at her sides and then felt for her pulse. Her hand was cold. She was quite dead.

After a moment he turned from the summerhouse and ran.

About three hundred yards away were the farm buildings of his neighbour, Mr Wilkinson. He hurried towards them, making for the cottage of Wickham, the coachman, running breathlessly into the garden and shouting out for him.

Inside the cottage was Mrs Annie Wickham, the coachman's wife who, earlier in the afternoon, had heard shots. She had been at the door with her daughter at the time. 'It was a very quiet afternoon,' she later told a reporter from *The Courier*, ' – one of the quietest I can remember, and we could hear every sound clearly. Not even the jays were making their usual noise. Suddenly the stillness was broken by a sound of a shot from the direction of the Casa. It was a peculiar kind of shot, as if it had gone through something. Then we heard two other shots fired in succession. I said to my daughter who was with me at the time, "My word! I don't know what they're killing up there, but they mean to make sure of it."'

She described also how General Luard came into the garden that afternoon. 'I thought no more of the matter,' she said, 'until I saw the general come down to my gate.

He was looking like to die himself. He was groaning and gasping for breath.' To the obviously distraught man, Mrs Wickham said concernedly, 'God bless us, sir, you do look bad. Is there anything I can do for you?'

The general didn't answer her question but asked where Wickham was. When she said that he was at the stables he simply said, 'Oh, dear,' and hurried off. As he moved away from the gate Mrs Wickham turned to her daughter. 'Something dreadful must have happened,' she said.

On the Wednesday following the killing, Mrs Wickham's husband, the coachman, would tell reporters of his own part in the drama.

'The general rushed into the stable yard where I was cleaning harness,' he said. 'He was breathing heavily, and it was obvious that he had been running hard. He was greatly agitated and couldn't speak. I said, "What's the matter?" but still he couldn't speak, although he tried to reply when I questioned him. I took him by the arm and led him to the harness-room box, telling him to rest a moment and get his breath. At last he gasped out, "Dead! Shot!" "What are you talking about?" I asked, and he repeated the words, "Dead! Shot!" Realizing that there was something very wrong I sent for the butler . . .'

Harding, the butler, told *The Courier*'s reporter how at just before six o'clock he was summoned from Frankfield House to the stables. Arriving in the harness room, he said, he found the general 'almost frenzied with grief' and barely able to tell of the terrible discovery he had made. Said Harding, 'He just kept gasping out, "My wife is dead. My wife is dead." I could make nothing of it; he was almost incoherent with grief.'

Harding said then that he asked the general whether Mrs Luard had perhaps fainted. Said Harding, 'I fancy he replied, "It's worse than that."'

'It was no time to ask for explanations,' Harding

continued. 'I gave him my arm and he took me to the wood. At times I almost had to carry him. He told me nothing. He sobbed and sobbed.'

As the general, the butler and the coachman started off through the trees they were followed by two more of Mr Wilkinson's employees, Daniel Kettel, and another gardener on the estate. Harding later described the walk through the wood, with the general groaning and gasping at his side as they went. 'The brutes!' the general cried out at one moment, ' – they've killed her!'

'We made the best of our way to the summerhouse,' said Harding. 'It was terrible for all of us. The general, in his distress, would walk quickly for a few steps, and then would stop as if paralysed by the thought of the loss he had sustained. As we got through the wood to the bungalow I saw the body of Mrs Luard lying in a pool of blood. The general's terrier was with us and it dashed ahead of us and licked Mrs Luard's face. Immediately that happened the general threw himself loose from my arm and rushed to the body. He knelt beside it, felt his wife's heart, and then, sobbing bitterly, took her hand and cried out her name over and over. I told some men whom I saw to run for the police and a doctor. Before they came the vicar, the Rev. Shaw Hill Scott, arrived, and he knelt down by the dead woman's side and comforted the poor general.'

When a policeman, PC Marsh of Seal, appeared on the scene shortly afterwards he at once sent word to his senior officers at Sevenoaks. Superintendent Taylor received the call at seven o'clock and, assisted by Sergeant Paramour, immediately set off. In the meantime the vicar managed to persuade the general to leave the scene and accompany him back to Ightham Knoll.

The police officers from Sevenoaks appeared at the summerhouse just a few minutes after the arrival on the scene of a doctor, also from Sevenoaks, Dr Mansfield. It was about 7.50 by then, and quite dark.

Word of the murder, meanwhile, had been spreading through the neighbourhood, one who heard it being the representative of the *Sevenoaks Chronicle and Kentish Advertiser*, who reported:

On hearing of the murder our representative drove to the spot. Going through Seal groups of villagers were standing about discussing the shocking discovery, it not then being known who the victim was. It was not until the *Sevenoaks Chronicle* reporter returned to Seal that it became known that the wife of General Luard had been discovered shot dead.

Driving with all speed to the Seal Chart schools, our representative made his way through a winding bridle path, and suddenly came across a summerhouse, the path in question leading right on to the verandah. Dr Mansfield, of Sevenoaks, was then bending over the body, which was lying prone on the verandah . . . It was a weird, ghastly spectacle, as night was closing round, and all the light available was a motor lamp from Dr Mansfield's car, and two or three candles . . .

While the doctor and the police were examining the body General Luard returned and asked if it could be taken home to Ightham Knoll. The police concurred, and when they and the doctor had completed their work Superintendent Taylor gave instructions for the body to be taken inside the summerhouse until a conveyance arrived. It was discovered, however, that the doors were locked, and a window had to be broken before the door could be opened. That done, Mrs Luard's body was carried inside and laid on a mattress on a camp bed.

A little while later Wickham arrived with a horse-drawn van and Superintendent Taylor directed that the mattress be brought out and laid inside it, after which Mrs Luard's body was placed upon it again. Then, slowly, the van was drawn through the dark woods to Ightham Knoll. Behind it, following in 'a dazed, aimless way', walked the general, accompanied by the vicar. They were followed not long afterwards by Dr Mansfield who, once arriving at Ightham Knoll, proceeded, with the assistance of another doctor, Walker, to carry out a *post mortem* on the body.

In the meantime, the darkness having made any real attempt at investigation almost a waste of time, Superintendent Taylor posted men at various entrances to the woods. He would get the search really under way in the morning.

The investigations began again at daybreak, some of the police officers beginning a search of the surrounding trees and thick bracken while others did what they could to build up a picture of the events of the previous afternoon.

The murder, for murder it clearly was, was a very terrible one, and even more shocking for the fact of its having taken place in a quiet spot like Seal Chart. Very swiftly several police officers from surrounding towns were seconded to the area to assist Superintendent Taylor. Colonel Warde, Chief-Constable of Kent, had been a close and personal friend of the Luards, and he was determined that everything possible would be done to find the killer of his friend's wife.

All the police had to go on at the start were those factors that were immediately discernible at the scene of the crime, and what they gained from their observations and those of the general, the doctor and others who were there in the vicinity at the time or just prior to it.

Mrs Luard had been shot twice in the head, once behind the right ear and again at a spot just above the cheekbone, low in the left temple. She was found lying prone on the balcony, her head in a pool of blood. From head to waist her clothing was saturated with blood. Her hat had come off and was lying two or three feet from her head. Her dress had been torn, the flounced skirt having been ripped from the waistband. Afterwards, it was clear, an attempt had been made to rearrange the dress, for the skirt had been pulled down tightly over the heels. On examination of the dress it was found to have a hole in it, and it was realized that the pocket had been cut away. The left-hand glove of the woman had been pulled off and was found lying partly inside-out. The three rings Mrs Luard had worn on her left hand were missing. On two of the fingers there were abrasions.

One of the first things the police did was to get from the general a description of the missing rings and circulate it to the Press. Promptly the newspapers carried the description:

One plain gold wedding ring, one gold ring with 'Ishi' on blue enamel; and one diamond ring set with a large diamond in the centre, encircled by eight smaller diamonds.

Apart from the rings, the dead woman's pocket was also missing, and also the purse it had presumably contained.

The investigations by the police soon found evidence to fix, within a few minutes, the time of the murder, discovering that Mrs Annie Wickham, the coachman's wife, had heard the shots at 3.15 while she was standing at her door. She had heard no cry of any sort, however, she said. Daniel Kettel, the gardener, supported her story, saying that at 3.15 he had distinctly heard shots – three of them.

With the time of the killing established, Superintendent Taylor then sought evidence to support General Luard's alibi, and subsequently found several witnesses who had seen him near the golf links very shortly after the shots had been fired.

Unfortunately no firearm had so far been found near

the spot, nor even the spent cartridges, in spite of careful searching. In a search for footprints the officers did find a track through the bracken leading towards the Wilkinsons' stables, but it didn't go very far. It had been very much hoped that they would find footprints immediately around the summerhouse. Unfortunately, however, much of the ground was carpeted with pine needles, added to which, by the time they got to searching it a number of persons had already tramped about the area.

There was one find, however, in which much hope was invested: close to the verandah one of the constables found a number of scraps of paper. A piece of paper had been torn up. The fragments were carefully gathered up.

While newspaper reporters converged on the area the investigators continued their search among the trees while other policemen had to be maintained at the different entrances to the woods, keeping away the large numbers of villagers and other sightseers who had come to view the scene of the crime.

What, everyone wondered, was the motive for the killing? Was it robbery, as the initial reports suggested? The fact of Mrs Luard's rings and purse being missing pointed to such a supposition. Some newspapers carried reports of the police being informed of a man having been seen leaving the summerhouse at the time of the crime. They were the first rumours of many, and had no foundation in fact.

Other newspapers stated the belief that the killer was very likely to have been a hop-picker. It was the beginning of the hop-gathering season, and in spite of the very wet weather which was beginning to spell ruin for the hop harvest, the villages of Kent were, as usual, visited by very large numbers of regular seasonal workers, along with hawkers, tramps and gypsies, many of whom found shelter in the woods. With regard to the latter groups, the regulations provided that they should not camp for more than twenty-four hours on one spot, and must leave at the end of that time. Practice, however, denied the rule, and the gypsies and other transients were said to remain in the district for much longer periods.

There were numerous stories circulating illustrating the dangers to be found in the woods at certain times. One came from the son of the Wilkinsons, the owners of the summerhouse. For quite a long period when the weather was suitable, he told one newspaper reporter, he would frequently sling a hammock in Fish Ponds Wood. Upon one of these occasions, he said, he was attacked by a gang of poachers. He was calmly sleeping in his hammock when he was disturbed by the gang, one of whom was armed with a knife. Before the young man had time to defend himself one of the gang aimed a blow at him with the weapon. Fortunately, the blade caught the support line of the hammock and instead of the knife injuring him he fell to the ground. As he did so his assailants made off through the wood. They were never identified. It was within ten yards of this spot that Mrs Luard met her death.

Following the *post mortem* Dr Mansfield said that the examination had revealed a wound at the back of the head of the dead woman, and he was of the opinion that the wound had been inflicted with a large-headed stick or bludgeon. The doctor's theory was that Mrs Luard was standing on the verandah, or sitting on the verandah rail, when she was struck from behind with a stick or bludgeon, felled to the ground and then shot twice.

The Courier had a reporter on the spot who obviously spent a good deal of time seeking out and interviewing various members of the local populace, and on the second day, 25 August, he interviewed the Rev. R. Cotton of Shipbourne, near Sevenoaks, who had an interesting story to tell. On the Monday afternoon, said *The Courier*, the Rev. Cotton 'was motoring with a party of ladies who were out on a photographic expedition, and while passing the woods in which the summerhouse is situated, just before four o'clock, saw a man emerge from the timber. The man was about forty years old, with "a low type of face". He appeared to bear the stamp of an East-End loafer. He was dressed in a grey and blue suit, and was by habit clean shaven, but had three or four days' growth of sandy hair on his face. His eyebrows and hair were very light, and he had a cast in both eyes. Mr Cotton thinks he could identify the man if he saw him again.'

While the police continued to search, the populace continued to wait and wonder, and although there was no shortage of conjectures and theories nothing seemed to add to that which was already known.

Under the command of Colonel Warde, Superintendent Taylor was swiftly given the assistance of Superintendent Ford of Malling and Detective Inspector Fowle of Maidstone. Such a force still proved insufficient, however, and observing the lack of progress and fearing that any trail would grow cold before they had found it, Warde went to Scotland Yard on the morning of Wednesday, the 26th, and, placing details of the case before the superintendent, asked for the assistance of a Scotland Yard detective. The request was granted at once and subsequently Chief Inspector Scott of the Criminal Investigation Department, accompanied by an assistant, Detective Sergeant Savage, set off for Sevenoaks.

On that same afternoon, the 26th, the inquest into Mrs Luard's death was opened in the dining room of Ightham Knoll under the direction of Mr Thomas Buss, the Kent County Coroner. Also present were Colonel Warde, Major Lafone – Deputy Chief Constable, Inspector Scott of Scotland Yard, Superintendent Taylor and Detective Inspector Fowle.

Seventeen jurors had been summoned, and were seated with their backs to the large mullioned window that looked out over the well-stocked flower beds. Only three members of the press were present, word having been sent out to the crowd of journalists at the gate that only that number would be admitted. Immediately afterwards this would lead to journalists' complaints against the coroner, Mr Buss, and he would write a disclaimer, saying that the order to exclude them was given completely without his knowledge, that no reporter had been kept out of his courts in the past, and that he regarded such 'unwarrantable action' as 'a gross interference with his powers and discretion'. Now, though, unaware of the resentment at the gates among the waiting press, the coroner took his place beside his clerk at a square table covered with a red cloth in the middle of the room. After the jury had been sworn and had elected their leader they were led upstairs to a room above where they viewed the body of the dead woman. On their return they were seated once more. Then General Luard was called.

Supported on the arm of a friend, the general came unsteadily into the room and sank into the witness's chair beside the coroner. To the reporter for *The Daily Chronicle* he 'seemed oppressed by the sense of his great affliction, and sat with his head bowed on his breast while the coroner was arranging his papers'.

In answer to questions the general said in a low voice that his wife was fifty-eight years of age and that they had lived at Ightham Knoll for the past twenty years. As he spoke the general's Irish terrier came into the room and stopped beside his master's chair. The general turned to him and with a sad smile, 'as though appreciating his fidelity, fondly patted him. Then with a sigh he looked up to answer the coroner's next question.'

'What was your wife's general health?' the coroner asked.

'Very good,' the general replied.

'And you were on good terms with her?'

'The best.'

In response to the coroner's questions, the general told of his leaving the house with his wife at 2.30 on the previous Monday afternoon and of going through the Fish Ponds Wood. It was about half a mile from the house, he said, adding that he and his wife went up through the woods past the summerhouse, which was on the estate of their neighbour, Mr Wilkinson.

'How far did your wife accompany you?' asked the coroner.

'She accompanied me as far as some gates at the top of the narrow lane which leads upwards from Mr Wilkinson's coachman's house. We parted near St Lawrence's School.'

At this point the coroner produced a chart of the neighbourhood, and the general, putting on his spectacles, traced with a pencil the route that he and his wife had taken. At the same time the jurymen studied a chart which had been published in *The Daily Chronicle* the previous day – this can't have been of much assistance as the route indicated upon it as having been taken by the general and his wife was quite at odds with the one they had actually walked.

'When you parted at St Lawrence's School,' went on the coroner, 'your wife went back? I think she was expecting someone to tea?'

'Yes.'

'Did you notice which way she went towards home?'

'I could only watch her for a few yards. There is a bend

in the track leading from the gate and you lose sight of anyone.'

The general then said that he went on to the links to get his clubs and returned home, arriving at 4.30. On entering the house, he said, he found his wife had not yet returned, though the visitor had arrived. He gave her tea, and afterwards suggested that they walk along the road to meet his wife. 'I thought it would be a most likely thing for her to return that way,' he said, ' – and the lady went with me. She said she particularly wanted to see my wife.'

Continuing, the general said that he and Mrs Stewart parted at a spot known as Seven Wents, near the Crown Point Hotel. It was then 5.15. 'I know that was the time,' he said, 'because the lady had to meet someone coming by train, and she looked at her watch.'

The coroner: 'You went by the path you thought your wife would return by?'

'Yes – being exactly the same path we had gone through in the afternoon.'

'You didn't see her on the road, so you went to the summerhouse?'

'Yes, I had expected to meet her on the road but did not.'

'Did you see anybody on the road?'

'Not from the time I left the high road at Seven Wents – not on the high road nor in the woods.'

In a matter-of-fact tone the coroner proceeded to ask whether the general saw his wife when he got to the summerhouse.

The general 'seemed to shudder at his recollection of the spectacle', and answered, 'Yes, I've written it all down – what I saw.' Then he said to the coroner in a plaintive tone: 'Read it, and I will say if it's correct, will you?'

The coroner then consulted several sheets of notepaper

containing the general's account of his movements. As the coroner went through it step by step, aided by General Luard, the story emerged of how the general had gone to the summerhouse and found his wife lying on the verandah, her head in a pool of blood. He could not see her face, he said, as she was lying face down. He took her hand and tried to feel her pulse. Her hand was quite cold.

Said the coroner: 'You then concluded that she was dead?'

The general nodded and in a scarcely audible whisper answered, 'Yes.'

It was then established that the general had noticed that the pocket of her dress had been cut open. Then he told of finding that one of her gloves had been pulled off her hand and partly turned inside-out, 'as though it had been wrenched off'. His wife had been wearing both gloves when she had left him, he said.

'Did you notice that her rings were missing?' the coroner asked him.

'Yes,' said the general, adding that he didn't notice whether the fingers were cut or bruised. 'I know she had her rings on when she left home with me,' he said. 'She always wore those rings except when she washed her hands.'

Asked about the rings that were taken, the general said that one of them must have been about a hundred years old; it had been given to his wife by her mother. 'It had an old design of mounting,' he said.

The coroner then asked whether Mrs Luard had any money when the general had left her.

'I cannot say,' answered the general. 'After I returned home I examined the bureau where she always kept her purse, and it wasn't there. I can only conclude that she had her purse with her, but how much she had in it I don't know.'

The general went on to say that when he had examined his wife's body at the summerhouse he had at once come to the conclusion that she had met with foul play. He was then asked whether he or his wife owned a revolver, and he replied that there were several in the house but that he didn't think his wife would be likely to take possession of them.

'Did you make any examination of the bungalow to see if anyone had been about?' the coroner asked.

'No.'

'You didn't take much notice?'

'No, I didn't trouble about anything else. I had seen quite enough.'

'About this walk,' said the coroner, ' – I think you take it every day?'

'Oh, no, but we had taken it very often.'

'You often go by the summerhouse?'

'Yes.'

'As far as you know,' said the coroner, 'had your wife anyone who was likely to do anything of this sort to her? Was she unfriendly with anybody? Had she any enemies?'

In tones of some incredulity the general replied emphatically, 'I have no idea of anybody.'

With the coroner's formal examination of the general at an end, he inquired of the jury whether they wanted to put any questions.

One of the jurors asked whether there was any ammunition in the house. 'You mean revolver ammunition?' asked the general. 'Yes,' the juror replied. Turning to the coroner, the general said with an awkward little laugh, 'It's a strange thing, but I don't know where it is. I mean, I had some ammunition for one revolver which I kept in my cupboard upstairs. I kept it there just for burglars. I never used it. There was a little packet of cartridges but I can't find them.'

'Since this affair,' said the coroner, 'have you missed a revolver?'

'Oh, no, both the revolvers are in the same place as usual.'

Asked then what bore the revolvers were, the general said that perhaps he had better get them. The coroner concurred, and the general, accompanied by a police sergeant, left the room. The two men returned shortly, the sergeant carrying one revolver in a case, the general following up with the other which was wrapped in paper. The police officers sitting around the table took up the weapons – both service revolvers – and examined them. 'It's not in the least likely,' volunteered the general, 'that anybody could have got access to those revolvers.'

A juror then asked the general what time he had arrived at the golf clubhouse. 'I don't think I could tell you,' the general replied. 'I didn't look at my watch. I got home at 4.30.'

After saying, in reply to a further question, that he did not hear any shots, the general was asked a question by a juror to which, hardly surprisingly, he reacted with great surprise.

'Had your wife,' asked the juror, 'any relative in an asylum who had been put away and might have owed her a grudge?' Plainly staggered, the general replied, 'None whatever.'

This completed the general's evidence and, again leaning on the arm of his friend, he left the room.

The next witness was Daniel Kettel, gardener to Mr Wilkinson of Frankfield Park. He testified to distinctly hearing three shots coming from the direction of the summerhouse. 'There was an interval between the first and the two others,' he said, and in answer to further questions said that the shots had come from the direction of the summerhouse, but that he had put them down to a farmer shooting squirrels. It was quite usual to hear such sounds, he added.

After stating that he had seen nobody about he told Superintendent Taylor that he sometimes had charge of the summerhouse. 'There was nobody in it at the time of the tragedy,' he said, adding that it was locked up and that 'nobody would have any business there'. After stating further that he had often cleaned out the summerhouse but that he had never seen a revolver there, Kettel stepped down.

The next witness was Mrs Annie Wickham. After affirming that she lived at Frankfield Farm, about three hundred yards from the summerhouse, she deposed to hearing the shots. She was standing at the door of her cottage with her daughter, she said, when she 'heard a very strange sound, as if something had been struck at close quarters'. A few seconds later she had heard two other sounds, shots, in quick succession. No, she said in answer to a question, she did not go to investigate, and she saw no one until about 5.30 when she saw General Luard, 'apparently in very deep trouble'.

The coroner: 'What time did you hear the report?'

Mrs Wickham: 'At a quarter-past three exactly.'

Questioned, she said she had heard no cry.

Following Mrs Wickham, Herbert Harding, the Wilkinsons' butler, was called. He stated how, at about 5.55, he was called to the stable where he found General Luard almost in a state of collapse and saying that his wife was dead. The witness then related how he accompanied General Luard to the summerhouse where he saw Mrs Luard lying on the verandah. After describing the appearance of the dead woman, the butler was asked about the position of the verandah and said that in his opinion it was impossible, when standing upon it, to see more than thirty yards down the path in either direction. It was an absolutely private path, he said, and added that the nearest point on the public road was Crown Point, which was a third of a mile away.

Following Herbert Harding came Dr Mansfield.

A young man, clean-shaven, the doctor began by saying that he practised at Sevenoaks and had never attended the deceased professionally during her life. 'I was summoned by a telephone message from Seal,' he said, 'asking me to go to Frankfield to see a woman who had been found dead.' He then proceeded to describe 'with a minute and scientific detail – that was so terrible as to cause the coroner to turn away his face from time to time in horror – exactly how he found Mrs Luard's body, and what was revealed by the *post mortem*'.

The dead woman, said the doctor, was lying prone on the verandah with her right cheek on the ground, her arms lying by her sides. Her feet were turned to the left, towards the edge of the verandah. Her head was about a foot from the steps leading into the bungalow. The head was lying in a pool of blood which was draining to the left and running off the verandah. At a distance of a foot or eighteen inches to the right of the edge was a large clot of blood about the size of a saucer, and mixed with it was some vomit. There was also a smaller clot of blood connecting the larger with her head. She had no hat on, but her clothes were orderly, save that there was a hole in her dress where the pocket had been removed. There was much blood on the left temple, and on turning the head over there was blood to be seen behind the right ear where was visible a hole apparently made by a bullet. There was another hole on the left temple, situated an inch and a half behind the corner of the left eye.

The *post mortem* had further revealed, the doctor said, that there were bruises on the right cheek, the chin and, to a slight extent, the nose. Around the bullet hole behind the right ear there was a scorched and blackened area two inches in diameter, and a similar mark of two and three-quarter inches around the wound on the left temple. There was, however, no trace of powder in the eye, suggesting that the eye must have been closed at the time of the shot. Both bullets were found in the head – one in fragments, and the other whole. Other signs of injury were found on two of the fingers, which bore abrasions. The left-hand glove, which was found half inside-out, had marks of blood inside which corresponded with the abrasions on the fingers. Also, there were blood marks on the hat, and a dent in it. Holding up the dead woman's old straw hat he demonstrated how a portion of the crown of the hat could be more easily dented than the rest, and that the weak part of the hat coincided with a mark on the head apparently inflicted by a blow. The removal of the scalp, he said, disclosed an effusion of blood on the upper part of the head, which corresponded exactly with the soft part of the hat, possibly the result of a blow with some blunt, large, round instrument.

The doctor then exhibited the dead woman's dress and said that he had found two small fragments which were formerly part of the pocket. These presented irregular edges which were evidently cut, the line of severance being against the grain of the material. He suggested that the pocket had been cut out with a knife.

Following this the coroner said to him: 'We have been told there were three shots.'

'Well,' said Mansfield, 'only two entered the skull.'

The coroner: 'Would the fragments found be equivalent to three bullets?'

'No, the fragments when weighed together corresponded exactly to the weight of the whole one.'

When Mansfield had stated that the bullet wounds had

caused the woman's death the coroner asked whether the wounds could have been self-inflicted.

'I think it is not *impossible*,' the doctor replied. 'Though for the righthand wound the head would have had to be turned to the left, and for the other wound to be turned to the right. The wounds might have been self-inflicted if the woman had had two pistols, one in each hand, and fired simultaneously – but I think in that case the areas of blackening by powder would have been smaller than they actually were.'

The doctor then gave his opinion that the first shot fired was the one that entered behind the right ear. 'It did remarkably little damage,' he said, 'and that only to the cerebellum, and it may not have caused very much disturbance beyond upsetting the balance of the lady, but the second shot entered the brain.'

In answer to a question from Chief Inspector Scott, Dr Mansfield made it clear that although it was possible for the gun-shot wounds to have been self-inflicted, it was highly improbable that they had been. Moreover, he added, he believed that the second shot was fired when the deceased was lying down in a prone position.

'It is advisable,' said the coroner, 'to clear up the evidence about the hat and the mark on the back of the head. Could it have been from a blow?'

Mansfield: 'It is consistent with a blow having been struck from behind.' Questioned as to whether the blow could have been struck with the butt of a revolver, the doctor said he believed it was possible.

'Would the blow have been struck before or after the shot was fired?' asked a juryman.

'It is difficult to say, but as there was a good deal of blood effusion it is probable that the blow was struck first, while the heart was beating strongly. My theory is that the lady was hit on the head; she fell and the blow made her sick. She was then shot behind the right ear. This did not kill her, and then the other shot was fired.' There was, he added, no attempt at sexual outrage.

A juryman: 'Would the blow on the head have been enough to kill her?'

'It is extremely difficult to say, as some people could stand a more severe blow on the head than others.'

Dr Walker, who had assisted at the *post mortem*, was called next, and while he corroborated the details of the examination as given by Dr Mansfield, he disagreed with him as to the cause of the wound at the back of the head. Not appearing to attach much importance to it, he said he was of the opinion that it was not inflicted by violence but was the result of a fall against one of the pillars on the verandah. Otherwise, he said, it could have been caused by one of the bullets inside the skull. With regard to the bullet wounds, he said that in his opinion they could not have been self-inflicted.

When Dr Walker had stepped down the inquest was adjourned. It would be resumed, said the coroner, on 9 September, at the George and Dragon Hotel, Ightham.

On the day following the inquest the missing pocket of Mrs Luard's dress was found at Ightham Knoll. Unseen when Mrs Luard's body had lain on the verandah, the pocket had evidently been caught up in the folds of her dress when her body had been taken up and carried from the summerhouse to Ightham Knoll. Later, following the *post mortem*, the housemaid, Jane Pugmore, had discovered it lying in the folds of the sheets in which Mrs Luard's body had lain.

That same day, Thursday, at the suggestion of Chief Inspector Scott of Scotland Yard, bloodhounds were brought in to supplement the efforts of the police in searching the woodland and the undergrowth about the summerhouse. Their owner, one Major Richardson of Carnoustie, had been reluctant, protesting that after the time lapse any trail that might have existed would have grown cold. The animals should have been brought in at the earliest opportunity, he said. Still, he agreed to the request and, along with two hounds, arrived at Wrotham Station just after eight o'clock that Thursday morning.

Met by Major Lafone, the Deputy Chief Constable of Kent, and Superintendent Ford, Major Richardson and his hounds were conveyed by wagonette to a spot some distance from the summerhouse. There they alighted and entered the woods where Major Richardson took a cross-bred blood-foxhound, Solferino, and Sergeant Paramour took charge of Sceptre, a pure bloodhound. *The Times* published an interesting account of what transpired, as told by one of the investigating party:

We struck into the woods, pushing and stumbling through bracken and bush, and climbed the hill till the summerhouse was reached. Here Chief Inspector Scott joined the company and, after a consultation, a plan was agreed on. A local motorcar agent named Hall, who is very familiar with the ground, acted as guide. The dogs were first taken round to the summerhouse and given a smell of the blood which still remains on the verandah. They sniffed the spot and Solferino immediately showed signs of excitement. Starting off round the verandah, it closely sniffed the doors and corners, lingering at certain spots. It then took a line to the southwards, through a gate in the higher ground and on to a field, where it continued, nose to the ground to show that it was on a trail. Making a tortuous passage along the field and among some heather, it finally reached a staked fence, which separated the field from the dense wood on the east. It led Major Richardson through the fence, and, in hot scent, entered the wood, where it continued the trail for a considerable distance. This did not satisfy Major Richardson, however, as he did not want to go away on a false trail picked up by the dog on the spur of the moment. He stopped the animal's career and with evident reluctance the dog was brought back to the summerhouse. Again it was given a sight of the blood and for the second time sniffed round the verandah, passed through the gates, and again led the major up to the hedge, through which it passed only a few yards' distance from the place where it first entered. The dog then quickly took up the original scent in the wood. Still not satisfied, Major Richardson took Solferino back again to the verandah, and the exactness with which it repeated its former movements was too striking to justify any interference from those in charge of it. We now went deep into the wood, the dog straining at its leash and almost breaking into a run. Its course never deviated from the straight, and, after traversing about five hundred yards in this manner, Major Richardson called a halt and sent back for Sceptre, which had been left behind.

Colonel Warde now joined the party, and the search was resumed. We made an ascent and struck a pathway. Traversing this at a good pace, both dogs led on without further incident, but still hot on the scent, to the Tonbridge road. Here the dogs came to a pause and appeared to be puzzled. The road seemed to have swallowed up the scent . . .

After trying to aid the dogs to pick up the scent again at various points, the handlers reluctantly gave up. Said *The Times*'s correspondent: 'It was evident that the hunt had failed. It was now past noon and, man and beast being thirsty, a visit was made to the inn.'

Afterwards Major Richardson expressed his surprise at the result of the search, telling a representative of the press:

I do not believe that a dog can be expected to get on a trail after, say, twelve hours, and it was certainly rather an extraordinary coincidence that the dog followed exactly the same trail as the local police say they followed in the early dawn after the murder. I am of opinion that the man who walked along that track had blood-stained boots. Dogs can only find their quarry by scent in the wind. I think in this case that person, after committing the murder, first of all, according to the dogs' theory, stayed on the verandah for a short time. Then he went across the fence into the field, crossed another fence, then turned on to the path which led to the main road, and eventually turned into the bracken. After that he went on to the main path, hesitated about going on to the road, and remained there till nightfall, when he went on to the main road and disappeared. I should be sorry to say positively that there was a scent there, but it is certainly extraordinary that the dogs should so persistently follow the trail.

Chief Inspector Scott is later said to have expressed the view that the theory of the murderer's having escaped by the Tonbridge road under the cover of darkness was the most practicable one on which to work. Also the local police officials laid some emphasis on the fact that the hounds travelled over a course almost identical with that which they concluded, on Tuesday morning, the murderer had taken after shooting Mrs Luard. There was, at that time, a distinct track of someone having walked through the bracken for some distance from the summerhouse.

For all that the dogs might have supported the beliefs of the investigating officers, however, those investigators were no further along in their hunt for the killer. All the hoped-for leads were coming to nothing. Rings like those stolen from Mrs Luard were supposedly being handed in all over the country, while one which was said to answer the description of one of those stolen was found at Tonbridge and sent by messenger to General Luard. He, however, declared it to be of much less value than his wife's. Furthermore, the torn scraps of paper found near the verandah of the summerhouse, and to which the police had attached importance, disappointingly turned out to contain merely the names of a number of villages. It was, police believed, simply a list torn up and discarded by a cyclist who had stopped to rest in the wood.

If the investigators were showing signs of desperation in their hunt for the killer it was hardly surprising, and it is clear that such feeling was being exhibited by other

LEFT: Georgina Moore. Taken from the engraving published in *The Penny Illustrated Paper*

BELOW: The River Medway near Yalding station as it appears today. The arrow indicates where Georgina Moore's body was found. *Copyright Bernard Taylor*

THE PIMLICO MYSTE...

THE MURDERED CHILD
GEORCINA MOORE FROM A PHOTO

JOSEPH SWAIN

THOMAS FREEDEN
P.C.S.S. YALDING

MR. MOORE
THE FATHER
OF THE MURDERED CHILD

THE PRISONER

THE GEORGE INN, YALDING
WHERE INQUEST WAS HELD

LINKS IN THE CHAIN OF EVIDENCE

LITTLE GEORGE'S HAT AND WRAPPER

THE PIMLICO MYSTE...
EXAMINATION OF THE PRI...
AT WEST...

GOSPEL GATE OF SCALDING

THE BOY
ARTHUR HARRINGTON

MR. POLAND

VIEW OF HOUSE, WHERE THE MOORES LIVE

MRS. MOORE IN THE WITNESS BOX

INSPECTOR MARSHALL
WHO ARRESTED MRS. PAY

ABOVE LEFT: Detail from the front page of *The Illustrated Police News* showing drawings, taken from life, of Stephen Moore and Esther Pay

ABOVE RIGHT: The house on the Maidstone Road which was once occupied by Esther Pay's parents and where Esther Pay was arrested. *Copyright Bernard Taylor*

BELOW LEFT: Part of the front page of *The Illustrated Police News*

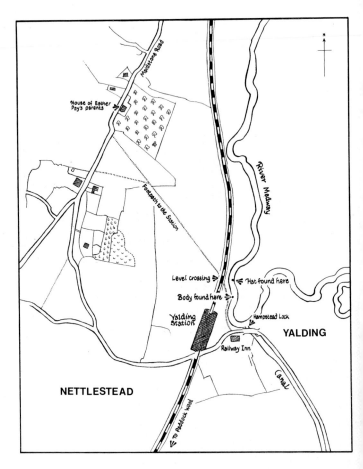

Section of a map of Kent showing the house of Esther Pay's parents in relation to the site of the discovery of Georgina Moore's body. Adapted from a contemporary map. *Copyright Bernard Taylor*

OPPOSITE ABOVE: Major-General Charles Luard
OPPOSITE BELOW: Mrs Caroline Luard

Views of the summerhouse where Mrs Luard was murdered with, inset, a photograph of the Luards' dog. In the lower photo X marks the spot where Mrs Luard was found dead

RIGHT: A policeman on watch at the wicket gate where Mrs Luard parted from her husband

BELOW: The rainy scene at the burial of Mrs Luard in the churchyard of St Peter's, Ightham. General Luard, hatless, is in the centre

ABOVE: Police conference on the Luard case. Inspector Scott (with bag) and Superintendant Taylor. The man on the left is unidentified

LEFT: John Alexander Dickman. From a contemporary drawing

ABOVE: The actor
Weldon Atherstone
(Thomas Weldon
Anderson). From a
contemporary drawing

RIGHT: Elizabeth Earl,
photographed in her
younger days

LEFT: Thomas Frederick Anderson

BELOW: Elizabeth Earl, sketched by a press artist as she appeared in the witness box at the inquest

MISS EARLE

OPPOSITE: The scene of the Atherstone murder. The sketch, taken from a contemporary drawing, shows the back of 17 Clifton Gardens, with the door at which the body was found, and the iron staircase leading to Elizabeth Earl's flat

Tony Mancini. *Photograph by permission of Photo Source*

LEFT: Violette Kaye. *Photograph by permission of News of the World*

BELOW: The body of Violette Kaye as it was discovered in the trunk. *Photograph by permission of J H H Gaute and Robin Odell*

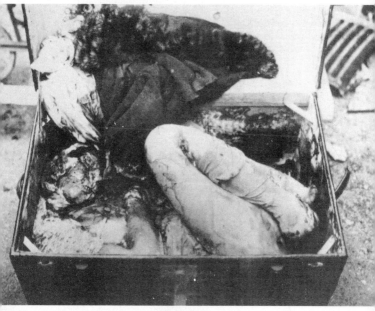

LEFT: Charles Walton

BELOW: Fabian of the Yard

OPPOSITE: Albert Potter

Helen Davidson and, below, her body as it was discovered in Hodgemoor Wood

parties. Wrote *The Daily Chronicle* on 28 August: 'A suggestion was made last night that the eyes of the dead woman should be photographed in the hope that it might reveal the image of her assailant, but no decision in that direction has yet been made.'

There were brief periods of Friday, 28 August, when the sun managed to get through the heavy clouds, but for the most part, in keeping with the general weather pattern, the day was grey and wet.

The funeral was set for 3.15, the exact hour when, the previous Monday, Mrs Luard had met her death, and well before that time people from Ightham and the surrounding villages were making their way through the drenching rain, trudging along the muddy roads towards St Peter's, the village church. Up at Ightham Knoll, the coffin, laden with wreaths, had been borne from the house in a hearse of black and gold to the narrow tree-lined lane which skirts the grounds and runs down to the Sevenoaks road. In the lane half a dozen carriages containing mourners were drawn up. Then, about three o'clock, the rain stopped and the sun struggled through the clouds. A few minutes later General Luard's carriage entered the lane and took up its position behind the hearse.

Through the rain the procession moved off down the lane and turned into the main road where a number of other carriages were waiting to fall in behind. As it passed through the little village of Ightham every blind was drawn. Men standing on the pavements bared their heads and many women were crying. On the hill near the church a large crowd of onlookers were gathered, waiting silently while the church bell tolled. Sympathizers also lined both sides of the avenue of limes which led up from the road to the church door.

Inside, the little church was packed. Every seat, except

for those reserved for the mourners, was occupied. Even the available standing space was taken up.

The coffin was carried inside by six bearers, the general walking immediately behind, wearing a black frock coat and carrying a small bunch of daisies in his hand.

After the singing of the 39th Psalm and a reading from *Corinthians* the Rev. J. Guise gave a brief address, recalling the time two years before when a service had been held on the occasion of the burial of General and Mrs Luard's younger son. Now, said Mr Guise, it was his sad lot to say a few words at the funeral of Mrs Luard. Everyone, he said, had lost a great friend. A deed of unspeakable cruelty had been done to one who herself was so gentle. Her good example stood out clearly before them. In Caroline Mary Luard they had a lady who served faithfully her generation, who went about doing good, who was wise in counsel and unfailing in sympathy.

After the address the congregation sang the hymn:

> Jesus lives. No longer now
> Can thy terrors, Death, appal us.

When the service inside the church was over, the funeral party left to move through the pouring rain to the graveside near the south wall where, beneath a yew tree, Mrs Luard was buried beside her son. At the graveside General Luard stood between his brother-in-law, Mr Thomas Hartley, and his late wife's sister, Maud. *The Daily Chronicle*, whose reporter was present, wrote: 'The general looked on sorrowfully as the coffin was lowered into the grave, but except for an occasional twitch of the muscles of his face he seemed quite self-possessed. At the committal sentence he tossed his bunch of daisies into the grave.'

After the Benediction had been pronounced the general

stood for a few moments, an isolated figure, gazing at the open grave. Then, suddenly straightening, he turned away and, head bowed to the rain, walked back down the avenue towards the carriage with his sister-in-law on his arm.

It was clear that Mrs Luard had been much loved. There were almost a hundred wreaths, a great many from titled friends. One bore the message: 'For dear Daisy Luard, with most tender pity and true love, from an old, old friend.' The inscription on another read: 'From her sorrowing servants, with sincere regret, Minnie, Huish and James.'

The People ended its account of the funeral with the words: 'This was the end of the tragedy – a service instinct with grief that left no casual stranger unmoved.'

The journalist was right with regard to the emotional effect of the proceeding. Not so when he stated that the funeral marked the end of the tragedy. The tragedy was by no means over.

With the inquest adjourned, the investigators, under the direction of Chief Inspector Scott, got back to work trying to find some clue that would lead them to the killer. So far there had been nothing – neither had there been any sign of those particular items the police sought, the revolver, the empty shells, the dead woman's purse and rings.

Following an interview with the young Mr Wilkinson, the police arranged to have the grass in the small field adjoining the summerhouse cut close and examined yard by yard. Likewise they cut down the bracken around the summerhouse and then had the deepest pond – the one nearest the summerhouse – dragged. Nothing was found.

Against the belief that the murder had been committed by a tramp or some other itinerant opportunist, it was argued that a common tramp would be unlikely to possess a revolver. Also, the papers asked, why kill for the sake of robbery when such a robbery could have been accomplished without it?

Day after day the newspapers gave reports on the case and the investigations, adding their own ideas and conjectures, much of it amounting to very little. *The People* was one of the many newspapers which had a reporter on the spot, who interviewed a number of persons in the area. Among those he talked to was Chief Inspector Scott. Following the interview, and after observing the mysterious comings and going of the various officers as yet again they tramped about the woods and over the scene of the crime, the reporter wrote:

I may state . . . that in their [police's] opinion the crime was a carefully planned one, and not the 'inspiration of the moment'. The theory that the murder was committed by a tramp has been entirely dismissed by the detectives, who are now endeavouring to find what motive the murderer could have for killing an elderly and highly esteemed lady beloved by all with whom she came in contact. The market value of the rings which were ruthlessly torn from the hands of deceased would be quite insufficient, they argue, to prompt a murder for the sake of robbery alone, and they are therefore compelled to seek for another motive. Herein lies their greatest difficulty.

On 5 September *The Illustrated Police News* wrote:

Theories by the dozen have been advanced as to the possible motive, but none bears analysis. Some trifling sum of money and some rings have disappeared, but the idea that robbery was the motive that actuated the deed may be dismissed. No ordinary thief, however desperate his condition, would be likely to risk his neck for so comparatively small a sum as Mrs Luard would possibly be in possession of, while no tramp is at all likely to have had a weapon such as was necessary to do the deed.

The discovery of the calibre of the bullets extracted from the dead woman's skull did nothing to further the inquiries. The Home Office expert, a Mr Edwin Churchill, to whom the bullets were submitted for examination, was unable to take the investigation any further. He was able to inform the police of the manufacturers of the bullets, but as the firm in question sold through agents in all parts of the world they were brought no nearer to finding a purchaser.

It was believed by some that Mrs Luard might actually have made an appointment with her killer. Otherwise, it was argued, she would have screamed, and Mrs Wickham had stated clearly that she had heard no screams that afternoon – yet due to the peculiarities of the acoustics of the place she said it was sometimes possible to hear voices coming from the summerhouse.

But was Mrs Wickham wrong? It is quite possible that she was. On Sunday, 30 August, *The People* wrote:

New witnesses have today come forward in the shape of two wood-cutters who were working only two fields away at the time of the murder. They heard the shots, but their information is important as throwing further light on the manner in which Mrs Luard met her death. They state that prior to hearing the shots they heard squeals. They took little notice of the fact at the time, thinking that the squeals came from a rabbit which had been seized by a weasel. It was only after the shots which followed almost immediately that they came to the conclusion that their theory was a wrong one. Even then they thought the shots were fired by a sportsman in the wood.

That they should at the time attach but little importance to the noise of firing is natural. They – men who have spent a long life in the open air – are used to hearing weird noises. Anyone living in this – one of the most wild and thinly populated parts of the south-eastern counties – marks little the squeal of a rabbit, the hoot of an owl, or the noise of a gun. They are everyday incidents, and call for no comment from the hardy sons of the land.

The Daily Chronicle reported that where motive was concerned the police were entertaining two alternatives. One was robbery and the other revenge. With regard to the latter, the newspaper said, '. . . if the murderer's motive was revenge one is left to wonder how a lady of fifty-eight, who had endeared herself to the whole district by her tender solicitude for the poor and ailing, could have been the object of anybody's animosity.'

In the meantime the police were receiving scores of letters offering suggestions in the case. A clairvoyant sent a description of the culprit, a little group of diviners came and tramped back and forth through the wood, nodding sagely and announcing that they had found the murderer's trail. One woman from the area reported to the police having seen a sandy-haired man on a road about three miles from the summerhouse. He was said to have had 'all the look of a hunted man at bay, unable to run any further'. A few moments later he was seen 'running up the road as fast as he could go'. A sandy-haired man? Could it be the same sandy-haired man as that seen by the Rev. Cotton? On the Monday the police detained at Dover a red-haired farm labourer who had been in the town for two or three days. He was found to have come from Ightham and, apparently, fully answered the description of a man seen leaving the Seal Chart woods on the day of the murder.

After admitting that he had once worked for General Luard, however, he was able to give a satisfactory account of his movements on the fatal day and was allowed to go free.

Sir Robert Anderson, erstwhile head of the CID, meanwhile offered his own comments to *The Daily Chronicle* on the lack of success in finding Mrs Luard's murderer. Asked generally as to the difficulties he had known to hinder crime investigations, Sir Robert spoke of the different status and powers of our own police, compared, for instance, with those of France.

'In Paris,' he said, 'if a murder were to take place, the house would at once be surrounded by a cordon of officers, the doors would all be sealed and the Chief of Police would be at once informed, and no one would be allowed to touch anything until he had completed his investigation. Everything would be left just as it was found; the most skilled police officers would see everything as the criminal left it; they would note the methods of his work by the evidence remaining, and would have placed before them all that would help them to unravel the story.'

After citing the unsolved murder of a Miss Camp[1], and those put down to Jack the Ripper[2] – in each of which case he believed that the destruction of evidence had aided the killer to escape – he turned to the current mystery.

As in this case of Mrs Luard [he said] . . . it appears that as soon as some of the police officers had seen the body it was removed, while a score of uniformed and other officers tramped around investigating every inch of the place and, perhaps, destroying clues that the experienced crime-investigating officer would find invaluable. I should have thought the proper thing to do was to leave everything as it was found, at least until the most expert men available had examined the scene with its setting and its surroundings.

On Wednesday, 2 September, the fire-arms expert from London, Mr Churchill, visited the summerhouse, where, in the company of some of the high-ranking investigators, he tried to form an opinion as to the position from which the shots were fired.

On the same day one more slender thread the

---

[1] Miss Camp was found murdered in a second-class compartment of a L&SW train from Feltham on its arrival at Waterloo on 12 February 1897. Her killer was never discovered.

[2] See Stephen Knight's book, *Jack the Ripper: The Final Solution.*

investigators had been following came to nothing. An inmate of the Tonbridge workhouse who was said to be suffering from loss of memory had been questioned and watched for some days by the police, their attention being all the more keen as they did not believe that his amnesia was genuine. Eventually at Tonbridge police court the man was charged with making a false statement for the purpose of obtaining relief at the workhouse. He pleaded guilty to making a false statement. A detective, Everett, said that following an initial interview with the prisoner several days earlier, he, Everett, and other officers were withdrawn from Sevenoaks in order to investigate the man, causing 'a great deal of inconvenience'. The Chairman remarked that the prisoner had put the county to much trouble and annoyance, and that he would have to go to Maidstone Prison for a fortnight with hard labour.

And the inquiries continued. Pawn shops were investigated in an effort to trace the missing jewellery and, as far as it could be done, the murder was reconstructed on the verandah of the summerhouse. With regard to the summerhouse itself, Mr Horace Wilkinson, its owner, announced that he had given instructions for the building to be pulled down once the investigations were completed – a move, apparently, to be undertaken purely for sentimental reasons.

Among the many, many letters engendered by the crime, a number were addressed to General Luard himself. One such came from Manchester and stated in an illiterate – or disguised – hand that the writer killed Mrs Luard 'for revenge after waiting for three years'. It was handed to the police. With so little to go on, however, they unfortunately had no way of tracing the sender.

On Thursday excited newsvendors in Tunbridge Wells were crying out that a confession to the murder had been made. Observed *The Courier*: 'The papers were easily disposed of, often at double the price of issue.' It appeared that on the previous evening a well-dressed man had gone to Bow Street Police Station in London's West End and informed the inspector on duty that he had murdered Mrs Luard and wanted to give himself up. He could give no reason for having committed the crime but merely said that he had been wandering aimlessly about for several days. The man was detained and Chief Inspector Scott was informed. By the time he got to Bow Street the man had retracted his confession, stating that he had never been to Sevenoaks in his life. After inquiries it was concluded that he could have had nothing to do with the crime and he was released.

As hope in one direction died, however, it sprang up in another. There was much talk in the papers about a man, 'agitated and trembling violently', who on the evening of 24 August had gone into a wayside public house in the village of Larkfield on the outskirts of Maidstone and called for brandy. News of the murder had not at that time reached Larkfield and no significance was attached to the stranger's offering a ring for sale for five shillings. Afterwards the man gulped down his brandy and left, striking out towards Maidstone. Following rumours that he had thrown a revolver into the River Medway whilst crossing Maidstone Bridge it was reported that the river would be dragged at that spot in an effort to find the weapon. Subsequently a diver, a Mr Rayfield, in the employ of diving apparatus experts of Westminster Bridge Road in London, offered his services to the police. His services said to have been accepted, he was then purported to have left London on Thursday, 3 September to make his search in the river. Whether the diver did indeed make the trip and search in the thick mud beneath the Maidstone Bridge was never reported. If he did, nothing of significance was found.

Further excitement flared for a time with the discovery on the banks of the lake in Regent's Park of a coat and a pair of boots. In the pocket of the coat was a letter which read:

My dear father,
I can bear the suspense no longer. The Ightham affair has preyed on my mind. I fired the shots while the devil was in me. By the time you get this I shall be beyond human aid.
Your unfortunate son
Jack Storm

The lake was dragged but no body was found.

As if hoaxes and wild fancies were not enough, the papers were full of strange tales about the murder and the investigations. However, said *The Kent Messenger*, 'seeing that forty or fifty London journalists have been established at Sevenoaks since the murder, each of whom is expected to write a readable narrative daily, it is not surprising that many strange stories have been worked up and given to the public . . .'

On Friday, 4 September, the police dug up a considerable patch of ground in front of the summerhouse to a depth of about a foot, in an effort to find the third bullet which was said to have been fired. Again, nothing was found.

On Wednesday, 9 September, at 3.00 P.M. at the George and Dragon Hotel, Ightham, the inquest was resumed, a long, panelled room being taken for the event, affording much more space than that offered by General Luard's dining room. Referring to the first part of the hearing when many members of the press had been kept away, the coroner, Mr Thomas Buss, said now at the outset, 'I hope the gentlemen of the press are accommodated on this occasion.' Assured that the arrangements for the press were satisfactory the coroner than read over the evidence previously given, after which the first witness, General Luard, was recalled.

Said one reporter, 'There was an air of quiet resignation about the general as he entered the room and made his way somewhat wearily to a seat beside the coroner.' The coroner began by asking whether there had been any incident in the lives of the general and his wife that would cause any person to entertain feelings of revenge towards either of them. After some pause for consideration the general replied that he could not think of anyone.

The coroner then asked whether the general or his wife had at any time received a letter from anyone that would indicate that bad feelings were entertained towards them. No, the general replied. 'Did your wife,' asked the coroner, 'recently before her death receive a letter from anyone making an appointment to see her?' 'Oh, no,' said the general,' she certainly would have told me if she had.'

The questions moving on to the last walk they had taken together, the coroner asked whether in their walks by the summerhouse General and Mrs Luard would usually go across the verandah or keep to the path. Replied the general, 'We would always go by the verandah.'

In answer to further questions, General Luard stated that he had never heard of anyone known to his wife who exhibited signs of insanity or homicidal mania. Neither, he said, had he carried a revolver that day.

One of the jurymen then asked whether the general had taken his dog with him after parting from his wife that day. The general replied that he had.

'As far as you are aware,' asked another, 'did anyone besides Mrs Luard and yourself know that you would be going near the Casa?'

'No, there is no reason whatever to suppose so,' said

the general, adding that they only decided to take that particular route after leaving the house.

Another juror wanted to know whether the dog barked as they approached the summerhouse, as though attracted by any suspicious character. 'No,' the general answered.

'Was the dog in the habit of barking if you passed anyone?'

'I think he certainly would have given us notice if there had been anybody there.'

After the general had reiterated that he had not heard any shots he was allowed to step down. With a bow to the coroner he left the room.

The next witness was Thomas Durrant, the manager of a Sevenoaks brewery. He stated that on 24 August he was at the top of Hall Hill, near Hall Farm, when he met General Luard. The general, with an Irish terrier, was walking under the fir trees at an ordinary pace, heading for the golf links. About ten minutes afterwards the witness said he looked at his watch and saw that it was 3.40. Durrant added, 'The general seemed very happy and contented, and smiled at me.'

After Durrant came Ernest King, a general labourer of Hall Cottage, Godden Green. He stated that on the afternoon of the tragedy he was at work near his home when he saw the general going towards the links. The time was between 3.25 and 3.30; the witness looked at his watch about a minute before the general passed by. He saw the general return about ten minutes later with his golf clubs. He did not speak to the general, he said, nor did the general recognize him in any way.

Henry Kent, sub-postmaster at Godden Green, told the court that about 3.30 on the afternoon of the 24th he was walking through the club-room when he saw General Luard walking across the eighteenth green towards the clubhouse. Later, he said, he met the general in the clubhouse; at which time the general spoke to him. The general seemed 'quite as usual', he added.

The next witness was Mrs Alice Stewart, a fashionably dressed woman of Battswood Cottage, Ightham, the wife of a retired solicitor. In reply to various questions she stated that she and her husband had been invited to tea at Ightham Knoll on 24 August, but that she went there alone, arriving at exactly 4.20, about five minutes before General Luard himself arrived.

She related then how she and the general waited for about five minutes and then had tea. 'Did the general say anything in reference to Mrs Luard's absence?' the coroner asked. 'Yes,' replied Mrs Stewart, 'he said he expected her any minute.' She added, 'After we had had tea the general suggested that we had better go and look for her.'

She went on to say that she and the general parted at Seven Wents at a quarter-past five. She had no doubt about the time as she had to go home to meet friends who were coming by train and were due at her cottage at 5.30.

Mrs Stewart was followed by Harriet Huish, parlour maid at Ightham Knoll. She stated that General and Mrs Luard left the house together on the afternoon of 24 August, that Mrs Stewart arrived about 4.15 and that General Luard returned about 4.30. She had been in the general's service for six years, she said. Asked on what terms the general and Mrs Luard had lived, she replied, 'Very happily, I should say.' And did they, she was asked, seem to be on good terms when they left on the afternoon of 24 August? She replied, 'Oh yes.'

The Rev. Cotton, waiting to be called as a witness, then asked leave to put a question and rather strangely asked the witness whether anyone or anything went out with General and Mrs Luard when they left home together on the 24th. The witness replied, 'The little dog went with them.'

'Did the dog live in the house?'

'Yes.'

'You are quite certain that the dog accompanied Mr and Mrs Luard?'

'Yes.'

The next witness was Jane Pugmore, housemaid at Ightham Knoll, who also said she had been employed by the general for about six years. Answering the coroner's questions she stated that after the doctors had concluded the *post mortem* examination she cleared up the room and shook out the sheets, at which time she found Mrs Luard's dress pocket rolled up in the sheets. It was lying loose in the sheets, she said; it was not concealed in any way.

The Rev. Cotton was now called as a witness, and the coroner asked him whether he had seen General Luard on the afternoon of Monday, 24 August. The reverend answered yes, and added:

'I was in the wood not very far from the scene of the murder – about half a mile or so away. I was with some ladies taking photographs in the wood when General Luard came towards me carrying his golf clubs and accompanied by a dog. I offered him a lift in my motorcar. He declined but put his golf clubs in the car, walking on in the direction of Ightham. We passed him on the main road as he came out of the wood. He then got into the car and we left him at his own gate when he took out his clubs and his dog. The time I saw him was five minutes after four o'clock. The general appeared at the bottom of the road about ten minutes after a lady with me looked at her watch. It was at half-past four that I dropped him at his gate. He looked hot and tired, but he chatted on the way quite naturally.'

After the Rev. Cotton came Mr Edwin Churchill who,

questioned with regard to the bullets extracted from the skull of the dead woman, said they were of .320 bore.

Said the coroner: 'You have had indicated to you the place in the head where the shots entered?'

'Yes,' said the witness, 'it was written on the box the bullets arrived in.'

'And in the case of the shot behind the right ear, how close would the weapon be held?'

'By the bruising of the bullet I should suggest it was held quite close – say about an inch behind the right ear.'

'And in regard to the other bullet wound, what would be the position?'

'Well, I should say that that might have been two or three inches.'

Mr Churchill was then asked whether he had tested the bullets found in the head of Mrs Luard with three revolvers – there produced – which had been kept in General Luard's house. The witness took up the revolvers and examined them. One, he said, was a Webley .450 or .455; the second a Colt double action, and the third merely a toy. The bullets that had entered Mrs Luard's head could not have been fired from any of them, he stated. The witness was then given an air gun which he also said would be incapable of firing the bullets.

In answer to further questions Mr Churchill stated that in the company of some of the senior police officers he had visited the summerhouse the previous Wednesday and examined the building, the pavement and the fences around. After saying that one of the pillars on the verandah had been used for target-practice from a weapon firing .22 cartridges, he was asked about an examination he had made of the cement floor of the verandah.

'Did you find any bullet marks there?' the coroner asked.

'I found one near the spot where Mrs Luard's head rested after she was turned over.'

'Can you suggest when the shot was fired?'

'I should suggest it was the second or third shot, when they were fired in quick succession. The first shot would have knocked the lady down.'

'I think you scraped the place the bullet had marked and found traces of lead?'

'Yes, and blood, in an exact line with where Mrs Luard's head had lain, as pointed out to me by Chief Inspector Scott.'

'Can you account for the sound of the first shot being so deadened?'

'Yes, a shot fired close to an object would be more like a thud than a sharp crack. The powder would cause a mark of burning of perhaps an inch and a half.'

'Have you any idea where a glancing shot would go to?'

'It might split up into smithereens.'

'The bullet might not be found intact?'

'No.'

'You have measured the distance from the bungalow to Mrs Wickham's house?'

'I think the police have done so. I interviewed Mrs Wickham and her statement confirmed my ideas that the second and third shots would have been much louder than the first.'

'Can you suggest at all whether these bullet wounds were self-inflicted?'

'They could not have been. Even if it were possible for the lady to have inflicted the first of them it would have been an utter impossibility for her to inflict the second.'

After the witness, at the coroner's request, had examined some ammunition found in General Luard's house he was asked: 'Would it be possible to shoot cartridges such as those from the weapon which was used to fire the shots which proved fatal to Mrs Luard?'

'No. Quite impossible.'

'Have you any doubt that three shots were fired?'

'None whatever.'

A juror then asked: 'Can you say from your observations at what angle the revolver shots were fired?'

'No, I cannot.'

Another juror: 'Is the size of the revolver used by the murderer a common size?'

'Yes, an ordinary type.' With this Mr Churchill smoothly took a revolver from his pocket, at which Superintendent Taylor asked, with a smile, whether it was loaded. Mr Churchill assured him it was not and then detached the chamber to show the size of bullet it would carry.

He was then asked whether such a revolver would be cheap or expensive, to which he replied, 'You can get a cheap one for about £1.'

'Would they take standard cartridges?'

'Yes. Unfortunately there are many cheap foreign pistols sold.'

Superintendent Taylor of the Sevenoaks Constabulary was the next witness. He described how he arrived at the summerhouse at 7.50 on the evening of 24 August, and how the following morning 'as soon as it was daylight' he and other police officers had made a thorough search of the surrounding wood and grounds.

'The only trace of any footprints or footmarks that I could discover,' he said, 'was one leading from the Casa through the gate towards the stables. A few yards beyond the end of the shed I could see where someone had broken down the bracken. It was quite plain. I traced footmarks for about thirty feet to the hedge, and there I lost all trace.'

He then related how in the course of his investigations he had walked from Ightham Knoll, through Fish Ponds Wood, on the route to the golf links described by General Luard, and that the journey had taken him a minute over an hour. The journey from the summerhouse to the golf links, he said, had taken him just over thirty minutes.

The coroner asked him then whether the investigations had been hampered by the wet weather. 'Yes,' the superintendent said, 'we experienced great difficulties from that cause.' To a further question he said that he and his fellow officers had followed up a great many suggestions and theories, 'but with no result'.

A juror then asked him: 'In what direction would the broken bracken marks lead?'

'Towards the fish ponds, a route which leads to the high road.'

'Can you give us any idea as to the size or character of the footprints you saw?'

'No, I could only just trace it in the bracken. There was no distinct mark. One could only say that a person had been there.'

In reply to another question Superintendent Taylor said that he took possession of the dead woman's hat and dress on the morning following the death, directly after the doctor had commenced the *post mortem* examination.

'Was there,' the coroner asked, 'any possibility that the pocket was in the clothes at that time?'

'I think there's no doubt that it was. You see, it was dark when we took the body home.'

'You think, then, that the pocket was with the dress at the very time that we were sitting here at the opening of the inquest?'

'Undoubtedly.'[1]

---

[1] The pocket could not have been with the dress when the latter was

'How is it, do you think, that the murderer put the pocket back?'

'I don't think he did. He must have taken the purse and left the pocket lying there, and when the body was removed it was picked up with the clothing.'

'How much money was in it?'

'I believe only a few shillings.'

A final question was asked of the superintendent: 'No one was seen to leave the woods?'

'No one at all.'

The final witness called that day was Chief Inspector Scott (referred to by *The Kent Messenger* as 'the famous detective'). He related how on the day following the murder he was sent down to assist Superintendent Taylor in his inquiries. Further, he said that having heard the superintendent's evidence as regards the time it took to get from Ightham Knoll to the golf links he corroborated what he had said. He added:

'I have caused every possible inquiry to be made by the Kent and Metropolitan police. A full description of the rings stolen, and a woodcut have been circulated throughout Great Britain, but up to the present without any good result. On Saturday, September 5th I stood on the spot where Mrs Wickham said she heard three shots, and on a signal given by me three shots were fired under the verandah of the summerhouse. I was accompanied by Inspector Fowle and we heard the shots. In fact they could be heard a great deal further away.'

'Have you noted any fingerprints?' the coroner asked.

'No. Clothing will not reproduce them, and I could find no traces of any on the verandah.'

---

exhibited at the opening of the inquest. Jane Pugmore had later found it 'lying loose in the sheets' in which Mrs Luard's body had been wrapped following the *post mortem*.

'Did you notice any spatters of bullets against the verandah?'

'No. The spot Mr Churchill indicated was covered with blood at the time.'

'How long since was it that the bungalow had been used?'

'I understood from Mr Wilkinson that it had not been used for some time. There is no indication of the bungalow having been used or the doors opened.'

At this Superintendent Taylor surprisingly intervened with the request that there should be further adjournments in order to enable the police to continue their inquiries. His words caused some excitement among the journalists there.

After a brief consultation with the police officers the coroner addressed the jury, saying that in the interests of justice he was adjourning the inquest in the hope that further evidence should be brought before the court. On this note of optimism the inquest was then adjourned until 23 September.

Following the inquest's adjournment the newspapers were full of comments hinting at renewed hope of finding the culprit. At the same time appeared the news that General Luard had decided to leave Ightham Knoll and had advertised available for transfer the remaining eight years of the lease: 'House, stables, cottage and eight acres. Rent £200.' The furniture, it was advertised, would be sold by auction on 24 September. Clearly, he had had enough.

At the same time a letter from General Luard, dated 8 September, appeared in most of the newspapers. To each of the editors he had written:

Dear Sir,
    I should be very much obliged if you will permit me, through

your columns, to acknowledge the very large numbers of telegrams, letters and cards which I have recently received expressing such deep sympathy for me. The public at large has been deeply stirred by the awful crime, and I may have some right to ask if the time has not arrived for clearing away from our roads, our lanes, and our woods, the many thousands of unemployed people, many of them in a desperate state from want, who may give way to temptation and commit the worst of sins.

I am, dear sir, yours truly,

C. E. Luard, Major-General.

General Luard's sentiments were echoed in some other quarters. There was a great deal of unrest in the country. Unemployment was at its highest level for forty-five years, strikes were threatened in five major industries, and in Glasgow there had been riots of such threatening character that, in order to deter the rioters, police had been brought in with drawn batons and soldiers with fixed bayonets. Further south the wet weather was continuing to wreak havoc with the crops, throwing many more out of work. *The Penny Illustrated Paper* on 19 September, in an article headed, 'The Menace of the Miserable', wrote of hordes of half-starved "out-of-works"' constituting 'a grave peril', and went on:

The wet autumn has meant ruin to the hop crop of the country, thus setting at large many thousands of the poorest of the poor who had anticipated work at good wages for several weeks to come. With no money to pay their fares back to London from the Kentish fields, they are now tramping back along the roads in their thousands, filling the workhouses to overflowing at each town they pass.

Belief that the murder was the result of a robbery, however, continued to be generally an unpopular view in the press. *The Tonbridge and Sevenoaks Standard* of Friday, 18 September stated what seemed to be a belief shared by most reporters of the investigations, saying:

'The idea that the murder was committed for robbery has been abandoned, and the energies of the police are directed to finding someone who had feelings of animosity against the Luard family.'

It was while the residents of Kent were reading the above words that the sorrowful story of the Luards was entering its final chapter.

From the time of his wife's death General Luard had not spent a single night at Ightham Knoll. Unable to stay in the large house without his wife he was spending his nights at the homes of various friends who were doing their best to keep him from brooding on his loss. His situation, however, was becoming increasingly difficult. The letters, cards and telegrams he had written of in his own letter to the press – those expressing sympathy for his loss – were not the only ones he received. He was also the recipient of a number of anonymous letters accusing him of his wife's murder. In addition to the letters against him, there was also a great deal of whispering.

Soon after Mrs Luard had been found dead the general had informed his son in South Africa, Captain Charles Luard of the Norfolk Regiment, who had immediately cabled back that he had booked passage on the *Norman* and was setting sail for England. His ship was due to arrive at Southampton on the morning of Saturday, 19 September and the general planned to travel to Southampton on the Friday in order to meet him. Afterwards, he had arranged, the two of them would go on to the house of a friend at Dulverton in Somersetshire for a protracted stay interrupted only by the resumed inquest on the 23rd, for which the general would have to return to Ightham. In the meantime, while the lease of the house was disposed of and he dealt with its contents ('I'm packing everything up . . .') he made his plans for the future. He would never live in Ightham again, he told his friend Colonel Warde, but would take two furnished rooms at his club.

In the week following the adjourned inquest Colonel Warde asked the general to visit him before going away from the area for good, and on the Thursday evening the colonel drove in his motorcar to Ightham Knoll where he found the general making final arrangements for his departure. Said Warde later, 'As we left the house there was a most brilliant sunset – the most brilliant I have ever seen, and the general remarked on it two or three times.' Together they set off to drive to the colonel's home, Barham Court, a huge hilltop mansion at Teston, near Maidstone. There the general planned to stay overnight and return to Ightham the next morning in time for an early lunch before taking the 1.40 P.M. train from Wrotham to Southampton. Colonel Warde was pleased to find his friend in fairly good spirits, although in a weak state of health. 'I thought he was bearing up marvellously,' he said later, 'but I noticed that he seemed more broken and aged.'

As they drove, General Luard mentioned the fact of his having to return to Ightham for the resumption of the adjourned inquest on the coming Wednesday. He didn't want to go, he told his friend, and he had written to the coroner to ask if his presence could be excused. The coroner had written back saying that as new evidence might crop up which might require information from him, he could not be excused.

Thinking back to the adjourned inquest the week before, the general remarked feelingly to the colonel that the questions the coroner had put to him had been scandalous. Colonel Warde concurred and they spoke of the matter no more.

General Luard ate a good dinner that evening.

Afterwards he yawned once or twice and the remark was made, 'How tired your packing must have made you.' 'I *am* tired,' the general replied, 'but I cannot sleep.'

He was then asked whether he was wise 'to pack up in such a hurry'. He replied that his brothers- and sisters-in-law were unanimous in agreeing that it was 'the best thing that could be done'.

The two men sat up smoking and talking for a while after Mrs Warde had gone to bed, then the colonel accompanied the general to his room and wished him goodnight.

In the morning just after eight o'clock the butler took the general some tea and bread and butter. Soon afterwards one of the maids saw the general up and dressed and leaving the house by the garden door. On previous visits to Barham Court it had been his practice to go for a stroll before breakfast so no significance was attached to his departure from the house that morning.

From Barham Court the general crossed the road and took a footpath that led him across a field to the South-Eastern and Chatham Railway line. At the footpath crossing, at a point between the Wateringbury and East Farleigh stations, he stopped and waited, concealing himself near the gate beside the line.

On the nine o'clock train from Maidstone the driver, Frederick Bridges, was aware of nothing untoward until the train was close upon the crossing. Then all at once an elderly man appeared at the side of the track, raised his arms in the air above his head, and threw himself in front of the rushing engine. Said the driver later, 'I gave two sharp whistles and applied the brake, but the gentleman was underneath. He was too sharp for me.'

When the train had been brought to a halt the driver and his men made their way back along the track to the body, mangled and almost cut in two by the wheels. From marks upon a handkerchief and the name inscribed upon a ring they discovered that the dead man was General Luard. In one of the pockets was found an envelope on which had been written the words, 'Please take my body to Barham Court.'

In the bedroom used by the general letters and telegrams were found. One letter bearing that day's date, 18 September, was addressed to Colonel Warde. General Luard had written:

My dear Warde,
  I am sorry to have to return your kindness and hospitality and long friendship in this way, but I am satisfied that it is best to join her in the second life at once, as I can be of no further use to anyone in the future in this world, of which I am tired, and in which I do not wish to live any longer. I thought that my strength was sufficient to bear up against the horrible imputation and terrible letters which I have received since that awful crime was committed which robbed me of my happiness. And so it was for long, and the goodness, kindness, and sympathy of so many friends kept me going. But somehow, now in the last day or two something seems to have snapped. The strength has left me, and I care for nothing except to join her again.
  So goodbye, dear friend, to both of us,
                    Yours very affectionately,
                                        C. E. Luard
P.S. I shall be somewhere on the line of railway.

The following morning at Southampton Captain Luard disembarked from the *Norman* to be greeted with the news that his father also was dead.

The Luard tragedy was now complete.

Following the shocking news of the general's death the newspapers had little more to report. At the inquest on the general's death the coroner said:

'The matter of [Mrs Luard's] death is still under investigation, but even now I think it is my duty to make some kind of reference to the many reports – the many base insinuations, I will call them – in the shape of anonymous letters which have been sent to General Luard, suggesting almost that he was responsible for the death of his wife. Those letters are innumerable. They have also been received by the police and myself in numbers. I was disgusted when I heard of these suggestions. And . . . I will say this: that those persons who have been prompted to write these letters, instead of sympathizing with General Luard in the great trouble he had undergone, added to the poignancy of his grief; and, since the death of his wife, I imagine that to the sensitive and honourable man that he was, they made his life almost unbearable.

'That, no doubt, was a great factor in inducing him to rid himself of his present life, and if those writers have any conscience at all they will reflect and feel, at any rate, that they must have contributed more or less to the doom to which the general sent himself. Let us hope that, although they treated him so badly in the last remaining days of his life, they will respect his memory now, and utter no more of these baseless and unfounded insinuations.'

Then referring to the general's remark, reported by Colonel Warde, that the questions put to the general by him, the coroner, had 'been scandalous', the coroner said:

'With regard to the questions which were asked General Luard at the inquest . . . having regard to the rumours which were in circulation after the first inquiry, and the suggestions that General Luard knew something about this unfortunate affair, I deemed it my duty to call evidence at the resumed inquiry which clearly showed – by the mouth of half a dozen witnesses – that the General accounted for his movements on this unfortunate day, and that he could not have been present on the occasion. That was the reason I asked the questions, and I thought it was only due to General Luard, and to the public, that, so far as he was concerned, he should be cleared as regards my court. Therefore, so far as the evidence goes . . . I need hardly say that he could not have been present and committed this terrible act.'

On Monday, 21 September, General Luard was buried beside his wife and son. On the stone, beneath the dates marking his life and death, is the inscription,

> The souls of the righteous are in the hand of God
> And there shall no torment touch them.

Two days later the inquest into the death of Mrs Luard was resumed. No new evidence was offered and it was soon over. Appearing to disregard the possible motive of robbery, the coroner in his summing up spoke of the great difficulties experienced by the police owing to the absence of any motive for the crime, the disadvantage suffered owing to the isolated spot where the death occurred, and the fact that darkness had set in before the police-superintendent from Sevenoaks could reach the summer-house on the night of the murder. Afterwards the jury, as expected, brought in a verdict of 'Wilful murder by some person or persons unknown.'

Was the killer some person or persons unknown?

There were those, as evidenced by the many anony-mous letters received by General Luard, the police and the press who believed that he, the general, was guilty of the murder. The evidence is all against such a supposition, however. He could not have committed the murder at the time accepted, 3.15, and then have been seen by various witnesses at such distances from the scene of the crime. Leaving Ightham Knoll together at 2.30, he and Mrs

Luard parted at the wicket gate about 3.00 or 3.05, Mrs Luard turning back towards the summerhouse and the general walking on to the golf club, a mile or so further on. He was subsequently seen by three witnesses at various stages of his journey, between 3.25 and 3.30, then, a few minutes later, in the clubhouse itself. Each time he was seen to be walking at a normal pace, and there was no evidence that he was exhausted or short of breath from exertion. If the general had indeed shot his wife at 3.15 that afternoon then immediately afterwards he managed to cover a mile and a half in less than fifteen minutes and not be in the least breathless. He was said to be a fit man, granted, but it must be acknowledged that he was almost seventy years old.

Apart from the evidence with regard to the general's movements, however, there are also the factors of his lack of motive, and of his behaviour following the murder. No one ever came up with any realistic motive for his having murdered his wife. And as for his behaviour following Mrs Luard's death, judging by reports it was in no way the behaviour of a guilty man; he appeared to have been genuinely affected by his wife's death, and as far as is known there was none who met him who believed otherwise. With regard to his behaviour following the discovery of his wife's death, one has only to look at the evidence of Harding, the Wilkinsons' butler, to see at once that the general's behaviour was that of a genuinely distraught and shattered man.

So, if one discounts the general as a suspect – as did the police – one is left – as were the investigators – with the mystery.

Colonel Warde, not giving up the search for clues to Mrs Luard's killer, was instrumental that November in having a £1,000 reward offered for information leading to a satisfactory arrest and charge. The reward notices, he wrote in a letter, should be posted at all police stations and 'in the vicinity of Unions, common lodging houses and other places where they would be seen by the tramping class, seafaring persons etc.'

Following the broadcasting of the offered reward, the Kent police received numerous letters putting forward various suggestions as to the identity of the murderer. A number of these, received that November, were to the effect that Mrs Luard's killer had been a *woman*.

The suggestion must have been the result of a swiftly spreading rumour, for the letters came from all over the country.

In essence the letters were to the effect that some twenty years earlier in India, Mrs Luard had withheld evidence at a trial at which an Englishwoman had been charged with the murder of her husband. As a result the woman had been found guilty and given a life sentence of penal servitude, which sentence she had been repatriated to England to serve. After being released from prison in 1908, so the story went, she had set out to have revenge on the woman she held responsible for her sentence, catching up with Mrs Luard at the summerhouse on the fatal day.

Could there be something in it? Warde wondered. At once checks were made on recently released female convicts – but without result; the CID could find no record of any woman having been discharged in England following such a crime within the past seven years. Inquiries were then made of the Director of Criminal Intelligence in Calcutta asking for information 'as to any at all parallel case which has occurred in recent years'. Continued the letter: 'The murdered Mrs Luard was a Miss Hartley, but I believe there were several ladies of the name of Luard in India at one time.'

The reply from India came in the negative; there was

no record of such a case. In the meantime inquiries in England had established that Mrs Luard had never been to India in her life. So another theory – albeit an improbable one – came to nothing.

The time went by and then, in September of the following year, 1909, a man was arrested and charged with the murder.

He was a certain David Talbot Woodruff, a tramp who had just finished serving a four-month sentence in Maidstone Prison. Due to be released at seven o'clock on the morning of Saturday, 18 September, he had nevertheless been kept in custody, and was still there at three o'clock that afternoon when Superintendent Taylor arrived from Sevenoaks with a warrant for his arrest on the murder charge. The reason behind the charge was that Woodruff, when originally arrested, had been carrying a revolver.

Protesting that the charge was a nonsense and that he had never been to Ightham in his life, Woodruff was brought into the Maidstone Police Court on Monday, 20 September.

The reporter for *The Illustrated Police News*, who was present at the time, described the scene as farcical. Expecting to see some powerful ruffian brought into court, he said, he saw appear instead a 'miserable old man', a 'mean and shrivelled old gentleman with a rheumy eye and a countenance scared into a pathetic picture of sheer bewilderment'.

The chairman of the bench asked first of all how it was that Woodruff had been held in prison for hours after he should have been released. Superintendent Taylor said he didn't know.

In answer to further questions Taylor said that although Woodruff had been in prison for four months it was only recently that facts had come to the knowledge of the police giving cause for further inquiries to be made.

Said the chairman: 'But there is no more evidence, you say, Mr Taylor?'

Taylor: 'No, sir, there is not.'

Nevertheless Colonel Warde asked for a remand of the prisoner, saying, 'I can give certain facts that caused us to have the prisoner arrested, but I should be loath to do that at this period. The hands of the police are very much tied, and we want to make certain inquiries before these facts are made public. If you were to ask what grounds I have for this man's arrest it would militate very much against us.'

Warde's plea did no good. After retiring for only three minutes, the bench came back saying that no evidence against the prisoner had been produced to warrant his further detention and that he should be released forthwith. And so he was.

So, set free, Woodruff shambled out of the court and back into obscurity, and with his going went Warde's last hope of success.

In searching for clues as to who murdered Mrs Luard, perhaps the nearest one can get is by speculating on the motive for the killing.

Was the motive robbery? And if so, who would kill for such a paltry prize as three rings and a few shillings? No casual robber, it had often been said (and still is – notwithstanding that Woodruff carried a revolver), would carry a gun; there had to be another motive, a stronger one. Then what? Revenge? But revenge for what? General Luard said his wife had no enemies, and certainly the accounts of her life do not present a picture wherein she was likely to make enemies.

Since the time of its occurrence almost eighty years ago, not a great deal has been written on the crime, though a dozen writers have touched upon it. Edgar

Jepson, writing in the book *Famous Crimes of Recent Times*, stated that the two doctors, Mansfield and Walker, were of the belief that the rings had been torn from the woman's fingers not at the time of her death but much later, as much as an hour afterwards. If Jepson's statement was true then it suggests that robbery was not the motive – for what was the killer doing, hanging about for an hour after committing the murder? Jepson was mistaken, however. One particular newspaper did make such a report, but *only one* newspaper, and nothing hinting at such a thing was ever said at the inquest. On the contrary, Dr Mansfield said (and Walker concurred) that there was a little blood on the inside of Mrs Luard's glove corresponding to the main injury to her fingers. This would indicate that while she was still wearing her glove the killer very roughly pressed the rings into her fingers – probably in an effort to determine whether she was wearing rings. Then, realizing that she was, he pulled the glove from her hand and removed the rings. If Mrs Luard had been dead for any length of time her fingers would not have bled when the rings were removed, and clearly they did.

Jepson also makes a curious statement with regard to the manner in which the glove had been torn off the hand, it having been pulled off so that it lay partly inside-out. 'This,' says Jepson, 'is the way in which a woman takes off her gloves; a man pulls them off by the fingertips.' This, according to Jepson, indicated that a woman might have committed the crime – out of revenge. (Did he believe there was truth in the rumours about the released female convict?) His suggested theory doesn't hold much water, though; for one thing, as most women will readily admit, they do not invariably remove their gloves in such a way.

So – revenge or robbery?

As Mrs Wickham heard no screams it indicated to many that Mrs Luard knew her killer, but that she could have had no idea that he was harbouring thoughts of revenge. Perhaps, it was thought, she had made an appointment to meet him, or perhaps he had lain in wait for her, killed her and then stolen her purse and rings to cover up the true motive.

In examining the revenge theory, however, one must account for the killer being in the right place at the right time in order to carry out such an act. But the walk by the summerhouse was not a daily occurrence, carried out at a particular time, so there was no way in which anyone could have known when the couple would pass. Further, it is hardly likely that the killer would have been in the area *in the hope* that Mrs Luard would chance by; he might have had to wait days. Is it likely, then, that she had arranged to meet someone at the summerhouse – as was suggested by some contemporary journalists?

Such a supposition does not stand up to examination. Mrs Luard left her husband at the wicket gate around 3.05 to return home. It was an arbitrary time, though, depending only on the hour at which they had set out from Ightham Knoll – which hour had not been planned in advance. The idea of an appointment on the verandah of the summerhouse can therefore be discounted – which in turn would appear to do away with the theory of premeditated revenge. Against such a theory there is also the unanswered question: revenge for what? Mrs Luard appeared to have no enemies. She was known as a kind, gentle woman, one who had shown so much good will to those less fortunate than herself. It is difficult to imagine, then, exactly what she could have done that would have brought upon herself such a brutal death.

It is also difficult to understand at this remove why the press seemed to be so eager to accept the motive of revenge for the killing, and so loath to accept the motive of robbery. Most of the newspapers put forward the revenge theory at some time or other – and many stuck with it. And if the press is to be believed they were only echoing the beliefs of the police investigators. Be that as it may, the press will frequently eschew a prosaic story in favour of a more exotic one, an obvious, mundane, motive in favour of one more thrilling. And certainly there is much more promise of excitement in the idea of a gentle, elderly woman being stalked by someone burning with a resentful, murderous hatred than there is in the more banal one of that same woman being mugged for no other purpose but that of stealing her purse from her pocket and the rings from her fingers.

It is nonsense, also, to assert that no man would kill for such small reward. There have always been men who would kill for peanuts.

The Daily Graphic of 1 September, 1908 published an interesting piece with regard to Mrs Luard being molested in the woods that summer. It told of a former servant of the Luards, a cook at Ightham Knoll for seven years, who called to see her erstwhile mistress only a few days before the murder. The cook later told the reporter for *The Daily Graphic* that during her visit Mrs Luard said to her, 'You remember how fond I used to be of walking in the woods? Well, I'm getting quite nervous about going there now, as I've been molested and asked for money two or three times.' Says the *Graphic*:

The obvious comment upon this is: Would not Mrs Luard have told her husband if she had been molested? It appears to be not at all certain that she would. General Luard is known to retain the disciplinarian attitude of mind common to retired officers. As a county magistrate, too, he would most probably have made an outcry and taken measures to keep the neighbourhood cleared of any persons likely to molest had he known that his wife had been thus interfered with in the course of her walks. And it is permissible to conjecture that he might also have prohibited his wife from walking in the woods alone. Mrs Luard, being a lady of resolute character, may not have cared for this prospect, and on that account may not have mentioned to her husband that she had been molested, or, if she did refer to it, may have made quite light of the matter to him.

While the police were investigating Mrs Luard's murder a man in the nearby village of East Farleigh, not far from Maidstone, was attacked by three men, knocked down and stunned, and robbed of his watch-and-chain, his tie pin and money. The assault was put down to hop-pickers. No one was apprehended, and it presented one more example of the relative ease with which one could escape justice when there were so many strangers in the area.

The writer Julian Symons, in his account of the case, suggests that Mrs Luard was killed by a resident in the neighbourhood, a man who hated her and who afterwards actively began the campaign of whispered and written accusations that drove General Luard to his death. To me it appears a highly improbable scenario and seems to be based mainly on the fact that Mrs Luard's killer was only inches away when he shot her, and the supposition that she would surely have screamed and run away if the man had been a stranger.

I find it inconceivable, however, that in such a small community a neighbour could have nursed such a murderous grudge without anyone else having an inkling of it. Such a thing could hardly have remained a total secret, least of all from the Luards. And if General Luard had had even the slightest suspicion of anyone he would have told the police. He, being on the wrong end of so much libel and slander, had more reason than almost anyone to want to see the killer apprehended.

There is fascination in the belief that Mrs Luard's

murder was the result of some bitter, long-held grudge, but it appears to me to be just too unlikely. I feel it is far more probable that her killer was someone who came to the district with the intention of committing robbery. Perhaps in some previous year he had come to work there, maybe as a picker of hops or fruit, and at that time had come to the realization that there were opportunities for easier money, particularly for someone who was not too dainty when the necessity occurred for a little violence. And certainly violence was not unheard of in the area at that time of year, as has been shown.

Also, as a stranger could move about the area with impunity at such a time he would have a good chance of getting the lie of the land, of seeing what opportunities were available. And, bearing in mind that there were several fine houses in the area, it is not unlikely that a would-be robber would be looking for a possible target. It must not be forgotten that Woodruff, regarded by many as nothing but a pathetic tramp, carried a revolver. There was no evidence to connect him with the Luard murder, but he is an illustration of the fact that some tramps and vagabonds carried firearms. And no one carries a loaded gun for no purpose.

So what happened on that day in late August? Did some rogue come across the summerhouse in the woods? It should be remembered that the summerhouse was furnished, so it might well have appeared to a casual observer as someone's home, with a promise, perhaps, of contents of value. If so, being so very isolated as it was and with no one about, it would have presented a golden opportunity.

Perhaps the stranger, the man, came upon the summerhouse a few minutes after General and Mrs Luard had gone past it. He can be imagined as, unseen, he moves steathily around the building, trying to find out whether there is anyone about. He sees no one. Then as he stands there, perhaps looking in at a window, he becomes aware of someone approaching along the path. Stepping quickly behind the corner of the summerhouse, he hides, watching as a well-dressed woman steps up on to the verandah. She stops on the verandah and rests against the rail of the balustrade. Unseen, the man takes a revolver from his pocket, slips out from his cover and creeps silently over the carpet of pine needles. The woman hears nothing until it is too late. He raises the revolver and brings it down . . .

In an alternative scenario she is walking on the verandah when she sees him coming towards her along the path. She comes to a halt and he steps up on to the verandah and stops before her. Although she is very uneasy, there is little that she can do. It is no use attempting to run from him. Nor is it any use screaming for help; she knows that; she is too far away for that to do any good. The best thing for her to do is keep calm; to try not to antagonize him. Perhaps he produces the gun, telling her not to make a noise or he will kill her. Reaching out, he snatches at her hand and roughly feels her fingers to find out whether she is wearing any rings. She whimpers in pain and fear and as she twists away from him he raises the revolver and brings it down . . .

The butt of the weapon catches her on the back of her head. She staggers and falls headlong, falling prone along the verandah, hands stretching out before her, her hat falling off. The blow only momentarily stuns her, however. She vomits, struggles to raise herself. As she does so the man, afraid that she will cry out, steps quickly to her side. He does not know that the closest help is too far away to be of any assistance; besides which, if he already has a criminal record he will fear identification. As she moves her head he stands astride her, puts the revolver close to her skull behind her right ear and pulls the trigger. With the blow of the shot she collapses again, her head now resting on the right cheek. He lifts her left hand, tears off the glove, then wrenches the rings from her fingers. As he straightens he realizes that she is moving, trying to raise herself once more. He fires again, the first shot missing, the second, closer and more carefully aimed, entering her left temple. This time he makes no mistake; in a moment she is dead.

Trying to turn her body over to get at her pocket he tears the flounces of her skirt. Locating the pocket, he feels the purse inside. Getting it free, though, is awkward, and taking a knife, he cuts it out. That done he rips the purse from it and tosses the pocket down. The job is finished. Swiftly he slips away into the cover of the trees. The whole operation has taken no more than a minute.

Between two and three hours later the general finds his wife dead. He pulls her arms down to her sides and feels for her pulse. Then, for the sake of decency, he straightens her skirt, pulling the hem down over her heels.

Almost certainly we shall never know now who killed Mrs Luard. Percy Savage, the assistant to Chief Inspector Scott of Scotland Yard during the inquiry, later himself reaching the rank of superintendent, wrote in his retirement of the Luard case: '. . . not a scrap of evidence was forthcoming on which we could justify an arrest, and to this day I frankly admit that I have no idea who the criminal was.'

Not everyone, however, believed that the Luard murder was such a mystery.

Some fifty years after the murder when Colin Wilson and Pat Pitman were writing their *Encyclopedia of Murder* they received a copy of a paper written by C. H. Norman, a sometime essayist who had at one time been employed

as the acting official shorthand-writer under the Criminal
Appeal Act. In his paper, *Memorandum on the Question
of Capital Punishment Submitted to the Gowers Commit-
tee*, Norman wrote on the doubt surrounding the conviction of John Dickman who in 1910 was hanged for the
murder of colliery cashier John Nisbet on board a train
travelling out of Newcastle. Nisbet was shot five times in
the head and the bag he carried containing £370 was
stolen. Dickman was convicted on circumstantial evidence, following identification on an identification parade
that was a disgrace, in that before the parade took place
two witnesses for the prosecution were invited to look at
him through a window. After his conviction there was an
outcry and the Home Secretary was petitioned for a
reprieve. To no avail, however; Dickman was hanged on
10 August, 1910, protesting his innocence to the last.

Four years after Dickman's execution an account of his
trial, edited by Sir S. Rowan-Hamilton, one-time Chief
Justice of Bermuda, was published in the *Notable British
Trials* series. Years later, in 1939, C. H. Norman wrote to
Sir S. Rowan-Hamilton with regard to the unsatisfactory
quality of the Dickman conviction. In his letter dated 26
October 1939 Rowan-Hamilton replied:

Sir,
Your interesting letter of the 24th August only reached me
today . . . Lowenthal was a fierce prosecutor. All the same
Dickman was justly [convicted?], and it may interest you to
know that he was with little doubt the murderer of Mrs Luard,
for he had forged a cheque she had sent him in response to an
advertisement in *The Times* (I believe) asking for help; she
discovered it and wrote to him and met him outside the
General's and her house and her body was found there. He was
absent from Newcastle those exact days. Tindal Atkinson knew
of this, but not being absolutely certain refused to cross-examine

Dickman on it. I have seen replicas of cheques. They were
shown me by the Public Prosecutor . . .
>   Yours very truly,
>   S. Rowan-Hamilton, Kt.

Ten years later Mr Norman wrote again to Sir Rowan-
Hamilton, prompted on this occasion by having just read
ex-superintendent Percy Savage's account of the Luard
murder and the investigations, in which Savage said that
he frankly admitted that he had no idea who the murderer
was. Rowan-Hamilton replied on 22 February 1949:

Dear Sir,
   Thank you for your letter. Superintendent Savage was certainly not at Counsel's conference and so doubtless knew
nothing of what passed between them. I am keeping your note
as you are interested in the case and will send you later a note
on the Luard case.
>   Yours truly,
>   S. Rowan-Hamilton, Kt.

Mr Norman's memorandum continues:

I replied, pointing out what a disturbing state of facts was
revealed, as it was within my knowledge that Lord Coleridge,
who tried Dickman, Lord Alverstone, Mr Justice A. T. Lawrence, and Mr Justice Phillimore, who constituted the Court of
Criminal Appeal, were friends of Major-General and Mrs
Luard. (Lord Alverstone made a public statement denouncing
in strong language the conduct of certain people who had written
anonymous letters to Major-General Luard hinting that he had
murdered his wife.) I did not receive any reply to this letter, nor
the promised note on the Luard case.
   Mr Winston Churchill, who was the Home Secretary who
rejected all representations on behalf of Dickman, was also a
friend of Major-General Luard.
   So one has the astonishing state of things disclosed that
Dickman was tried for the murder of Nisbet by judges who
already had formed the view that he was guilty of the murder of

the wife of a friend of theirs. If Superintendent Savage is to be believed, this was an entirely mistaken view.

I was surprised at the time of the trial at the venom which was displayed towards the prisoner by those in charge of the case. When I was called in to Lord Coleridge's room to read my note before the verdict was given on the point of the non-calling of Mrs Dickman as a witness, I was amazed to find in the judge's room Mr Lowenthal, Junior Counsel for the Crown, the police officers in charge of the case, and the solicitor for the prosecution. When I mentioned this in a subsequent interview with Lord Alverstone, he said I must not refer to the matter in view of my official position.

Mr Norman's interest in the affair was primarily due to his dissatisfaction and unease over the conviction of Dickman – which dissatisfaction was warranted in that no matter how much *belief* there is in a man's guilt, unless there is sufficient evidence to *prove* that guilt then he must be given the benefit of the doubt.

However, what concerns us here is the question of whether Mrs Luard was killed by John Dickman.

Clearly Sir S. Rowan-Hamilton believed so, for apart from informing C. H. Norman of his belief, he had earlier conveyed it to the writer H. L. Adam, who, in his book, *CID: Behind the Scenes at Scotland Yard*, wrote:

When Dickman was arrested there was found in his possession a letter from Mrs Luard at Sevenoaks. It transpired that some time before the murder at that place occurred Dickman had put an advertisement in the paper of the 'Reduced Gentleman' type, appealing for help. It was seen by Mrs Luard [who] responded to it by sending the advertiser a cheque. This Dickman forged, making the amount much larger, converting it from tens to hundreds. When the forgery subsequently came to the knowledge of Mrs Luard she wrote to Dickman, asking him for an explanation, and intimating that unless he came to her and made a satisfactory one she would place the matter in the hands of the police. This was of course a serious threat to a man like Dickman. He would certainly not be slow in adopting means of

preventing this step being taken. The inference is that he went
to Sevenoaks for that purpose.

If there is any truth in this story it is more surprising
that no mention of it was ever made at the time by the
police or other authorities, particularly as Dickman's
execution had not been a popular one and the powers
would have been glad of any factor that supported them.

The writer H. L. Adam, however, was a most unreliable writer and is a most unsatisfactory source – which my
own researches into other murder cases prove. With
regard to his statement above one has only to look at the
facts. Mrs Luard was murdered in the summer of 1908
and Dickman was arrested for Nisbet's murder in the
spring of 1910. Can one seriously believe that Dickman,
having committed the murder of Nisbet, and having done
all he could to cover up all the traces of that murder (even
the stolen money was never found) would carry about
with him for *nearly two years* a letter which was powerful
evidence of a *previous* murder? It doesn't make sense. *If*
Dickman had killed Mrs Luard he would surely have
destroyed any incriminating evidence, not carried it about
with him to be found by anyone who chose to look in his
pocket.

Also, the business about Dickman forging the cheque
doesn't stand up to examination. H. L. Adam said that
on the cheque Dickman altered the tens to hundreds,
which implies that the cheque was made out for £20 at the
very least. This, though, was a considerable sum of money
in 1908 – about ten weeks' wages for the average man. Is
it likely that Mrs Luard would have sent such a large sum
to some unknown man simply as the result of his asking?
But, if she did, and forgery did take place, then General
Luard would surely have known of it in some way. It is
highly unlikely that Mrs Luard would have tried to handle

the matter of the forgery on her own – particularly when the Chief Constable of Kent was one of her husband's best friends.

There is further evidence of H. L. Adam's being mistaken, however – evidence showing that *he himself* knew he was wrong. His book *CID: Behind the Scenes at Scotland Yard* was published in 1931. Four years later in *The Fifty Most Amazing Crimes of the Last Hundred Years* (published 1935) he wrote again of the Luard murder. In this later account, however, obviously having thought better of it – or having received further information – he makes no mention whatever of any letter found in Dickman's possession; indeed, he does not mention Dickman at all, either as a suspect or in any other connection. On the contrary, Adam states categorically, 'It is the writer's firm conviction that Mrs Luard was killed by a homicidal lunatic.' At the end of his account, after dwelling at length on the vagaries of homicidal lunatics, Adam returns to the murder of Mrs Luard, saying, 'Nothing has happened since to throw any additional light on this poignant and impenetrable mystery and in all human probability never will.'

Although there is no evidence to connect Dickman with the murder of Mrs Luard and the newspapers carried no word of any possible involvement on his part, there might well be reason to believe that he may have been involved in another killing of the time. Certainly some members of the press believed so.

After Dickman's execution a reporter wrote an item connecting Dickman with the death in 1909 of Hermann Cohen, a moneylender who was found battered to death in his office in Sunderland. In *The People* of 14 August 1910, the journalist asked:

Was John Alexander Dickman, the slayer of Nisbet, a double murderer? It will be recalled that twelve months before Nisbet . . . met with his tragic end on the NE Railway a Sunderland moneylender, named Hermann Cohen, was brutally butchered and robbed. From inquiries I have made there seems – to put it mildly – a possibility that Dickman could have helped the police in their efforts to solve a crime as mysterious as it was brutal.

Hermann Cohen was killed on 8 March 1909, his head savagely battered in with a series of eight blows, any one of which would have been sufficient to kill him. Also, the little finger of his left hand had been cut off. Had the killer, not content with stealing money, also been determined to steal the diamond ring that Cohen usually wore? In spite of careful inquiries by the police no one was arrested for the crime. Then came the murder of Nisbet, following which the police made a careful search of Dickman's home, even to the point of digging up the garden, emptying the water cistern and taking the piano to pieces. According to *The People*'s investigating journalist: 'Although they found little to connect him with the train murder, they discovered certain facts which left no doubt that Dickman had had transactions with Hermann Cohen, and they also found certain jewellery.'

The writer goes on to say that the police inquiries took them so far that, had Dickman been acquitted of the murder of Nisbet, he would at once have been asked to explain his movements on the night of 8 March 1909. Continues the reporter:

Had his statement been unsatisfactory – and from what I know there could be little doubt that it must have been – he would have been kept in custody. Indeed, I may go further, and state that while the case was being heard on appeal in London, a detective was present and in a position to produce certain evidence which would leave but little doubt as to the need for Dickman's detention in custody . . . Police discoveries show that

Dickman had transactions with Cohen, and the possibility that his visits to the Sunderland moneylender were also to see the way the land lay is at once apparent. Again, the last man seen talking to Hermann Cohen prior to his untimely end was described by Mr Solomon Tamkelowitz as wearing a light or fawn coat. Dickman almost always used a coat that might be so described.

The reporter continued with the statement that a number of street robberies had occurred in the area of Dickman's home, for which Dickman might well have been responsible. And, he goes on:

There are several other offences against the law which, in the mind of some, may be laid at Dickman's door, but they are difficult to prove. One – a burglary – resulted in the loss of some very valuable jewels, but as, if the full story were told, it might more or less implicate others still in the land of the living it is best not published. Suffice it to say that by a clever trick a certain householder and his wife were persuaded to leave their house one evening, and upon their return they discovered the loss of practically all their jewellery.

However, says the journalist, 'No similar outrages have been reported since Dickman's arrest.'

A week later the same journalist was writing again in support of the theory that Dickman was guilty also of the murder of Cohen, saying that he was 'informed on authority' that on one occasion Dickman paid his rates with a £5 note taken from Cohen's rooms.

Continues the writer:

. . . In passing sentence on Dickman Lord Coleridge made use of the following impressive words: 'In your hungry lust for gold you had no pity on the victim that you slew, and it is only just that the Nemesis of the law should overtake the author of the crime.' Did Dickman's lust for gold drive him to commit another brutal, ghastly and callous murder? I know that those few persons who are in possession of the full facts think it did, and that by his execution last Tuesday the Nemesis of the law overtook a double murderer . . .

In spite of the unsatisfactory quality of Dickman's trial, there can't be much doubt that he was guilty of the murder of Nisbet. Accepting that, was he guilty also of the murder of Cohen? More to the point with regard to the subject of this brief study, was he also the murderer of Mrs Luard?

It is quite possible, even likely, that in the rumour that was evidently rife at the time the Luards were confused with that 'certain householder and his wife' whom the journalist from *The People* wrote of – the couple who were robbed of 'practically all their jewellery'.

However, what factors are there that might be seen to connect Dickman with the murder of Mrs Luard?

In all three murders – Nisbet, Luard, and Cohen – robbery took place following the murder. Nisbet was killed for the money he carried. Cohen was killed for money and jewellery. Mrs Luard was probably killed for money and jewellery.

And the methods used for the killings? Nisbet, on the train, was shot five times in the head with a .320 revolver, two of the bullets entering behind his ear as he lay on the floor of the train compartment. Mrs Luard was also shot in the head with a .320 revolver, one bullet entering behind her ear as she lay prone on the verandah.

It was also claimed by Dr Mansfield that she had been struck on the head with a heavy, blunt instrument. Cohen, though, had not been shot; he had been killed solely by blows to the head. But it should be remembered that he was killed in his office, where the sound of gunshots would have attracted infinitely more attention from outside than the use of the bludgeon that killed him. (Also, if *The People*'s investigative reporter is to be believed, then Dickman was suspected of having clubbed *other* victims in the course of robbing them.)

In each case the murder was particularly vicious and ruthless: Nisbet shot five times; Mrs Luard shot twice and clubbed; Cohen clubbed eight times.

Robbery, however, is a common motive, and the calibre of the bullets used, .320, was among the most popular. It must be admitted that beyond the similarities evidenced there seems to be little else to connect Dickman with the murder of Mrs Luard. For one thing, although it is only twelve miles from Newcastle-upon-Tyne to Sunderland where Cohen was murdered, it is a distance of some two hundred and ninety miles to Seal Chart where Mrs Luard met her death. In view of that great distance one wonders why Dickman would travel so many miles when there were similar pickings to be had closer to home. Though it is quite possible, of course, that he had gone to the area for some other purpose altogether.

Further, in considering the likelihood of Dickman's guilt in the murder of Mrs Luard, although he might have carried it out in an opportunistic manner, it could not have occurred as Sir S. Rowan-Hamilton would have it – that Dickman had forged a cheque she had sent him and then murdered her to prevent her carrying out her threat to inform the police of his act.

Sir S. Rowan-Hamilton's story sounds highly implausible. For one thing Mrs Luard was not found dead outside her home as Rowan-Hamilton stated, but almost a mile away. Furthermore, it is very unlikely that she met Dickman there as the result of having made an appointment with him. On that fatal afternoon she left her husband about 3.05 to return home, but, as was made clear, that hour was arbitrary, depending only on the time at which they had set out from Ightham Knoll – which time had not been planned in advance and which had only come about as a result of a desire of the *general*'s – to go to the clubhouse to fetch his clubs. Furthermore, the general claimed that they did not decide upon the route they would take until they had actually left the house.

Also judging by what is known of the Luards, it is most unlikely that Mrs Luard would have made an appointment to meet a complete stranger at some remote spot in the middle of a wood – and particularly someone whom she had already discovered to be a criminal. And how would Dickman know about the summerhouse, anyway? How would he know where to go? If Mrs Luard had wanted to meet Dickman, knowing him to be a criminal, she would surely have told her husband. She would not have gone off alone and, unknown to her husband, have kept a secret rendezvous with the man. Also, it is extremely unlikely that any cheque of Mrs Luard's could have been forged and cashed by Dickman without General Luard knowing about it. All these points considered, the idea of an appointment on the verandah of the summerhouse can surely be discounted.

C. H. Norman, in his letter to Rowan-Hamilton, stated that it was within his knowledge that Lord Coleridge, who tried Dickman, Lord Alverstone, Mr Justice A. T. Law-rence, and Mr Justice Phillimore, who constituted the Court of Criminal Appeal, and Winston Churchill, who was the Home Secretary who rejected all representations on behalf of Dickman, were all friends of General and Mrs Luard.

The present writer, however, has been unable to prove any relationship between the Luards and any of the above named gentlemen. At the funeral of Mrs Luard almost a hundred wreaths were presented, more than a third of which number were listed in local newspapers. Among the names of the senders, however, there is no name corresponding to any of those above. C. H. Norman also stated that Lord Alverstone 'made a public statement denouncing in strong language the conduct of certain people who had written anonymous letters to Major-General Luard hinting that he had murdered his wife . . .' In spite of searching, however, no record of such a statement by Lord Alverstone has been turned up in any of the contemporary newspapers. There *was* a denunciation published in many papers of the time, but that came from Thomas Hartley, brother to Mrs Luard and great friend to her husband.

With regard to a friendship between Home Secretary Winston Churchill and General Luard, it is perhaps worth noting that at the time of the crime General Luard was within a few weeks of his seventieth birthday whereas Winston Churchill was only thirty-three. Experience tells one that close friendships across such wide generation gaps are not that common. At the time of the deaths of the Luards, Winston Churchill was preparing for his wedding. The late Lady Churchill, however, subsequently told the writer Stephen Knight in a letter in 1977 that she did not remember any General and Mrs Luard.

I firmly believe that the statements of both Mr Norman and Sir S. Rowan-Hamilton have to be taken with pinches of salt. Rowan-Hamilton stated in his letter that Tindal Atkinson, prosecuting counsel at Dickman's trial, would have cross-examined Dickman on the Luard murder, but did not do so as he was 'not absolutely certain' of the facts. This is an astonishing thing for Rowan-Hamilton to have said. Dickman was on trial for the murder of *John Nisbet*. He was never charged with the murder of Mrs Luard, so the question of his being 'cross-examined' on the case during a trial for a *totally different crime* would never have come up!

Also, further with regard to Rowan-Hamilton's scenario there must arise the simple questions of why, if the police had such strong evidence to connect Dickman with Mrs Luard's death, they did nothing at all about it, and, also, why Superintendent Savage later stated that the police at the time were completely baffled as to the identity of Mrs Luard's killer.

It is quite possible that somewhere in Rowan-Hamilton's improbable story there is a kernel of truth; perhaps apart from the misleading 'information' about forged cheques and secret appointments there is the simple fact that Dickman was indeed Mrs Luard's killer. It is possible. When I first heard of the Dickman theory I at once thought that the answer to the mystery had been found. However. after looking into the matter more thoroughly I found that there was not a single jot of evidence to support such a theory, added to which the suggested scenario for the crime does not stand up to the slightest examination.

I have been informed that the police files on the Dickman and Luard cases have been destroyed (in common with the records of many of the classic crimes) so from the official police records no answers will ever be forthcoming. Whether clues to a solution lie in records kept by the Home Office (which records at the present time are still being kept under wraps) or some other body, however, is a question that has yet to be answered.

There are few signs left now of the events of that tragic afternoon and their aftermath, although Fish Ponds Wood appears to be almost as unspoilt now as it must have been on the fatal afternoon. From the road a path takes one past the five ponds – situated on different levels and draining one into the other – leading upwards until, on the side of the hill to the west, one comes upon the narrow footpath leading from the bridle path. Nowadays that footpath leads to nowhere in particular; the summerhouse has long gone; now at the side of the clearing in the wood only bits of rotting timber lie in the undergrowth to show where the building once stood.

Those remaining traces of the summerhouse are a sad memento of the Luards' story, and as one stands in the sodden grass beneath the dripping trees of a wet summer day the memory of the tragedy adds to the melancholy atmosphere – an atmosphere, one imagines, that comes from the thought of the tragic event itself and also, perhaps, from the secret that is held there. It is a secret that has been well-kept.

Further away in the graveyard of St Peter's church in Ightham the grave holding the three Luards is untended and overgrown, the two low-standing stones partly covered with moss and trailed over with brambles and ivy. On the side of the stone marking the burial of Mrs Luard there is a hint of her brutal, tragic end. The inscription reads:

SACRED TO THE BELOVED MEMORY OF
CAROLINE MARY
WIFE OF MAJOR GENERAL C.E. LUARD
AND DAUGHTER OF THOMAS HARTLEY ESQ
OF GILLFOOT CUMBERLAND
BORN 27.8.1850 DIED 24.8.1908
'THE LORD THY GOD SHALL MAKE THY DARKNESS TO BE LIGHT'

The Battersea Flat Mystery

The Murder of Weldon Atherstone

BY BERNARD TAYLOR

The names of two particular members of the theatrical profession hit the headlines in the summer of 1910, though in neither case was the blaze of publicity due to the actors' talents or to any particular theatrical production. The pair concerned went by the professional names of Belle Elmore and Weldon Atherstone. Neither of the two found fame during their particular careers, but in their deaths they attained a kind of stardom – Belle Elmore when parts of her dismembered body were dug up from beneath the cellar floor of her home at Hilldrop Crescent, London, and Weldon Atherstone when he died on the doorstep of a flat in London's Battersea.

Belle Elmore is of course better known as the wife of Dr Crippen, and the subsequent discovery of the vanished doctor – in the company of his lover, Ethel LeNeve – on board the SS *Montrose* bound for Quebec, his repatriation to Britain and trial and execution, made for sensational reading, and ensured him a permanent place in the annals of British crime and household mythology.

In her chosen career as an actress the American Belle Elmore had not met with any degree of success. Weldon Atherstone's theatrical career had been a little more notable, although at the time of his death he was out of work. His last engagement had been for a six-week period doing 'sketch-work' in music hall, one of which sketches, in a piece called 'The Grip of the Law', was at the Battersea Empire. At the climax of the sketch he would throw the villain into a cauldron used for bacon-curing and then cry out, 'Thank God, my father's murder has been avenged!'

His words seem imbued with a strange touch of irony in view of his death and the mystery that surrounds it to this day.

The strange and mysterious crime took place at the rear of 17, Clifton Gardens, Prince of Wales Road, Battersea, in southwest London, on the night of 16 July 1910. Number 17 was comprised of three flats, only one of which – the first floor, middle flat – was occupied on that night; the ground floor flat was empty and up for sale, while the owners of the top flat, by the name of Butcher, were away for the weekend.

A chauffeur by the name of Edward Noice was driving his car along Rosenau Road in Battersea at about 9.30 that summer night when two shots rang out from the direction of the rear of the houses in Clifton Gardens, and looking across he saw a man breaking through a tree in the garden of Number 19, the house next door to Number 17. A few moments later the man appeared on the top of a wall, leapt down on the pavement of Rosenau Road – narrowly missing a woman and two boys who were passing by – and ran off down the street towards the river. Noice wasted no time but drove at once to Battersea Bridge Road Police Station where he reported the incident.

In response to the report Police Sergeant Buckley was despatched to investigate, and was driven by Noice to Clifton Gardens. On entering the main door of Number 17, Buckley tried the door of the ground floor flat but found it secure. Going up the stairs he knocked at the door of the flat on the first floor. It was opened to him by its owner, Miss Elizabeth Earl[1], a teacher at the Academy

---

[1] In many contemporary newspapers her name was spelt Earle.

of Dramatic Art (now the Royal Academy of Dramatic Art, or RADA) in Gower Street.

'After telling Miss Earl that he had received information that shots had been fired at the rear of the building, Buckley asked if he might go through her flat and make a search. 'Yes,' she replied at once, adding, 'I heard the shots fired, and saw a man climb over the wall.'

Entering the flat the sergeant headed for the back door and on going into the kitchen found a young man there. He was Thomas Anderson, a twenty-one-year-old warehouseman. On seeing the police officer Anderson also said that he had heard the shots, and as the sergeant went out onto the fire escape Anderson said that he would go down with him and show him where the man had scrambled over the wall.

Both Anderson and Miss Earl, the sergeant said later, appeared quite calm and unperturbed.

With the woman Elizabeth Earl standing watching at the head of the stairs the two men stepped down to the lower level and walked to the end of the garden, the police sergeant leading the way. Seeing nothing, they turned and headed back, the sergeant coming to a stop mid-way to look over the garden wall. As the young man continued on and drew closer to the building he heard the sounds of heavy breathing coming from the shadows beneath the iron staircase. It sounded to him, he would say later, like the breathing of a dog, and on hearing it he called up to the woman to ask her whether the dog belonging to the Butchers was still in the flat. She replied that it was not. At her answer the young man stepped into the shadows, struck a match and saw lying in the doorway of the downstairs scullery the body of a man. He appeared to be unconscious and badly wounded. At once Anderson called to Sergeant Buckley: 'There is a man lying here.'

The sergeant came at the summons, looked at the man, and then asked Anderson to get him a light. The woman called down, 'I'll get you a lamp.' As she went back inside the sergeant asked Anderson to go out to the chauffeur, Noice, who was waiting in his motorcar, and ask him to fetch a doctor.

While the young man was gone on his errand the woman came part-way down the stairs and handed to the sergeant a small brass lamp with a single globe. By its light the sergeant took one more look at the unconscious man, then immediately said to the woman that if she was nervous she had better not come down any further. 'This man's been cut to pieces,' he said. Thomas Anderson returned then and held the lamp while the sergeant further examined the injured man.

The latter was lying on the scullery steps, his legs touching the yard. He lay on his back with his head turned to the left. There was blood on his face, and Buckley saw that he had been shot in the right side of the face, by his mouth. Then on turning the man's head he discovered another wound in the left temple. One eye was hanging out on his cheek. Turning to Anderson, Buckley asked him whether he knew the man. No, Anderson replied, he did not. The sergeant then pointed out that the man was wearing carpet slippers. On lifting the lamp higher, Buckley noticed in the open door's window pane a hole the size of a man's hand – as if from a gunshot. Anderson then asked if, while the doctor was being brought, they could do anything to help the wounded man. 'Perhaps,' he suggested, 'we could lift him into a sitting position . . .' No, the sergeant replied, it was better to leave him as he was. Throughout this Elizabeth Earl had been standing on the iron staircase and the young man called up to her to go back into the flat.

Soon afterwards a Dr Marriott arrived, soon to be

joined by Dr Kempster, the divisional surgeon. They were unable to do anything for the injured man, however, and he died at 10.20 without regaining consciousness.

Led by Detective Inspector Badcock, the man who was to take charge of the investigation, other members of the police force were soon on the scene. Following their arrival it was quickly discovered that although the ground floor flat was empty and locked – it was in the course of being decorated prior to being sold – it was quite an easy matter to make entry, for the decorators had tied a string to the catch of the latch inside, which could be activated by reaching through the letter box.

On searching the dead man's clothing the police made a surprising discovery. In his hip pocket they found a piece of insulated electric cable, seventeen inches long, wrapped in brown paper and wound around with wool, a loop attached to one end of it forming a wristband. It was a homemade example of what was known as a life-preserver, a kind of cosh. Also found in the man's pockets were an empty spectacles case, several letters addressed to Weldon Atherstone at 14, Great Percy Street, WC, and a small red diary containing business cards. In a waistcoat pocket were found two keys and a watch and chain, and in other pockets some loose change, a pipe, tobacco pouch, box of matches and empty cigarette case.

When examination of the body at the scene had been completed it was taken to the mortuary while the officers turned their attention to the scene of the crime. In the sink in the scullery were found two pieces of a bullet, and on the floor some pieces of a crushed spectacles frame and the crushed glass of their lenses. In a copper in the scullery was found a small quantity of blood, and on the mantelpiece above the fireplace in the kitchen a pair of boots wrapped in brown paper. There was no sign of any gun, however. It looked like a case of murder.

As the police officers continued with their investigations Thomas Anderson went to Detective Geake to ask if he was wanted any more as he would like to leave and go home. The inspector replied that he could not be allowed to leave yet and the young man went back up the stairs to Miss Earl's flat. An hour later he made the same request, explaining that he had to be in by 11.30 or he would be locked out for the night. Geake again refused him permission to go, telling him not to worry – 'I'll see to that' – and the young man went into the kitchen of the ground floor flat where he was interviewed by Inspector Badcock. During this time Badcock asked him if he had recognized the dead man. He said he had not. After some time Anderson went out into the front garden where he found Inspector Geake talking to Dr Kempster.

'I came out to get some air,' Anderson told the inspector. 'I feel sick.'

Geake, who was holding some of the dead man's belongings, called Anderson to one side and, having inadvertently misread the name on the business cards, asked him if he knew anyone of the name of *Atherton*.

'No,' replied the young man, 'but I know someone of the name of *Atherstone*.'

'Who is that?'

'My father.'

The inspector then showed the young man a business card and asked him if he recognized it. On it was written:

Weldon Atherstone
Leading Character Actor
14 Great Percy Street, W.C.

Anderson looked at the card and said, 'That is my father's card.'

He was then told that he was to be taken to the station

and soon afterwards he was escorted to the Battersea Bridge Road Police Station. On arrival he was asked if the dead man was his father.

'I can't think that,' he replied. 'My father doesn't wear a moustache.' Then he added, 'Was he wearing a *false* moustache?'

'No, he has no moustache,' Geake replied. 'He's clean shaven.'

'Do you mean that that man was my father?' Anderson asked.

'I don't know,' Geake said. 'But I want you to understand that you're being detained while inquiries are being made – nothing else at present.'

After a few moments the young man asked the inspector to describe the dead man.

'He has a long, thin face, like yours,' Geake said.

At the words the young man burst into a fit of sobbing and, covering his face with his hands, cried out, 'Good God, it's my father! I saw my father die.'

In the early hours of the morning Thomas Anderson was taken to the mortuary where he saw again the body of the dead man. There, without hesitation, he identified it as that of his father.

The real name of Weldon Atherstone was Thomas Weldon Anderson.

As far as is known no photograph of him survives. All that is available is a drawing taken from a photograph, and which appeared in some of the newspapers following the murder. It shows a fairly good-looking man with a strong brow and jaw.

At the time of the killing he was forty-seven years old. His wife, from whom he had been separated for some years, had been a Miss Monica Kelly, the orphaned daughter of a law clerk. She had been an actress, and it is likely that she and Atherstone had met when working with the same theatrical company. They were married in Salford, in the early autumn of 1888, both giving their address as 20, Barlows Road, Salford, and describing themselves as 'comedians'. During their marriage they had four children, two boys, two girls.

After separating from his wife in about 1900, Atherstone had come to live in London, the only place in England for anyone seriously wishing to pursue a theatrical career. His two sons, Thomas Frederick and William Gordon, left home at a later date, also coming to London, and both getting jobs as warehousemen and taking lodgings together in Wood Street, near St Paul's Cathedral.

It was at the lodgings shared by the Anderson brothers that the younger, the sixteen-year-old William Anderson, was informed at two o'clock on the Sunday morning of the tragedy that had befallen his father. Afterwards he was taken to the mortuary, following which, along with his brother Thomas, he was allowed to return home.

At the first floor flat at Clifton Gardens, Elizabeth Earl was told the identity of the dead man. Hitherto she had appeared quite collected and not unduly disturbed by the events. Now, on learning who he was, she went into hysterics and had to be treated by a doctor.

Later, when she had recovered sufficiently, she gave Inspector Badcock a statement in which she revealed that she had known Weldon Atherstone for many years, and that they had been lovers.

At the time of Atherstone's death Elizabeth Earl was about forty years of age. Once an actress, she had given up the stage to become a teacher at the Academy of Dramatic Art. A photograph of her, taken in her earlier years, shows a not-unattractive, round-faced young woman with a longish nose, wide eyes, a small mouth and a mass of wavy hair.

She had been living at 17, Clifton Gardens, Prince of Wales Road, for eight years, four years in the first floor flat, and the previous four years in the flat below. In earlier times her mother and invalid brother had also lived there. Four years before, however, her brother, who suffered from tuberculosis, had gone abroad to Australia. Her mother had since died.

In the statement she gave to Inspector Badcock in the early hours of the morning following the shooting she stated that she had met Weldon Atherstone a number of years before and had 'since been on intimate relations with him', adding that he had stayed with her 'when he liked'.

She further stated that she had known the actor's son, Thomas Frederick Anderson, from a boy, and that he had made an appointment to call on her on the Saturday night. They had heard the shots while they were taking supper in the kitchen, she said, and immediately afterwards had seen a man scrambling over the wall from the alley into the garden of Number 19. Further, with regard to her relationship with the deceased actor, she said that he had been very jealous of her and had accused her of seeing other men. Following a quarrel as the result of his accusations, she added, he had left her and found other lodgings, telling her that their relationship was over.

Dr Kempster, the divisional surgeon, who saw Elizabeth Earl in the early hours immediately following her having been informed of the identification of the dead man, found her to be in a state of nervous collapse. 'She was trembling in every limb,' he was later to report, 'and complaining bitterly of the cold. She was almost pulseless.'

When daylight came the police were able to effect a

more thorough search of the flat and the gardens at the rear of Numbers 17 and 19, between which was a narrow walled alley, a tradesmen's way, leading from Prince of Wales Road at the front. It was clear that the assailant had had to climb three walls to make his escape. In their search of the garden of Number 19 the police found footprints leading from the wall bordering the alley, traces of a passage through the shrubbery, and marks on the inside of the opposite wall where the supposed assailant had scrambled over into Rosenau Road. Of the revolver that had caused the actor's fatal wounds, however, there was still no sign.

There were, however, various witnesses to the man's leaping over the garden wall of Number 19 into Rosenau Road and his dash down towards the Thames.

Noice, the chauffeur, when questioned about the man he had seen leaping over the wall into Rosenau Road, said he could not describe how he was dressed, though he was certain that he was not wearing an overcoat. The impression he had of him was that he was about 5'6" tall and not of the labouring type. He did not think, he said, that the man had been carrying a gun as he had used both hands to get over the wall. One thing he was certain about, and that was that young Thomas Anderson was *not* the man. When faced with him at Battersea Bridge Road Police Station at one o'clock on the Sunday morning he stated categorically, 'That is not the man that got over the wall. Of that I am positive.'

Young Thomas Anderson had been wearing a new blue serge suit when Sergeant Buckley first saw him in the flat, and later examination of his hands and clothes had revealed them to be quite clean.

These factors also ruled him out as the escaping man as far as another witness was concerned. She, Mrs Lewis, of nearby Juer Street, told police that she was returning home along Rosenau Road when she heard two pistol shots in quick succession, and on looking over the wall in the direction of the sounds saw a man spring onto the wall only a step from where she was standing. On leaping down onto the pavement he ran away along Rosenau Road, quickly disappearing from sight. He was about 5′6″ in height, she said, and was wearing a dark-jacketed suit and a bowler hat. He had nothing in his hands and wore no gloves. She thought she would be able to recognize him again, side-faced. With regard to the state of his clothing, she said that the back of his jacket appeared to be covered in mud or dust.

A third witness, Arthur James, a salesman from Ilford, said he was passing along Rosenau Road on his way from work when a man ran past him, breathing heavily. The man ran down towards Petworth Street. James said that he caught a passing glimpse of his face, that the man was wearing a peaked cap and carried nothing in his hands. He thought, he added, that the man was wearing light boots as he made little noise in his running. Judging by the man's dress, James said, he would think he was more likely to be a clerk than a labourer. He would be about twenty-five or twenty-six years old.

Later, the two boys who had also been passing by at the time would be traced. They would describe the man as between twenty-three and thirty years of age, and about 5′3″ tall.

The press wasted no time in trying to get their own exclusive stories in connection with the case, and on Monday a representative from *The Daily Chronicle* interviewed Thomas Anderson at his lodgings in Wood Street, during which the young man 'spoke frankly upon the matter, only once or twice answering evasively when a question went too closely to family matters that he felt had no direct bearing upon the tragedy'.

'I have no idea why anyone should take my father's life,' Anderson said, 'or why anyone should feel enmity towards him. He was of a lovable nature, kind and sympathetic, and I should say the last in the world to make an enemy. He made friends everywhere.'

Questioned about the relationship with Miss Earl, Anderson said, 'We have been friends for years. We had known Miss Earl and her late mother for a very long time, and the friendship was continued after her mother's death.' Presumably unaware of Elizabeth Earl's statement to the police regarding the intimate nature of her own relationship with the actor, he insisted that she and his father had been nothing more than friends.

He then went on to say, 'Let me tell you exactly what was the position, also, as between my father and myself. He had not the slightest objection to my visiting her – in fact we often went together. Nor was there the slightest secrecy as to the visits we paid. He knew I was going there on Saturday, although I did not expect that he would meet me there at the time he came. But it would not have surprised me in the least to see his face at the door at any moment. As to his taking off his boots and putting on slippers in the bottom flat, I can only say that I cannot understand his motive. But I would rather not discuss points of that kind, because the police have warned me not to talk about what took place, and I do not want to interfere with their efforts to find the murderer.'

With regard to events at the time of the killing, when he and Miss Earl had heard the shots, he said:

'She wanted to go down to the yard and see what was the matter. I persuaded her not to, because I knew the recent burglaries had made people nervous, and that if there was someone half silly with fright and carrying a revolver she might get a bullet. We looked out of the back window after a bit, and then could see the crowd gathering in the side street, so that we knew there was no need to inform the police of what we had seen.'

Asked why the police had taken him away for interrogation, he replied he did not know the reason.

Inspector Badcock continued with his investigations, interrupting them only to attend the inquest which was opened on the Tuesday afternoon, 19 July by the Battersea coroner, Dr Troutbeck. Only one witness was called. She was Miss Harriet Anderson, a sister of the dead man. After she had given formal identification of the body the inquest was adjourned until 11 A.M. on Saturday, the 23rd. The police hoped that by the time the inquest was resumed they would have come up with some answers. Until that happened they must continue to search diligently for any clue that would lead to an unravelling of the mystery.

And it *was* a mystery. All that was really known were those facts that had become apparent soon after the revelation of the happening: a forty-seven-year-old actor had been shot and killed in the rear doorway of an empty ground floor flat while in the apartment above his young son and erstwhile mistress had, so they claimed, been dining together, unaware of the man's presence. The fact that the dead man, dressed in ordinary walking clothes, was found to be wearing carpet slippers while his boots stood on a nearby shelf, wrapped in paper, suggested that he had wanted to be able to move about without making a noise and being detected. Also, the discovery of a homemade life-preserver in his back pocket indicated that he had prepared himself for the possibility of a violent encounter – the violence either being instigated by himself or by some other person.

Whether Atherstone was expecting to meet any

particular person was a fact that had yet to be discovered. The only certainty was that he had met *someone* – and that that someone had killed him. But who? That a man, probably aged in his mid-twenties, had been seen desperately running from the scene of the crime had been testified to by no fewer than five passers-by. But who the man was and what motive he might have had for killing the actor was anybody's guess.

Dr Felix Kempster, who examined Atherstone's body, revealed that there were two gunshot wounds in the man's head, one in the left temple and the other in the upper lip. Both of the wounds, said Kempster, were bleeding when he arrived on the scene shortly before the man's death. One bullet was later found in the skull, the other – apparently having been deflected by striking the man's teeth – was found in pieces in the scullery sink. There was every indication of a struggle having taken place before the shots were fired, there being fingernail marks on the dead man's face and wrists, and abrasions on his chest.

The Daily Chronicle set out some of the questions to which the police were hoping soon to find the answers, among them:

Had the deceased reason to believe that someone might come to the back premises, and if so, for what purpose?

Was he anticipating an attack from anyone upon himself, or his son, or Miss Earl?

Who is there with whom he has at any time quarrelled who might bear him ill-will enough to take his life personally, or by an agent or friend?

Who is there who anticipated a possible meeting with him and an attack by him, and for what reason?

What was the motive for the attack?

Who is there in the whole wide world who bore him animosity, or was doing something of which he knew the deceased would disapprove, and who knew that if detected in what he was doing he would run a serious risk?

Who was the man in the back yard who fired the shots, and what was his motive?

In a search for answers there was no shortage of theories put forward by the press.

Said one newspaper: 'It is almost impossible to avoid the conclusion that the man who was murdered and the man who fired the fatal shot were known to each other, and were, moreover, aware of the fact that they might meet at the flat at any time.'

It was further suggested that the motive for the murder might be revenge, or alternatively that perhaps Atherstone had had reason to believe that someone intended 'to annoy Miss Earl by unasked intrusion' and that he had 'resolved to lie in wait for the intruder'. It was also suggested by *The Daily Chronicle* that when Atherstone arrived the intruder was already there and had begun to ascend the iron steps with the intention of spying on Elizabeth Earl and whoever might be with her. 'Such a spy,' it was said, 'would rightly fear violence and go armed.'

This latter statement is nonsense; there is no reason to suppose that a man intent on spying would go armed with a loaded revolver. Besides which, one would have to assume that Atherstone, on finding the intruder on the stairs, first stopped to change into his slippers before trying to apprehend him!

A theory carefully being considered by the police was that the killing was the result of an attempted robbery by a would-be thief who, on entering the ground floor flat, happened to encounter Atherstone. There had been a number of burglaries in the area, and obviously such a theory was a definite possibility.

According to one paper, the police later hinted that they believed 'that three men were directly or indirectly concerned in the tragedy, and that Miss Earl was the innocent cause of a passionate feud that had arisen between two of them', the outcome being that Atherstone, believing – mistakenly or not – that his rival intended to be at the flat at a certain time, went there to confront him. Regarding that violent confrontation, *The Daily Chronicle* said:

In view of the struggle which there is now practically no doubt took place between the dead man and his assailant, it is almost certain that the latter must have received some injury. Indeed it is probable that he only fired the shot as a means of escaping from the grip that the actor had fastened upon him. It is stated that the police have detected bruises round the dead man's mouth that exactly correspond to the thumb and four finger-marks of a 'spread' hand, such as would be left if the murderer had tried to close it, and prevent an outcry.

It was . . . stated that an examination of the footprints in the garden of Number 19 showed that the individual who had passed over it to the back of Miss Earl's flat had made the double journey. As against this statement it may be said that an investigator who scrutinized the ground very closely came to the conclusion that the two sets of footprints, one of which was very indistinct, had not been made at the same time.

There is another fact that makes it extremely improbable that anyone went over from the Rosenau Road side, and that is that he would have to scale the wall in the full light of an electric standard and a street lamp. It would have been much less likely to attract attention if the intruder had climbed over the gate of the tradesman's passage of Number 17 in Prince of Wales Road.

Whatever was said, however, the only thing that clearly emerged was that no one seemed to be any nearer to finding the answer to the mystery.

Atherstone seemed to have had no enemies. Granted his marriage had failed – which was said to have caused him great unhappiness – but nevertheless it is hard to imagine that in such an event lay the seeds of his murder. With regard to his wife, it was reported that on his death she was much affected and wrote 'a very womanly letter of sympathy' to the dead man's sisters in Tufnell Park Road.

Neither could the police investigators find any trace of hostility between Atherstone and his two sons, Thomas and William. On the contrary, it appeared that they had been affectionately close, in support of which contention was the fact that William had spent his annual two weeks' summer holiday at his father's lodgings in Great Percy Street, the fortnight's vacation only coming to an end on the day of the actor's death.

Inquiring into Atherstone's past, it was found that over the preceding year he had spent between four and five months living and working in London and the remainder of the time in other parts of the country. For years past when in London he had lived for most of the time at Elizabeth Earl's flat, the situation changing only two months before his death when he had moved into the lodgings at Great Percy Street.

While the police continued their investigations there appeared in the stage paper *The Era* an obituary to Atherstone, describing him as 'a quiet, reserved man, and a sound and useful actor', going on to name some of his more notable appearances in various theatrical productions.

Atherstone's funeral took place on Friday, 22 July, the cortège forming at the house of his sisters in north London. Chief mourner was his elder son, Thomas, who was accompanied by his brother William and his two sisters. Neither the dead man's widow nor Elizabeth Earl was present. Reported one of the daily newspapers:

The funeral had been arranged to take place at Abney Park Cemetery, and as the time of its departure had not been publicly announced there were but a dozen or so onlookers, as many more being gathered at the graveside.

Many who had known and loved the dead man who were unable to be present sent wreaths of the flowers of which he was a lover, while the son Tom laid at the head of the coffin, with affectionate care, the offering of himself and his brother and sisters, to which was attached a card, 'To our darling father, from his children.' Anxious to show a last token of affection for his father, the elder son assisted in carrying the body from the hearse to the grave and in lowering it into its resting place.

The Daily Chronicle on Saturday, the 23rd, after reporting on the funeral, wrote:

Today the coroner's jury will resume their inquiry into the tragedy, but unless the unexpected happens they will have no evidence upon which to base any other verdict that that the deceased met his death at the hands of a person unknown . . .

Miss Earl, the dead man's intimate friend, will be the chief witness, if the latter is well enough to go through the ordeal. At the time of writing she was so prostrate that there were grave doubts whether she would be able to attend. Indeed, her absence from the funeral was eloquent testimony to the extreme weakness from which she is suffering as the effect of the crime. She had also had the worry of close examination by the police, with a view to discovering whether there was anyone whose association with Mr Anderson [Atherstone] was of a nature to lead to suspicion that he or she could throw light upon the crime.

As the hour of the resumed inquest approached the press eagerly looked forward to seeing in the witness box Elizabeth Earl, the woman in the case. One paper, following up reports of her 'extreme weakness', said that on the previous day, the Friday, her doctor had certified that she was too ill to attend. But, said *The Daily Graphic* on the morning of the inquiry: 'Miss Elizabeth Earl . . . has recovered from her nervous prostration, and it is expected that she will be able to attend the inquest when it is resumed today.'

And so she did. Reported *The Daily Chronicle* later:

'It had been thought that Miss Earl would be unable to attend the resumed inquest . . . but just before the inquiry was opened she drove up in a cab, accompanied by three other women, and was assisted into the court. She seemed, however, exceedingly weak.'

The first witnesses called were Edward Noice and Mrs Lewis – two of those who had seen the unknown man leap from the wall of Number 19 Clifton Gardens. They were followed by Arthur James who had passed the man as he had dashed towards the river. After the latter came Sergeant Buckley who testified to going to Number 17 and, in the company of Thomas Anderson, finding the dying man lying on the back steps of the ground floor flat. When he had asked Anderson whether he knew the injured man he had been holding the lamp close to Atherstone's face, he said. Questioned by a juryman, he said that when Miss Earl had answered the door to his knock and he had told her what business he had come about, she 'did not seem agitated'.

Buckley was followed by Inspector Geake who related how, after finding Atherstone's business card, he asked Thomas Anderson whether he knew anyone named Atherton. 'No,' Anderson had replied, 'but I do Atherstone.' Shown one of the deceased's cards Anderson had said, 'That is my father's card.' After this, said Geake, Anderson was taken to Battersea Bridge Road Police Station for further questioning. The young man was not shown the body again, he said, until it was in the mortuary.

At the police station, went on Geake, the son had asked if it was his father who had been shot, and afterwards had asked whether the man had been wearing a false moustache. He had then been told that he was to be detained while inquiries were made. The young man, he said, had 'burst into a fit of sobbing, covered his face with his hands and cried out, "Good God, it's my father!"'

Detective Sergeant Purkiss testified to searching the dead man's pockets and finding, among other items, the homemade life-preserver. He was also present, he said, when Thomas Anderson had been questioned at the police station. There, in answer to a question from the young man, the deceased was described. 'Good God,' Anderson had said, weeping, 'I saw my father die.' Purkiss further testified to accompanying Thomas Anderson to the mortuary where he identified the body as that of his father.

After Purkiss came Inspector Badcock who said that after thoroughly searching the premises he had interviewed Miss Elizabeth Earl and taken from her the following statement:

I am a teacher of the Academy of Dramatic Art, Gower Street, and occupy a flat at 17 Clifton Gardens, Prince of Wales Road, Battersea. I have lived there and at the flat below for about eight years.

Thomas Weldon Anderson, lying dead, was an actor whose stage name was Weldon Atherstone. He was married, and lived at 14 Great Percy Street, King's Cross, in lodgings, having been separated from his wife before I knew him. He had four children, whose names I give.

I first met deceased when on a theatrical tour upwards of eight years ago, and have since been on intimate relations with him, and he has come and stayed with me when he liked.

With regard to the events of the night of the 16th, her statement read:

About 8.30 or 8.45 tonight the son, Thomas Frederick Anderson, called upon me by an appointment made on a postcard asking if he might call. I had known him from a boy and he had always visited me. I replied that he might call and he did so. On his arrival, about 8.40 P.M., we sat and talked in the front sitting room until about nine. Then I showed him some decorations that I had carried out in my bedroom, and then went to take supper in the kitchen. While doing so we heard two shots in quick succession, and on going into the scullery adjoining, opened a door leading onto the back stairs. Looking out, we saw a man scrambling over the wall dividing our back from the adjoining one to the right of us. I wanted to go down to see what the matter was, but Anderson would not let me. We resumed our meal, thinking that someone might have fired to scare a thief. A few minutes later a knock came at the door, and I admitted Sergeant Buckley.

Further, with regard to her relationship with the dead actor, she said:

I last saw Thomas Weldon Anderson about seven weeks ago when he called with his son, Thomas Frederick. They stayed to tea, and through the evening, and we were happy together. The time before that I saw Mr Thomas Weldon Anderson was about eight weeks ago. He called before I came home, and I believe was let through the back by one of the other flats. He stayed with me that night, but seemed sulky. At breakfast the next morning we quarrelled, because he said I had had another man in the flat. I denied it. He then pointed to the sofa and said that it was indented and had been laid on. He struck me. I called for help. I went out and into the park. On my return he said, 'It is all over', meaning our friendship. As he had been frequently jealous because I had my pupils, I gave them up a year ago, and had got used to his jealousy. After the quarrel he called in my absence and left my latchkey with a note asking me to forward his letters to an address he had written, and this made me think he might not come again. My home was always open to him, and he knew it. I know of no one who had any feeling against him. I had behaved like a mother to his boys, the eldest of whom I had taken great interest in, and had instructed.

Questioned by the coroner, Badcock said that he had examined Thomas Anderson and that his answers had agreed exactly with what Miss Earl had said.

Producing a small red diary, the inspector said it had

been taken from Atherstone's pocket and that entries in it indicated the deceased's jealousy of Miss Earl. The coroner, on examining the diary, turned to the jury and said, 'These are intimate entries, gentlemen.' In answer to further questions, Badcock said Miss Earl had been shown the diary and had been questioned respecting it. 'Does she know it?' asked the coroner. 'She does not say she knows it,' Badcock replied.

The coroner handed copies of some of the entries in the diary to the jury who made an inspection of them. While this was going on the inspector said that on searching the rear of the premises in daylight he had found footmarks of boots, about size nine. The footprints, he said, did not match the boots of the deceased man.

Asked by a juryman how Atherstone had entered the ground floor flat, Badcock explained the arrangement of the piece of cord which protruded through the letter box and was attached to the latch inside. The latchkey found on the dead man, Badcock added, opened the front door to Miss Earl's flat. At this the coroner said, 'So had he tried to he could have entered into Miss Earl's flat by means of his key?'

'Yes,' answered Badcock.

An adjournment was called at this point and the public and press filed out to wait in the street. As they went past the witness room they tried to catch a glimpse of Elizabeth Earl as she waited to be called. The reporter for the *News of the World* later wrote that in glancing into the room as he passed by, he 'caught sight of the weary, troubled form and the haggard, drawn features of one of the central figures in this mysterious drama'. He added, 'Robed in deep black, and her pale, wan face thickly veiled from the gaze of the crowd, sat Miss Earl. Beside her stood the two sons of the murdered actor . . .'

On the inquest's resumption a little later Dr Felix

Kempster gave evidence as to the deceased's wounds, saying that Atherstone had lived until 10.20, though had been unconscious. At that time, he said, the man's face was not much disfigured. Said Kempster:

'Young Anderson came up as I was examining the body. He was there for some considerable time. The features were quite placid, and when the body was seen next morning, and recognized by the son, the body was exactly in the same state.'

'Was there a good light?' asked the coroner.

'A splendid light.'

After relating that he had found Elizabeth Earl 'in a state of nervous collapse', he said she had told him that the actor had had a severe accident two years previously, and that since that time he had been jealous of her.

With regard to the wounds found on the dead man, Kempster said that the revolver must have been fired at very close quarters, and that beforehand there had been a struggle. No one, he added, appeared to have heard the sounds of any shouts during the struggle.

'When you saw the wounds,' said the coroner, 'were there any powder marks or burning?'

'Yes,' replied the doctor, ' – well marked over the region of the wound near the eyebrow, and less well marked over the region of the wound in the face.'

After a second doctor had corroborated Kempster's evidence the coroner sent a police constable to interview Elizabeth Earl – who was waiting in another room – with regard to the accident sustained by Atherstone to which she had referred in her statement.

On his return the constable said he had been informed by Miss Earl that Atherstone had been knocked down two years before by a motorcar. He had been very much bruised, and suffered from slight concussion. He had been taken to a hospital where he had remained for about three hours.

The final witness of the day was the sixteen-year-old William Anderson. In answer to questions he said his father had 'had no fixed address, as being an actor he had to travel about the country a good deal, though when in London he stayed with Miss Earl and at 14, Great Percy Street'. He then said that he himself had been staying for his holidays with his father at his lodgings in Great Percy Street for the last two weeks of his father's life. He had last seen Miss Earl three or four months ago, he said. Questioned, he said he knew of no reason why he had not seen her since; he had not had the time. At this the coroner said to him: 'You could have gone to see her during the last fortnight.'

'Yes,' said the boy, 'but I didn't think of it.'

The coroner: 'She speaks of her relationship as if she were a mother to you boys.'

'Yes, she was. She took a great interest in us.'

In reply to the coroner William Anderson said that he had last seen his father on Saturday, the 16th, about 12.30 midday, in his lodgings. Asked whether it had been intended that he should spend the afternoon with his father on that day, he said no.

The slippers, the boots, and the peaked cap found beneath the body were produced and he identified them as belonging to his father. His father had seldom worn a cap, he added.

His brother, he said, was a greater friend of Miss Earl than he was. Further, he said he was told by his brother that he was going to see Miss Earl on the Saturday.

He had heard of no 'estrangement' between Miss Earl and his father, he said. Asked if he had any idea why his brother had not at once recognized the unconscious man as their father, he replied that his brother had said that the reason was because there was a blood mark on the upper lip, and that their father was the last person he expected to see there.

'Recently,' he said in answer to further questions, 'my father had been troubled about his business. It was getting well on in the autumn season and he had not fixed any engagements.' His father was a man of sober habits, he said.

Questioned about his father's recent movements, he said that on the Wednesday night before his death his father had been away all night, saying he had 'private business', and on returning the following morning said he had had 'no luck'. 'He came home by workman's tram.' Here the ticket was produced, showing that it had been issued in the Battersea district.

Asked whether he had any reason to believe that his father was on bad terms with anyone, he answered that he had not. 'Do you know anything of a quarrel between Miss Earl and your father?' asked the coroner. 'No,' the boy replied.

After William Anderson had been dismissed the coroner said there was considerable further evidence, and the police desired time in which to follow up inquiries. He didn't wish to interfere with the holidays, he said, but it would be necessary to have a further adjournment. Finally it was agreed to adjourn the inquest until 17 September.

The press and the public must have left the courtroom feeling somewhat disappointed at the anti-climactic ending to the day's proceedings. They had heard some fascinating revelations – of Elizabeth Earl's love affair with the actor, his jealousies, and his diary with its 'intimate entries' – but Elizabeth Earl herself had not been called.

* * *

Following the closing of the second part of the resumed inquest, information was given to some of the newspapers regarding the notes written in Atherstone's little red diary. There were, it was said, a great many entries under the heading 'B', which was later discovered to stand for 'Bessie', the name by which Atherstone had known Elizabeth Earl. Said *The People*:

'. . . Extracts from the diary of the dead man . . . show how deep-rooted was his jealousy. Certain entries, which it is not advisable to publish, show that he had been watching Miss Earl's flat for some months past in the expectation of meeting a visitor, and others show that he was fast losing his reason. No sane man would write such sentences, even in a private pocket-book.'

Two entries under a date about the middle of July, it was said, showed how Atherstone had watched the house at Number 17 and 'acted as an amateur detective in his endeavours to find out who was the man he imagined to be paying attentions to Miss Earl'.

Read one entry: 'Watched the house until 11.30, when lights were turned out.' Another entry ran: 'Found bunch of flowers in the ashbin.' In connection with the latter entry Atherstone argued in his diary that someone had evidently made Miss Earl a present of the flowers, a conclusion which she herself denied.

Another entry, apparently quoted from some published work, ran: 'Friendship is but a substitute for love, and cannot exist beside it, unless the lover and friend be one and the same person. They suppose that a man can love a woman with the best kind of love, and may have at the same time a friend with whom he is in entire sympathy. Why not? Because he cannot serve two masters – either his friendship or his love must be imperfect.'

Another of the several entries on the subject of love ran: 'The prime essence of love is that it should be complete, making no reservation, and allowing of no check from the reason. When the heart gets the mastery it knows neither rest nor mercy. If the heart is good the result will be good; if bad, evil.'

The report in *The People* added: 'Certain of the notes scribbled in his diary by the murdered actor are of too personal a character for production here. Every item of the daily life of Miss Earl that came to his notice was entered and commented on in such a manner that the police could only conclude that he was fast going out of his mind.'

With regard to the state of Atherstone's mind, the diary held a note of the accident he had suffered, and after which, Elizabeth Earl had stated, his behaviour had changed. Under the date January 14, 1908 was written: 'Knocked down by motor-bus. Slight concussion of the brain.'

It was stated that the police had hoped they would find in the diary some clue to the name of the man whom Atherstone hoped or expected to meet on that fatal Saturday night, but, said *The People*, 'so many names were mentioned that it was of little use'. One man, it was reported, against whom Atherstone's suspicions seemed to have been greatest, was on tour in America, while most of the others referred to were in the provinces.

It was later reported that Elizabeth Earl was about to undergo an operation, and that upon her recovery intended to leave the country to go to Australia to join her brother. 'Her departure, however,' it was stated, 'will not take place until the inquest on her one-time lover has been concluded.'

Shortly afterwards Elizabeth Earl was found to be absent from her flat and rumour went about that she had already left the country to join her brother. The rumour was untrue; it was revealed that with the permission of the police she had gone to stay with friends 'a long way from London, in order to prepare herself for the ordeal of the resumed inquest on September 17th'.

While the police were trying to gather new evidence in preparation for the resumed inquest the newspapermen were doing their best to keep the case alive in the face of a lack of any new development, and to find new information on the case. One reporter, commenting on Atherstone's state of mind, said he appeared to have been 'an unusually jealous man, and several actors who have appeared with him tell me that he was ready to fly into a temper directly the least thing upset him'.

Writing on what might have happened on that Saturday night, one paper wrote that the fact that Atherstone had not taken his life-preserver from his pocket during the struggle gave 'colour to the suggestion that he had also armed himself with a revolver, and that it was with his own weapon, drawn against another man, that he was shot'.

With regard to who Atherstone's adversary was, one paper reported that the police were 'entirely satisfied' that he was shot by a burglar whom he had met casually at the flat. Another paper stated: 'One of the most experienced Scotland Yard men throws over the "burglar theory" absolutely and without reserve,' adding that it was the belief that 'the murderer was some acquaintance of the dead man, or Miss Earl, or both'.

Then, in support of the belief that the burglar theory had by no means been discounted, there came the news in mid-August that a man had been arrested and was being held at a police station 'on the other side of the Thames' in connection with the crime.

According to reports certain documents found on the man indicated that he might have had some connection with the Battersea crime. He was not named in the newspapers, but it was stated that his physical description tallied closely with that given of the man seen running from the scene of the crime. In addition to this fact was the knowledge that he had been seen in the Battersea area on the day of the crime and at the time had only recently been discharged from prison. His known history, it was said, encouraged 'the belief that he might be engaged in petty housebreaking exploits, and certainly that he would defend himself with the utmost disregard of consequences if in danger of assault'.

A statement by one reporter in the press ran: 'The man still refuses to give any detailed account of himself, and maintains a sullen demeanour, resenting even the presence of the usual visitors to the prison . . . He has evidently lived a very irregular life, and is suffering somewhat from privation, although he seems possessed of a considerable share of physical strength. His arms and body carry a number of bruises, some of them of large size, and very badly discoloured. But they are of recent origin, and none of them, as I understand, likely to be old enough to carry back to the date of the Battersea tragedy.'

Said *The People*: 'It is not suggested that the man now in custody was known to Anderson. Although he is an educated man, there is no reason to believe that they were even mutually cognizant of each other's existence. On the contrary, there is every reason to believe that the fatal encounter, whoever it was with, was entirely fortuitous, that burglary would seem to have been the intent of the perpetrator of the murder.'

Unfortunately for the investigating officers, however, the promising lead fizzled out. The apprehension of the unnamed man failed to lead to any charge and he was subsequently released. The police appeared to be as far from a solution as ever.

* * *

17 September. Battersea Coroner's Court. Elizabeth Earl kept the veil of her large, fashionable hat lowered over her face when she walked into the courtroom that morning, and only lifted it after taking a seat in the witness stand. Then she sat in such a position that only the coroner could clearly see her face. Speaking in 'a tragic voice, which was not always easily heard', she gave her name and then, in answer to questions, proceeded to give information about her relationship with the late actor.

She and Atherstone had lived on good terms until the last four years, she said, when they had begun to quarrel due to his jealousies. 'Of any particular person?' asked the coroner, to which she replied, 'He was jealous of every man I knew.'

'Did you ever give any reason or cause for jealousy?'

'No.'

'Did you continue your intimate relations notwithstanding these quarrels?'

'Yes.'

'Up to when?'

'Eight weeks before his death. They ceased when Mr Anderson said I had someone staying with me. I denied it and he struck and left me.'

'Was the separation by his wish?'

'Yes.'

'And by yours also?'

'No.'

'Did you see him after that occurrence?'

'Yes. He called that night and brought the key back and left his address for letters to be sent.'

The letter, read out in court, ran:

'Dear Bessie, – Just to enclose latchkey and give my address to which you can forward any letters if they turn up. I am sorry I hurt you, very sorry. Of course you can but deny. That was the ground you were forced to take. I am sorry.'

The coroner then asked whether she knew whether Atherstone had ever been into her flat in her absence since they had separated. She replied that from the entries in his diary she surmised that he had. 'How did he get in?' asked the coroner, to which she replied that he had another key. It was then stated that the key had been found on Atherstone's body, and the coroner observed that he might have had it specially cut. Elizabeth Earl then said that it was not necessary for him to have a key at all as the back door was never locked.

The coroner: 'I understand there have been burglars in the district. Have you been visited?'

'Yes. I had my gas meter broken open last year. They broke in at the front door.'

'You did not think it necessary to shut your back door after that?'

'No.'

After repeating that there was no foundation for the deceased's suspicions concerning her, she was asked her opinion as to his mental state. She replied: 'I think he had got this idea into his head, and it had become an obsession.'

In answer to further questions she said that the two sons had not been aware of the true relationship between the actor and herself, and that since the rupture in the relationship she had had no male visitors, only female. Asked to give her story of the night Atherstone had died, she said, 'The son came about 8.30 and we sat talking in the sitting room. At 9.30 or a little before I suggested supper, and went out to the kitchen to prepare it, and he came out and watched me. We sat down and heard two shots fired very close together.'

'Did you hear anything first? Did you hear any scrambling?'

'No.'

'What did you do?'

'I thought they were shooting cats, and I jumped up and looked out at the scullery door and Mr Anderson followed. We saw a man scrambling over the wall of the garden next door. I started to run downstairs and Mr Anderson said I had better not. I said, "Someone has fired a shot to scare off a prowler." We sat down and a policeman came and said someone had heard two shots and seen someone running away, and he wished to see if there was anything wrong.'

She went on to relate how Thomas Anderson had followed the policeman down the stairs into the yard where they had found the wounded man. When she got the policeman a light, she stated, he said to her, 'You go upstairs; this man is cut to pieces.'

Later, she said, she had told Thomas Anderson that he had better go or he would be late and get into trouble at his business. 'He went downstairs and came back and told me the policeman said he must wait as it was very important.'

At a later time, she said, she went downstairs where there were a number of policemen and asked if they had identified the dead man. 'One of them said they did not know. Then the inspector turned to me and asked me if my name was Bess. I said, "Yes," and he said, "Do you know the name of Atherstone?" and I said, "Yes." He said, "He is dead."'

'What did you do then?' asked the coroner.

'I don't remember.'

'Did you see him?'

'No.'

'You have been interviewed by the police a good many

times, and have given every information in your power? You have answered all their questions?'

'Yes.'

'Sincerely?'

'Yes.'

Further questioned she said that she had no idea of the identity of the person who had committed the act, and went on to say that she had no idea whether Atherstone, in his state of mind, might have got on bad terms with anyone besides herself. 'I think he had mentioned several men in connection with yourself?' said the coroner. 'Yes, but there was no reason.'

'Did he ever attack or question any of these men?'

'Not to my knowledge.'

'Have the burglaries been quite recent?'

'I don't know how recent. The bottom flat was broken into and the meter was broken open.'

'Have you any suggestion as to why the deceased had this weapon, this piece of electric cable, upon him?'

'No, I have no idea.'

'He had been violent to you once?'

'More than once.'

'Dangerously violent towards you?'

'No; he struck me.'

'Was that in a sudden rage, or very deliberately?'

'It was in a rage.'

'Has he ever threatened you?'

'He once threatened to cut my throat. That was last summer.'

There was an interruption in the questioning then to establish that there had been serious robberies in the district. Miss Earl's questioning resumed, she said that she had obtained the appointment at the Academy of Dramatic Art about four years before, and, having to keep her invalid brother in Australia, had found it necessary to take private pupils in addition to her work at the academy. At first, she said, she had had private pupils of both sexes, but she had given up the male pupils some fifteen months previously. Asked why she had given up her male pupils, she replied that she 'did not want to do anything to offend' Atherstone.

'Did you do this because of his threat, or were you frightened?'

'No, I was not frightened, but I didn't want to make him unhappy.' Atherstone, she said, had felt, 'without reason, that he was being shut out' and that her interests were being diverted from him. Her taking pupils, she added, was the beginning of his unreasonable jealousy. She then added that two years earlier the deceased had met with a motor accident and injured his head.

'Was there any noticeable alteration in his manner after the accident?'

'Yes. There was a noticeable increase in his fits of jealousy.'

Elizabeth Earl's testimony was finished and she was allowed to step down. A few minutes later her place was taken by the other principal witness in the inquiry, the dead man's son, Thomas.

A photograph of Thomas Frederick Anderson appeared in the press the following day, and judging by it one might well suppose that it was taken at the courthouse. He looks intense and appears to be chewing his lip. Although smartly dressed, he cannot by any means be described as a handsome young man. Photographed in profile, he is seen as thin-faced, with a receding chin and a very large and prominent nose.

In his evidence, however, he seemed to come over as an intelligent young man, and to show a certain dignity.

After giving his name, occupation and address, he said

that he had been on terms of affection with his late father and had seen him frequently when his father was in London. Over the past eight years, he said, when his father had lived in London he had resided at Miss Earl's flat.

'Do you ever see your mother?' he was asked.

'I saw her at Easter last year.'

After saying that he did not know, and had not suspected, the nature of the relationship between his father and Miss Earl, he was asked whether he could recall anything his father had said about Miss Earl in the last few weeks of his life. He answered:

'When I went to see him he suggested we should go over to see Miss Earl, and we went. That was shortly after his return to London.'

'Did you think there was any serious quarrel between them?'

'No, I did not.'

'It has been mentioned on a previous occasion you wrote to Miss Earl to go and see her? Do you remember when you did so? It was the same week, was it not?'

'Yes.'

'Do you remember the day?'

'I think it was on Thursday or Friday.'

'Was there any reason for making the appointment?'

'No, I usually did so.'

'Did she reply?'

'Yes, she said, "By all means," and she was eager to hear an account of my holidays.'

'You told your father that?'

'I told him on the Tuesday and on the Thursday.'

'Apparently he said he might come?'

'I don't remember it. Possibly. I didn't notice.'

'Did you think it likely he might come?'

'I didn't think it likely, but I wouldn't have been surprised.'

Requested to relate what had happened on the night of Saturday, 16 July, the young man said:

'We sat together in the drawing room talking for some time, and then she said she would get the supper ready. This would be a quarter to nine. While out in the kitchen she called to me and showed me the new fittings in her bedroom. We came back from there to the drawing room and talked a little longer.'

'What were the new fittings?'

'The room had been new-papered and there were new curtains.'

'Had you been in her bedroom before?'

'Yes.'

'Go on.'

'We returned to the drawing room, and following that we went into the kitchen for supper. That was about nine o'clock. Miss Earl prepared supper and we sat down. That would be about a quarter past nine. We had been seated at supper for a short time when we heard two loud reports.'

After being asked to describe the location of the kitchen and scullery windows, he was asked, 'What else did you hear?'

'Nothing more. Miss Earl got up first and went to the back door. I followed. She opened the door and looked out, but could see nothing, except a man who had just jumped from one wall to another.'

'Did you see him?'

'Yes.'

'What was he doing when you first saw him?'

'He was lying almost full-length upon the trellis work erected on top of the higher of the two walls. Then he dropped down into the garden of Cambridge House [No. 19], and we saw nothing more of him.'

'How were you able to see at all?'

'It was just light enough to see, but I think there was a moon.'

'Not very much moon?'

'No, but it was at any rate enough to see a man. We could hear a noise too. The crackling of the bushes and the trellis work.'

'Did you hear anything before the shots?'

'Nothing whatever.'

'No sound of a struggle?'

'No.'

'What did you do then?'

'Miss Earl moved forward as though to go downstairs. I called her back and told her not to go down. She came in and closed the door and went into the back room which overlooks the end of the garden.' He added that this room was used as a sitting room, and had once been his father's bedroom.

He then said that on looking out they had seen nothing in the garden. 'We saw a few people in Rosenau Road who had evidently been attracted by the shots. We then went back to supper, thinking some householder had surprised a burglar and had fired two shots to frighten him off, and that it was the burglar whom we had seen escaping. About a quarter of an hour after that Police Sergeant Buckley knocked at the door and Miss Earl admitted him.'

He described then how he had followed the police sergeant down into the yard and how from the shadows under the iron staircase he had heard the sounds of heavy breathing. 'I thought at first it might be a dog,' he said.

'Why did you think that?'

'Because there was a dog in the upper flat, and I did

not want to believe it was anything worse. I called out to Miss Earl to ask if the dog was still in the flat. She replied, "No" and then I knew something was wrong, and went forward and found my father.'

'Tell us what your sensations and beliefs were then. You did not then know it was your father?'

'No, I had no idea.'

'What did you find?'

'I found a man lying unconscious and apparently badly wounded. I struck a match, for it was too dark to see anything. Then I called for Police Sergeant Buckley. He came to my call and looked for himself.'

He then related how Miss Earl had brought a light while he himself went to send the chauffeur for a doctor. Later, he said, when other police officers were on the scene and it was getting late, he asked permission to leave, but was refused. Some time afterwards, he said, when feeling 'the strain of the whole thing', and going into the garden to get some air, he was asked by Inspector Geake whether he knew anyone of the name of Atherton. '"No," I said, "but I know someone of the name of Atherstone." He said, "Who is that?" and I replied, "My father." He then showed me a business card asking me if I recognized it. I said, "Yes, it is my father's card." Then he and another officer took me at once to Battersea Police Station. It began to dawn upon me then that they supposed the man whom I had seen – the dying man – to be my father.'

'Why did you then think that? Did you then know whether the card had been found on the deceased man or elsewhere?'

'I knew they had been through the pockets of the dead man.'

'Did you know it had been found in a pocket?'

'I assumed so.'

'But you were not told?'

'No. I felt sure, however, that it was not my father.'

'Why?'

'Because my father was the last person in the world I expected to see in such a condition, wearing carpet slippers.'

'How did you know he was wearing carpet slippers?'

'I saw them in the first place. Police Sergeant Buckley pointed them out to me.'

'Why did you assume the card was found in the pockets of the dead man and not on the ground nearby?'

'That occurred to me also.'

'Why did it occur to you that the dead man might be your father and not the man who was running away?'

'That is what occurred to me in the first place. When Inspector Geake was taking me to the station his manner was such as to suggest that I knew something of the affair – and he had found a business card belonging to my father.'

'These circumstances made you think in the first place it might be your father running away?'

'Yes, and also I was convinced the [injured] man I had seen was not my father.'

'What convinced you of that?'

'Because he seemed to be wearing a moustache, and my father was the last person I expected to see there. I saw the dying man before any suspicion of having anything to do with the matter occurred to me at all. All these notions came to me as I was being taken to the police station.'

'Have you any explanation for the suspicion there was a moustache?'

'Yes. There was a black mark on the side of the face. I only got a sort of general impression.'

'How long do you think you were looking?'

'I was down with Inspector Badcock for a long time, but only glanced once or twice in all that time. When he asked me if I recognized him, well, it was the sort of thing – I should hardly trouble to look again.'

He then related how Inspector Geake had asked him whether the man was his father, and how in turn he himself had asked whether the man was wearing a false moustache. Geake had replied, he said: 'He has no moustache.'

'It was a great surprise to me,' Anderson told the coroner, 'because I had assumed he had a moustache, I having thought I had seen one. Had he said that the man had had a moustache I should have said it was *not* my father, because I knew he was clean-shaven. I asked for a description and he said the dead man had a long, thin face, like mine, and then I began to think it was my father. That was confirmed later on by Inspector Badcock, and next morning I identified the body at the mortuary.'

The coroner, wanting clarification of Thomas Anderson's statement that at first it had occurred to him that the man seen running away was his father, asked him to explain what he meant. Said the young man:

'It occurred to me that Inspector Geake knew more than he said. He seized me and took me to Battersea Police Station, and I could only conceive the officers had good reason for doing so, and then, of course, there was the incident of the card. The whole thing was a nightmare, and was more or less fantastic to me.'

After saying that he knew nothing of the life-preserver his father had carried he was asked whether he had known that his father was a very jealous man. 'No, sir, decidedly,' he answered.

'The information now is apparently to that effect?'

'Yes.'

'Did you know much about his affairs?'

'I knew a little. He was always reticent about his business affairs, but I knew a good deal of his private affairs, though he seldom confided in anyone.'

'In trouble or worry he would never confide with a view to seeking sympathy?'

'He always kept it to himself.'

After some further questions which were mainly repetitions of earlier ones, Thomas Anderson was allowed to step down.

The next and final witness was Detective Inspector Badcock who said that since the last adjournment he had made full inquiries in connection with the case, and that there was no further evidence he could put before the court. Presenting what he considered 'an important point', he read from the dead man's diary a passage which, he said, had been taken from a publication called *The Smart Set*:

'If he had kept away from her, if he had broken from the spell of her fascination and remained out of reach, this would never have happened. He had no one to thank but himself.'

A great number of letters were found at Miss Earl's flat, he said, but none from men, other than on business matters. His subsequent inquiries, he said, had satisfactorily cleared up the movements on the night in question of every person named.

The coroner: 'As regards Miss Earl's statement, you have had an opportunity of seeing whether it can be corroborated?' Replied Badcock, 'I have thoroughly tested it, and I have found her truthful in every particular.'

'Can you say the same about the sons?'

'Yes. They have all appeared to be anxious to help me.'

In reply to a further question, Badcock said there had been a number of robberies from flats, principally thefts from gas meters, but, he said, he had found 'that often people robbed their own meters'.

The coroner then remarked that the case was as mysterious now as it had ever been, though perhaps some day there might be a clue. After a short consultation the jury then returned a verdict of *Wilful murder by some person or persons unknown*, following which the coroner thanked Inspector Badcock and his staff for the zeal they had displayed in dealing with the case.

And that was it. No one was ever charged with the crime, and the killer, whoever he was, went scot-free.

Following the closure of the inquest, the murder and the mystery surrounding it gradually faded from the public's consciousness, its fascination being, naturally, eclipsed by other events. And the police, with no further evidence, were left with another unsolved murder in their files. Someone, the assailant, had managed to keep to himself all the answers to the mystery.

But who was he?

H. L. Adam, writing in his book, *Murder by Persons Unknown*, believes in the theory that the killing was not a murder at all, but that the revolver used was carried by Atherstone – 'It seems improbable that the life-preserver was the only weapon he had with him' – and that in Atherstone's struggle with a petty thief who had come upon the scene the gun was accidentally turned upon himself. According to Adam the thief then dropped the gun into his pocket and made off.

It is possible, of course, though it seems highly improbable. Why should Atherstone bother to make himself a life-preserver if he already had a gun? The former weapon would seem to be a little superfluous. Also, what reason is there to suppose that the thief would 'automatically drop the [revolver] into his pocket before making off'? It doesn't add up. There has to be another answer.

When I first read a brief account of the crime my initial reaction was one of great suspicion towards Elizabeth Earl and Thomas Anderson. There was the dying man's mistress in the flat above, entertaining his twenty-one-year-old son, added to which the son, when faced with the dying man, claimed not to know him. Yes, I thought, a likely story!

Both Elizabeth Earl and Thomas Anderson were only yards from the actor at the time of the crime, so naturally they came in for some examination by the police. But did they, in truth, have a hand in Atherstone's death?

Obviously the writer Jonathan Goodman feels they did. In his recent book, *Acts of Murder*, in which he writes on the case, he appears to believe in their guilt – and not only the guilt of Elizabeth Earl and Thomas Anderson, but of William Anderson too.

He advances several possible theories and as these might well be favoured by some readers an examination of them here will serve in the search for some of the answers.

Writing, mistakenly, as if Inspector Geake, and not Badcock, had been in charge of the investigations, Goodman states that Geake couldn't accept the theory that the killer was a burglar; one reason for this being the 'Sunday-best' clothing worn by the man seen running from the scene of the crime, which, Geake believed, was not that usually worn by a burglar. Whether or not Geake actually entertained such beliefs, apparently he arrived at the conclusion that Atherstone had been murdered by his two sons – with Elizabeth Earl involved as an accessory.

Goodman says the trio had at least three possible motives for the killing and gives the three following:

1. Elizabeth and young Thomas had fallen in love and,

aware that Atherstone was jealously spying on Elizabeth, and was prepared to use his home-made life-preserver on a rival, had to be killed.

2. Thomas Anderson and his young brother William, devoted to one another and to their mother, had murdered their father in revenge. The motive given is that he deserted their mother and left her alone to rear the four children, and for this the sons could not forgive him.

3. Elizabeth Earl and the Anderson brothers chose to kill Atherstone in order to prevent him living *with* them and *off* them for the rest of his life.

Jonathan Goodman further suggests that after the murder had been carried out the gun was taken away by William. Thomas's slowness in 'recognizing' the victim, he suggests, was in order to provide his younger brother with sufficient time to make good his escape. Goodman finishes his account by saying that perhaps after the crime the three met together to congratulate each other on the success of the enterprise and to drink to the good riddance of the murdered man, Weldon Atherstone, an unsuccessful parent, actor and lover.

One thing that puzzles me is how Mr Goodman can be so convinced of the beliefs Geake held – particularly, as he himself states, the inspector was never able to make known his beliefs to the public. And I wonder also how Goodman is able to be so sure that Geake could not accept the burglar theory? As far as I can determine the police file on the case is no longer in existence, so access to any of the officers' reports containing notes on their thoughts and personal beliefs is no longer possible.

However, looking at Goodman's three possible theories one finds quite quickly that they do not stand up to examination.

One thing that is certain is that *Thomas* Anderson was not the man seen running away from the scene of the crime. Noice, the chauffeur, was quite certain of that – 'That is not the man I saw.' So *was* it young William who killed his father and made his escape? Goodman says the witnesses to the running man described him as 'young'. In fact the witnesses were far more specific in their statements. The consensus of their descriptions places the man at age twenty-three to thirty. William was sixteen: a boy, not a man. There is an approximate age difference of at least ten years. Further, the difference in appearance between a teenage boy and a grown man would be far more apparent than in a ten-year age difference in an older age group.

Another point in William's favour is that he would certainly have been seen later by some of the witnesses who came forward, and if there had been the slightest chance that he had been the 'man' they had seen running away they would have mentioned it.

It should also be remembered that a fierce struggle had taken place between Atherstone and his killer. It is hardly likely, therefore, that the killer escaped from the scene without some signs of the struggle on his body. William was seen by the police in the early hours of the next morning, and surely any marks of the struggle on him would not have been allowed to pass.

And what of Goodman's suggested motives for the brothers and Elizabeth Earl conspiring to kill Atherstone? To my mind his first theory – that the actor had to be eliminated as Elizabeth and Thomas were in love and knew that Atherstone was spying on them and quite prepared to use his life-preserver – is highly improbable. For one thing, it seems very hard to reconcile with the characters of the three as evinced by their court appearances. Also, if the trio had been intent on killing Atherstone, surely they wouldn't have chosen to do it almost literally on Elizabeth Earl's doorstep; they would have chosen some other spot, some place where it wouldn't advertise their involvement. And anyway, why choose to take such a drastic step as murder to get out of the situation?

In his second theory Goodman says the boys were devoted to each other, and also to their mother whom their father had deserted – so they killed him out of revenge. But what evidence is there for this 'devotion'? One can accept that the brothers were naturally fond of one another, but of some 'devotion' in the thrall of which they would not stop at murder – and simply out of revenge for their father's treatment of their mother – is never demonstrated.

Further examining this same theory, what evidence is there of any great devotion to their mother, as Goodman claims existed? Questioned at the inquest in September, Thomas said that he had last seen his mother at Easter in the previous year. *Sixteen months before.* Rather a long absence for a young man who was so devoted to his mother that he would kill to avenge her desertion. On the contrary, all the signs indicated that the brothers were more fond of their *father.* For one thing, young William had chosen to spend his two weeks' holiday with him, that holiday only ending on the Saturday, the day of the actor's death. Hardly the act of a son who hated his father to the point of being cold-bloodedly driven to murdering him.

Goodman's third theory, that Elizabeth Earl and the brothers chose to kill Atherstone to avoid the possibility of his being a parasite on them until he died, is also too improbable to be taken seriously. Atherstone was *not* sponging off them. Goodman says with regard to Atherstone's leaving Clifton Gardens that there was nothing to show whether Elizabeth Earl threw him out or whether he chose to leave of his own accord. However, she stated quite clearly at the inquest that he left her by *his* wish and *not by hers*, and the letter he later wrote to her when returning her latch key confirms this. (Incidentally, Goodman says that Atherstone moved out of the flat in Clifton Gardens near the end of 1909, when in fact it was clearly established that he left in May of 1910.)

Further, says Goodman, after leaving Clifton Gardens, Atherstone went to see his two sons who had come to London and were sharing a flat in Great Percy Street. According to Goodman's account, Atherstone begged them to forget the past and his mistreatment of them, their mother and their two sisters, and take him in – which they did.

If one regards the above account as fiction it makes interesting reading, but one is seeking the truth, and in this context, for a start, it was clearly established that the two brothers were in lodgings in *Wood Street*, EC, and that Atherstone went *alone* into lodgings at Great Percy Street.

Therefore, any theory based on a belief that Atherstone was 'sponging' off Elizabeth Earl and his sons can be dismissed. He clearly was not.

Mr Goodman's account of the crime and the events surrounding it contains a number of errors. Just in one paragraph, for instance, he states that both brothers 'had clerical jobs in the city', and that William was Thomas's junior 'by about a year'. In fact evidence given at the inquest shows clearly that Thomas was twenty-one and William sixteen, and that both brothers were warehousemen.

However, even if Jonathan Goodman's three particular theories of a conspiracy between Elizabeth Earl and the brothers don't stand up to examination, there is still the question as to whether they were nonetheless guilty in some other way, and, if so, what the motive was.

As stated earlier, when first reading a brief account of the Battersea flat mystery, years ago, my immediate reaction was to feel that Thomas Anderson and Elizabeth Earl were guilty and had somehow carried out the crime between them. However, after studying all the available literature – accounts in various books, and the main newspapers of the time – I find it impossible to sustain such a belief.

In the account in this book I have quoted all the relevant evidence given by the various witnesses, and, almost totally, that given by Elizabeth Earl and the two brothers. Not only do I think it will be of interest, but also it will help the reader to come to some kind of conclusion. Further, I feel that, specifically in the case of Elizabeth Earl and the Anderson brothers, their testimony has the ring of truth to it.

Granted, at first reading it appears extremely odd that Thomas did not recognize his father lying beneath the stairs. But I am convinced that had he been guilty his behaviour would have been very different. I am quite sure that he spoke the truth. A man, wearing carpet slippers, lies unconscious, shot in the temple and through the upper lip at very close range. On his face are bloodstains and the black marks of powder burns. One eye is hanging out on his cheek. Dr Kempster said in his testimony that 'the face was not much disfigured', but on the other hand Sergeant Buckley said to Elizabeth Earl in advising her to go upstairs: 'This man has been cut to pieces.' In any case, the doctors who examined the dead Atherstone had not known him before. Thomas Anderson had. Also, Thomas Anderson said that his father was the last person he expected to see there; which statement, to me, seems eminently reasonable and acceptable.

Take also the behaviour of Anderson and of Elizabeth Earl. Buckley said that when he went to Miss Earl's flat she did not appear to be at all agitated. He said the same of Thomas Anderson. It was only when Anderson was subsequently convinced of the identity of the dead man that he went to pieces. Similarly in the case of Elizabeth Earl. On being told that the man was Atherstone and that he was dead she went into hysterics. Granted she was an actress, but even an ability to act could not account for her physical state. As Dr Kempster testified, 'she was trembling in every limb', and 'was almost pulseless'.

Jonathan Goodman's account implies that the police were convinced of the guilt of Elizabeth Earl and the Anderson brothers but could not find the necessary evidence to support their belief. To my mind, however, events do not support such a hypothesis.

One indication of whether the police believed that Elizabeth Earl and either or both of the Anderson brothers were guilty is surely that of the investigators' behaviour towards the three. The police were not fools and if, for a start, they had seriously suspected Thomas Anderson they would have taken him to the station for questioning on more than the one occasion they did, which was immediately following the killing. At the inquest several references were made to his being taken to the station on that occasion, but there was no reference – made either by the police themselves, by Thomas Anderson, or any member of the press – to it ever happening again.

Where Elizabeth Earl is concerned, she stated at the inquest that she had been examined a number of times by the police, but this fact cannot be taken as an indication that they necessarily believed her to be guilty in some way. They would of course question her closely, for even if she had had no hand in the killing she was still involved in the crime. She and Atherstone had been lovers for many years, and quite clearly she was the reason for his being on the premises in the first place. If he had come to confront or spy on a rival who did exist, then she held the key to the mystery – the rival's name.

The question must still arise, of course, as to whether Elizabeth Earl was having a love affair with Thomas Anderson – notwithstanding that it is extremely unlikely that he had any hand in his father's killing.

I do not believe they were lovers. Granted, it is not at all uncommon for a mature woman to take a younger lover, but Elizabeth Earl had known Thomas for a number of years and it is doubtful that their relationship would have changed to that of lovers.

Was someone else her lover? It is possible. Early on in the investigations she was criticized in one newspaper for 'stonewalling', the paper implying that she was withholding 'material facts and important names'. The paper does not identify her, but it is clearly Miss Earl to whom the report refers.

And the question remains: Who did kill Weldon Atherstone, and for what reason?

I find it hard to accept that he was an unnamed lover of Elizabeth Earl. For one thing I cannot believe that a lover would carry a revolver with him while going to call on her. Unless he had been threatened by Atherstone the man would have no reason to believe that he might have to protect himself, and there was no entry in the diary to indicate that Atherstone was certain of any one man.

I believe that after all the available evidence is sifted only the burglar theory can be accepted.

In his writing on the affair Jonathan Goodman gives the impression that the police regarded as totally untenable the idea that Atherstone had been killed by a burglar. One reason Goodman gives is that of the man being armed, saying that armed burglars almost invariably go for rich pickings and that there was very little of any value in the flats at Clifton Gardens. But a burglar could not be sure that there was nothing of value in such a place. In any case, as is demonstrated over and over again in our newspapers, violence is often used in the acquisition of very slim pickings.

Also, proof that robbery was never ruled out by the police is the fact that a man was arrested and detained on suspicion in connection with the crime, a man who was believed to have been at the scene for the purpose of burglary.

I am convinced, when all the known facts are taken into account, that the burglar theory is the only one that holds water.

It was established at the inquest that there had been a number of burglaries in the area. As pointed out in the case of the Luard murder, which took place two years previously, unemployment at the time was extremely high, and it was before the days when the unemployed could turn to the Department of Health and Social Security for Unemployment Benefit or other financial help.

The iron staircase at the rear of the flats at 17 Clifton Gardens would be an open invitation to a burglar, and in all probability one paid a visit to the flats that night. He might well have chosen the venue by chance, just intending to try his luck, or it is possible that he had somehow learned that the Butchers, who lived in the top flat, were absent. It seems likely, however, that he chose 17 Clifton Gardens after seeing the *To Let* sign outside the house; seeing it, he would naturally have supposed that he would not be disturbed by any occupant.

He *was* disturbed, however. There was an occupant, albeit by chance. Atherstone had come there to keep his vigil.

Then comes the question: *Why* was Atherstone there,

and why was he armed with his home-made life-preserver?

Clearly he was obsessively jealous of Elizabeth Earl. His diary notes alone make that quite clear. It must be supposed, therefore, that his presence there was as a result of his jealousy and his suspicions. But was he waiting in the expectation of seeing a *particular* person or of *any* person he suspected of being a rival?

The answer is not known, but some interesting questions are raised.

It was stated at the inquest that Atherstone knew that his son was to visit Miss Earl on the Saturday. If so, then knowing this he went there also, unknown to them. If Atherstone *did* know that his son was to visit Miss Earl, then really the only conclusion one can draw is that he might have imagined that his son could be his rival for Elizabeth Earl's affections, and he wanted to find out for certain.

At the time Atherstone was not thinking rationally. Following his accident two years earlier he had become most irrational and obsessively jealous. And, totally convinced as he was that Elizabeth Earl was seeing another, perhaps at some time he would be almost bound to wonder whether his son, who sometimes visited her, was, in the absence of proof against any other man, his rival.

Up to that time, in spite of having kept a watch on a few occasions, Atherstone had not been able to catch Elizabeth out in any secret liaison. Therefore, when his son said that he was to call on her on the Saturday, the thought perhaps occurred to Atherstone in his irrational state that his son was the one. So he determined to go to Clifton Gardens and spy on them.

I believe that his possession of the life-preserver stemmed also from his irrationality. As he felt violent anger towards any possible rival, so he might well have expected to have to protect himself from violence in the possible event of a confrontation.

So, putting on a cap – which he never customarily wore – to aid his disguise, he wraps his carpet slippers in brown paper, puts the life-preserver into his back pocket and sets out for Battersea. On arrival at Clifton Gardens he lets himself into the ground floor flat by means of the cord attached to the latch inside the front door. In the kitchen he takes off his boots and puts on the slippers, afterwards using the brown paper to wrap his boots and so keep them together in the deepening gloom of the kitchen (it was stated in evidence that the kitchen and scullery were extremely dark).

Waiting quietly in the flat he would probably be able to tell from any faint sounds of footsteps coming from the floor above where the occupants of the flat were from time to time. He would probably have heard them in the kitchen above his head as Elizabeth moved about making the supper – but that would not be the time for him to creep upstairs and spy on them. He would wait until they had left the kitchen. Then, after a time, making no sound in his carpet slippers, he could creep up the staircase, open the scullery door – which was always left unlocked – and creep along the passage. Then, perhaps in the sitting room, or the bedroom, he would find them together . . .

He never has a chance to carry out his plan, however. As he waits – with the scullery door open for light – a man suddenly appears in the yard. Perhaps the thought that the man is a burglar never occurs to Atherstone. In all likelihood he sees the stranger as the rival he has long suspected. Without hesitating, and without pausing to take his life-preserver from his back pocket, he dashes out into the yard and seizes the man as he is about to start up the stairs. Violently they struggle together, in the course of which Atherstone's spectacles fall off and are trodden and crushed underfoot. Atherstone has a vice-like grip on the man who tries in vain to free himself, and in desperation the intruder takes a revolver from his pocket and fires point-blank into Atherstone's face. The bullet enters his upper lip, glances off his teeth and goes through the glass panel of the scullery door. The man fires again, the second bullet entering Atherstone's head at the temple. At this, Atherstone releases the man and staggers back. Free, the man leaps over the wall into the narrow alley, then over the other alley wall into the next-door garden, dashes across it, scrambles over the third wall into Rosenau Road, and so makes his escape.

While the man is running away, Atherstone, reeling from the bullet to his brain, staggers into the scullery. There he clutches at the sides of the copper, leaning over it, his blood falling. Then, reeling back towards the door, he staggers into the yard where he collapses, falling back upon the steps.

What became of the chief protagonists in the case is not recorded. As far as is known, Thomas and William Anderson faded back into obscurity, while in all probability Elizabeth Earl adhered to her plans and went to live abroad with her consumptive brother, to whom she was much attached. In all likelihood she had made the decision in view of the revelation of her love affair with Weldon Atherstone and the publicity surrounding it. Perhaps she felt that her damaged reputation could not be repaired and the only thing to do was to retreat into anonymity. This, it seems, while maintaining that dignity which like Thomas Anderson she had demonstrated throughout, she subsequently did.

And if Elizabeth Earl had all along possessed the key to the mystery's answer – then she took it with her.

The Brighton Trunk Murder

The Ordeal of Tony Mancini

BY STEPHEN KNIGHT
Additional material by Bernard Taylor

Two sensational unsolved homicides have come down to us under the *nom de journaux* of Brighton Trunk Murder. Both occurred in the spring of the same year, 1934, and both have since remained officially unsolved.

The second trunk murder, which rapidly overshadowed the first, is the subject of this chapter.

The background of the case is the seaside resort of Brighton in Sussex in the sunny spring of 1934. Crowds of holidaymakers were already beginning to fill the hotels and guest houses. The fun fairs, glittering façades cloaking sleazy reality, were peopled not only by jaded parents and tired city dwellers determined to get the most out of their yearly reprieve from factory and office; behind the flashing smiles and glib words of many a sideshow owner hid the hard, cruel personality of a creature of the criminal underworld. Brighton's own population of delinquents was swollen by hoodlums from London who fancied a sunny working season away from the capital.

Nineteen thirty-four. The holiday season was barely under way before Brighton had become in newspapers everywhere the 'Queen of Slaughtering Places'. No fewer than twenty women and girls disappeared from the town in the space of a few weeks. Several were found brutally murdered. Then, on Derby Day, a female torso was discovered in a suitcase in the left-luggage office at Brighton Railway Station. A medical examination showed that the torso belonged to a woman aged about thirty who had been approximately five months pregnant. The following day her legs were found in a suitcase at the left-luggage office at King's Cross Station in London. This second discovery provided detectives investigating the murder with only one positive fact – that the victim had recently attended a chiropodist.

The police were to be unsuccessful in their investigation of this first sensational trunk murder, and failed even to identify the corpse. But their inquiries led to the discovery of yet another murdered body stashed away in a trunk, the body of a woman called Violette Kaye. The irony of this discovery was that Violette Kaye's family had thought she was working abroad.

Kaye, a known prostitute, had been living in a basement flat at 44, Park Crescent, Brighton, with a man who called himself variously Jack Notyre and Tony Mancini. A petty crook from London, his real name was Cecil Louis England, and he had been working of late as a waiter in Brighton's Skylark Café. For several months before taking his job at the Skylark, Mancini had been living on the earnings of his mistress, Kaye. She was then thirty-eight and he was twenty-six.

About six weeks before the discovery of her body in July, her sister Mrs Olive Watts – who lived in London and had intended to visit Kaye for a holiday – received a telegram. It read: 'Going abroad. Good job. Sail Sunday. Will Write. Vi.'

The telegram was handwritten but did not appear to be in Violette's handwriting.

A week later Mancini moved from Park Crescent to a basement flat in Kemp Street, Brighton. He told several people that he had left his mistress because she was always nagging at him, and that she had found a job in Paris.

One of the belongings which Mancini brought with him to the flat in Kemp Street was a large cabin trunk containing something extremely heavy. He told his new landlady that it was mainly books and other possessions. Later, she complained that 'some fluid' was seeping from the bottom of it. He told her that it was French polish and that he would make sure it was cleared up. Other tenants of the house began to grumble about a foul smell . . .

Detectives investigating the case of the dismembered torso found at the railway stations visited Kemp Street for a routine search on 14 July, and there found Violette Kaye's body, doubled up and terribly decomposed, in Mancini's trunk. Mancini himself had disappeared. Later, a search of the flat at Park Crescent turned up a charred hammer in the cellar.

A call went out to all police forces in England to keep watch for the prime suspect, who at this stage the police felt had not only almost certainly killed Violette Kaye, but perhaps also the unknown woman of Trunk Murder Number One. A Kent policeman found Mancini wandering dazedly along a lonely part of the London–Maidstone road in the small hours of 17 July. He was asked if he was Jack Notyre and if he would answer some questions about the death in Brighton of a woman called Kaye.

'Yes,' he replied, 'I am the man. But I did not murder her. I would not cut her hand. She had been keeping me for months.'

Despite his protestations, he was returned to Brighton, where, after a lengthy interrogation by Chief Inspector Donaldson, who had been called in by the Sussex Constabulary to take charge of investigations into both trunk murders, he was charged with killing Violette Kaye. 'All I can say is that I am not guilty,' he replied.

Mancini's story was that he had returned to the basement in Park Crescent on the evening of 10 May and found his mistress 'laying on the bed with a handkerchief tied around her neck and there was blood all over the sheets and everywhere'. He had realized that one of

Violette's clients had killed her, he told the police, but he was frightened he would never be able to convince anyone. His statement reads:

I knew they would blame me and I couldn't prove I hadn't done it, so I just went out and tried to think things over, what to do . . . I hadn't got the courage to go and tell the police what I had found, so I decided to take it [the body] with me . . . There were always men coming to the house . . . I don't know who killed her. As God is my judge, I don't know . . . I am quite innocent, except for the fact that I kept the body hidden.

Sir Bernard Spilsbury, the country's foremost pathologist, was called in to carry out an autopsy. His report described the cause of death as a violent blow with some blunt object, possibly a hammer, which had caused a fracture on the right side of the skull.

Mancini was committed for trial by Brighton magistrates and remained in prison until the case came up at the Sussex Assizes at Lewes Assize Court in mid December. Meanwhile the most celebrated advocate in the land, Norman Birkett, had agreed to defend Mancini. Birkett's private judgement of Mancini was that he was 'a despicable and worthless creature', but that did not necessarily make Mancini a killer. His defence of the diminutive, Italian-looking crook was masterly and is generally considered the best of his triumphant career. An old friend later wrote of its ranking 'as one of the great defences in the annals of legal medical records and worthy of a Marshall Hall'.

At the trial, which opened on 10 December before Mr Justice Branson, Birkett was accompanied by Mr John Flowers, KC, and Mr Eric Neve. The prosecution was led by Mr J. D. Cassels, KC (later Mr Justice Cassels), who had Mr Quintin Hogg (later Lord Hailsham and Lord Chancellor of England) as his junior counsel.

The newspapers, both national and local, had seemingly gone mad in their coverage of the Brighton Trunk Murder and the committal of Mancini. Editors everywhere behaved as if their journals were starved of good hard news copy and sensationalized the case beyond recognition. The realities of the case were sensational enough. It is hard to imagine why journalists felt the need to go further. But go further they did. 'Facts' about Mancini, which had never existed anywhere but in the inventive minds of reporters, proliferated. Over the months as he awaited trial the story emulated Topsy and 'just growed'. He was transformed by the mighty work of a thousand conscientious hacks from a cheap and shabby crook into a loathsome monster. Long before Mancini was led handcuffed into the dock on 10 December the general public was convinced of his guilt. A months-long 'trial by newspaper', seldom equalled in iniquity this century, had done its work. All hopes of impartiality from a jury saturated with previous impressions seemed empty. Outside the court chanting crowds had booed, hissed and hurled abuse at him as he made his way inside.

He could hardly speak when the Clerk of the Assizes asked if he pleaded guilty or not guilty. 'I am not . . .' he began, but seemed to choke. After a long pause he said in a terrified whisper, '. . . not guilty.'

After several minor witnesses had been heard, the Crown called Mr Henry Snuggs, landlord of 44, Park Crescent. Snuggs testified that he had let his basement flat to the accused and a woman in March of the same year.

'I knew them as Mr and Mrs Watson,' said Snuggs. 'The prisoner said he was a clothes-presser, and gave as his reason for leaving where he had been the fact that people objected to the banging of his iron. As far as I could see he and the woman were very friendly.'

'Affectionate?' he was asked.

'Yes,' he replied.

'Did you ever hear any quarrels?'

'No.'

'When did you last see the woman alive?'

'On Monday, May 7th, when she paid the rent.'

Snuggs had never noticed anything unusual about the behaviour of either Mancini or Violette Kaye, except that one night in the week following 7 May he had heard Mancini run first up and then down the basement stairs, as if in a hurry. On 14 May he saw the prisoner with a young woman whom he introduced as his sister. On this occasion Mancini had said that he was leaving because his wife had deserted him and gone to France.

Birkett rose to cross-examine the landlord. 'On the occasions on which you saw the prisoner and the woman, they appeared not merely to be friendly, but to be affectionate?'

'Yes,' said Snuggs.

'I want to get this quite plainly before the jury,' said Birkett. 'At no time, from start to finish, did you ever see anything of any kind to the contrary?'

'No sir,' said Snuggs.

After the examination and cross-examination of several witnesses who spoke of Violette Kaye's visitors at Park Crescent and Mancini's purchase of a trunk for 7s 6d at a furniture stall in Brighton market, Cassels called Thomas Kerslake to the stand. Kerslake was a motor driver and the last of the Crown witnesses to have seen Kaye alive. He testified that he had had a brief conversation with her in the basement doorway at 44, Park Crescent on the afternoon of 10 May.

'Are you familiar with the effect of drugs on people?' asked Birkett suddenly as he cross-examined Kerslake.

'Yes,' the witness replied.

'Would you say that the appearance of the woman was that of somebody who was under the influence of drugs?'

'Yes. And drink. She appeared to be in a distressed condition over something or other.'

'Was she all agitated and twitching?'

'Yes.'

'Did she appear to you to be in an extremely frightened condition?'

'Yes.'

Violette Kaye's sister, Mrs Watts, swore that the writing on the telegram was nothing like her sister's. A graphologist later testified that in his opinion the telegram and a Skylark Café menu prepared by Mancini had been written by the same person.

The prosecution then introduced evidence of a row between Mancini and his mistress, which had taken place in the Skylark. The day after the quarrel, Mancini had gone dancing with a Skylark waitress and told her that Kaye had gone to France. The waitress later went with him to Park Crescent, where he introduced her to his landlord as his sister, and gave her some of Kaye's clothes. She told the court that she had washed some of Mancini's clothes, and had seen a bloodstain, 'the size of a farthing or something a little smaller', on a shirt. Mancini had told her that he did it shaving.

'Did you notice anything about the room?' asked the Crown counsel.

'Yes,' said the waitress. 'It smelt.'

Birkett made a dent in the prosecution's armour in his cross-examination of Miss Joyce Golding, a witness who euphemistically described herself as a waitress. Miss Golding had told the court that Mancini had spoken to her of quarrels between himself and Violette Kaye. She said that Mancini had even asked her, Golding, to live with him, but that she had refused.

'I have to suggest to you, although I am sorry to do so, that most of your evidence is quite false,' said Birkett.

'It is all true,' replied the witness.

Birkett cast doubt upon several statements made by Golding, and then said, 'Let me suggest to you that another matter is wholly false. He [Mancini] never suggested to you that he had quarrelled with his wife?'

'Yes, several times,' replied Golding. 'I can bring witnesses to prove it. There is one here.'

'Who is that?'

'Mrs Summers would tell you.'

But what Golding did not know, having been kept outside the court until called to take the stand, was that Mrs Phyllis Summers, a friend of Kaye's, had already testified that the prisoner and his mistress had always appeared to her 'to be upon the most friendly and affectionate terms'.

When Birkett informed Golding of this, she said lamely, 'It might have slipped her memory.'

Home Office analyst Dr Roche Lynch, a friend of Birkett's, was called by the prosecution to give evidence of his examination of Mancini's clothing, and the hammer discovered in the cellar of 44, Park Crescent. He told the court that he had scrutinized two shirts, two pairs of trousers and a handkerchief as well as the hammer. There were marks of blood on everything but the hammer. If there had been any blood on the hammer, said Dr Lynch, the burning to which it had been subjected would certainly have removed all traces.

Under questioning by Birkett, Lynch admitted that he had been unable to discover either the group of the blood on Mancini's clothing or the blood group of Violette Kaye because of the advanced state of decomposition of her body. And although the marks on one of the shirts indicated that blood had been *splashed* onto it, Birkett indicated that he would prove this shirt was not bought by Mancini until *after* Violette Kaye's death. Lynch admitted – as he had to – that if the blood on the shirt were that of the victim, it must have found its way onto the shirt after she had died. Birkett likewise promised to demonstrate that the blood-spattered trousers had not been in Mancini's possession when the woman died – and did so later with the assistance of a tailor who testified that the defendant had ordered the clothing from him in May but had not received it until June.

Dr Lynch told the court that he had made minute examination of the remains of the deceased's internal organs. In some of them he had found infinitesimal traces of morphine. The fact that any amount had been detected in such a badly decomposed body indicated that the quantity taken had been 'distinctly greater than a medicinal dose'. Drowsiness, and probably unconsciousness, would follow such a dose.

'Do you know that prostitutes are in the habit of taking opium or morphine?' asked Birkett.

'I do not know,' said Lynch.

'I am not speaking of law-abiding people. You will have known in the past that morphine was commonly used by prostitutes?'

'In the past, yes.'

'It may lead to sleep, and death in sleep?'

'Yes.'

'Are you clear in this case that there was not enough to cause death?'

'I am not prepared to answer that question.'

Referring to Lynch's earlier statement, Birkett asked, 'Do you mean by "more than a medicinal dose" a fatal dose?'

'It may have been. It is absolutely impossible to say.'

'Is it a matter of speculation that it was more than a medicinal dose?'

'No.'

'If somebody has taken morphine – not a lethal dose, but sufficient to dull the faculties and cloud the senses – and that person receives a head injury, would the presence of morphine accelerate or assist the death?'

'I don't think so, because it is a common treatment to give people, who have had a serious head injury, morphine.'

One of the most damning prosecution witnesses was a seventeen-year-old girl called Doris Saville. Crown counsel alleged that on the day Mancini had fled to London he had met Miss Saville and they had gone for a walk and bus ride together. She told the court that Mancini had asked her if she could keep a secret, that she had replied she could, and that he had then told her about a murder. He had said that if he was arrested for the murder she was to give the police a particular story he had concocted.

'He said I was supposed to have met him in Brighton on the sea front at the end of May,' testified Saville. 'We were supposed to have gone to tea with a woman in Park Crescent, and she told us she was expecting three men to come and see her. He said we left her alone with the three men and went for a walk. When we came back we found the woman dead.'

'Did he tell you why he wanted you to give that story?' asked Cassels.

'He said he wanted someone to stand by him and that I could save him.'

Birkett was on to her like an eagle, pointing out that the story she had told at Mancini's committal was materially different from the present one. According to her earlier evidence, Mancini had spoken about a murder but he had not said *which* murder. Her statement in the magistrates' court had read: 'He said that a murder was done and that he was innocent of it, and that I was supposed to have met him.'

'You did not tell us that today,' said Birkett. 'Do you intend to convey that he was saying, "There was a murder and I am innocent of it, and I want you to help me"? Is that what it was?'

'Yes,' said Doris Saville, with one word changing the entire implication of the alleged episode.

'Perfectly plain, is it not,' pursued Birkett, 'based on the fact that he was innocent of it?'

'Yes,' admitted the witness.

'Do you know what alibi means?' Birkett asked as a parting shot, and the discredited Saville admitted to the Crown's dismay that she did not.

A vital point was cleared up when Birkett cross-examined one of the last Crown witnesses, Chief Inspector Donaldson.

'Are you satisfied, Chief Inspector, that, so far as the prisoner is concerned, he had absolutely nothing whatever to do with Trunk Crime Number One?'

'Yes.'

This was a crucial point. Newspapers, hearsay and general suspicion had inevitably linked the two trunk cases.

Birkett then began a dialogue with Donaldson that made it seem, momentarily, that he had changed sides.

'Inspector,' he said, 'this man is a blackguard, isn't he?'

'Yes, sir,' said the inspector, slightly taken aback, 'I should describe him as such.'

'An idle, worthless man without morals or principles?'

'Yes, sir, I think that sums him up.'

'With previous convictions?'

'That is so.'

'But, Inspector, no conviction or charge of violence?'

'No, sir, none.'

'Is it within your professional knowledge, doing your duty,' continued Birkett, 'that there have been any false statements in the press relating to this prisoner?'

'Yes, sir. From the accounts I have read I am satisfied that many of the stories that were told in relation to this matter were untrue.'

Birkett then held up a copy of a national newspaper. 'So this paragraph, which says that the prisoner has been charged and convicted of violence, is completely untrue?' The scurrilous story Birkett referred to claimed that Mancini had been involved in a fight in Soho in which a woman had been stabbed.

'Yes,' said Donaldson, 'there is no foundation for it at all.'

Birkett had all but transformed a Crown witness into a witness for the defence.

He damaged the prosecution case even further when Sir Bernard Spilsbury took the stand. His first tactical advantage was to get Spilsbury to admit – albeit grudgingly – that his ideas about the cause of Violette Kaye's death were 'mere theories'.

He then referred to a piece of bone, produced by Sir Bernard for the first time in court that day, the third day of the trial. Spilsbury had earlier told the court that this piece of bone was the exact piece forming the fracture which in his opinion was the cause of death.

'Did it not occur to you,' said Birkett, 'that the defendant might have been informed that that small piece of bone was in your possession?'

'I am afraid it did not occur to me. The bone was not ready to produce at the time I gave evidence in the police court.'

'For a piece of bone which has been in existence all this

time to be produced on the third day of the trial does put the defence in some difficulty?'

'I do not think it would take anyone long to examine it and come to conclusions.'

A photograph of the entrance of the flat at 44, Park Crescent was then passed to Sir Bernard, who agreed that a drunken or drugged person could have tripped over a stone brace at the top of the steps. A human skull which Spilsbury had brought with him into the witness box was then passed to the jury, with the fragment of bone in its rightful position.

'I am suggesting plainly,' said Birkett to the witness, 'that if someone fell from the top step of that flight or the second step or thereabouts with violence onto the iron rail at the bottom it could produce such a depressed fracture?'

'I think it is impossible.'

'There was also a window ledge at the bottom of the stairs. If her head had struck this, could it not have produced a depressed fracture?'

The pathologist replied that the ledge would be too long for that.

'Are you really telling the members of the jury,' said Birkett, 'that if someone fell down that flight and came upon the stone ledge, he would not get a depressed fracture?'

'He could not get *this* fracture.'

'Could you get a depressed fracture of one-eighth of an inch, which was what this one was?'

'Yes.'

'The only thing in your mind is the shape of it?'

'Yes,' admitted Spilsbury, but repeated his opinion that the most likely cause of the fracture that had killed Violette Kaye was a blow from the small end of the hammer.

Doubt had been carefully sown in the minds of the jury by Birkett's questioning. Had the victim really died from a hammer blow? Or had it been morphine poisoning – or a fall down the basement step? Or was it, as Mancini had said, murder by one of her unknown clients?

'The Crown,' said Birkett to the jury in opening the case for the defence, 'has done nothing to explain or illustrate the evidence of Kerslake, who says that on May 10th, the day when the prisoner says he found the body, he, Kerslake, saw the dead woman in the late afternoon. He said that he suspected she was drunk or drugged. She was very frightened, leaning against the wall as though for support, her hands and face twitching, and in the basement flat were people whose voices he heard. Down those area steps at that self-same moment went another man. I cannot prove she died by another hand. That is beyond my power. But I submit that you can never exclude it. If that is so, every single thing in the case falls into its true place.

'There has never been the slightest breath of motive. If you believe that evidence, I do not think you will have any doubt that the morphine in the body of Violette Kaye was morphine which, in one way or another, she herself had obtained. Every chemist shop in London and Brighton is known, and, with all the resources of the police, if the prisoner had bought a spot of morphine the last detail of it would be known to you.'

Birkett then called Mancini himself to take the stand. As he took the oath, Mancini was seen to take some small object from his pocket.

'What did you take then out of your pocket?' asked the judge. 'What is it?'

Mancini held up a black rosary.

'Are you a Roman Catholic?'

'I was,' said Mancini quietly.

In a carefully rehearsed exchange between himself and Birkett, Mancini revealed details of his past life, from his birth at Newcastle-upon-Tyne to the day he started to live with Violette Kaye at 44, Park Crescent. Faltering at first, he gradually gained confidence until the natural showman in him prevailed. If he had not been on trial for his life he would doubtless have revelled in his centre-stage position.

Mancini was characteristic of the cheap little crook with a large ego. Even the awesome nature of the circumstances which thrust him into the glare of public attention could not detract entirely from the sense of having 'made the big time'. Having gently led him by the nose into this state of confidence, Birkett turned to matters central to the case. He asked first about Violette Kaye.

'Where did she get money?'

'She was a loose woman and I knew it.'

'Did men come to the flat?'

'Yes.'

'What did you do?'

'I walked out.'

'At 44, Park Crescent, Charlie Moores[1] used to come. Were there any others you knew?'

'I have heard of one and have seen him. He was known as "Hoppy" because he was lame.'

'Were there occasions upon which she showed you money?'

'Yes. I would be in the room with her. There would be a knock at the door. She would open the door and I would hear her speaking to someone. She would say, "Go into the other room, quick. There is someone to see me."'

Mancini turned to the judge. 'I know it was wrong, my Lord,' he continued, 'but I would go. I would remain in the other room until this other man went. Then I would

---

[1] One of her clients.

go back to the other room and she would show me the money.'

Later in his long examination of his client, Birkett asked this vital question: 'Did she appear to be in fear?' The jury was glimpsing a picture of the case quite different from that painted in the newspapers.

'Yes,' said Mancini. 'We were always moving, and she seemed to be in fear all the time.'

'What about Violette Kaye and the taking of drink?'

'She used to drink.'

'Were there many occasions when she was intoxicated?'

'Yes.'

'Did you ever buy morphine or give her morphine at any time?'

'Never.'

'During the whole time you lived with her as man and wife,' said Birkett, adding another crucial detail to the defence's picture, 'how did you get on together?'

'Strange as it is,' murmured Mancini, a look of sadness crossing his features, 'I used to love her. We were always on the most affectionate terms. There were no quarrels.'

'Did that cover the whole time?' asked Birkett.

'Yes, every second she was alive.'

After further questions, Mancini gave his story of Kaye's last hours. On the day of her death she had called on him at the Skylark. She was somewhat the worse for drink and 'staggered a little'. That evening, when he arrived back at the flat, the front gate was open. It was normally closed. He rang the doorbell and rapped the knocker. There was no answer.

'Nobody came,' said Mancini. 'I waited. Then I opened the window and got through. I called out, "Are you there, Vi?"'

'Why did you do that?' said Birkett.

'Because sometimes, if she was in, she used to hide behind the door and then spring out.'

Birkett nodded. Mancini went on:

'I went into the bedroom, and the first thing that met my eyes was her coat on the floor. I saw her lying on the bed with her knees almost touching her chin. She was clutching a handful of sheets in one hand. I thought she was asleep and shook her. She was not cold and she was not warm. Then I saw blood on the pillow. I said to her, "Wake up." Then I put my hands on her heart and it did not beat. I thought she must be dead.'

'When you realized she was dead, how did that affect your mind?' asked Birkett.

'I was crazy, my Lord,' said Mancini, turning to the judge.

The examination continued. To every question Mancini had a ready and confident reply.

'Why did you not go for the police?' asked Birkett at length.

'I considered a man who has been convicted never gets a fair and square deal from the police.'

'In what respect did you fear you would not get a square deal? Because of your convictions?'

'Because I thought they would say, "Very well, you must be the man. You have been living with her. She has been keeping you. You are a convicted man and you found her."'

The prisoner freely admitted that he had sent the telegram to Kaye's sister, but he denied that he had boasted of having struck his mistress with a hammer, or that he had begged Doris Saville to help save him.

'Were you in any way responsible for the death of Violette Kaye?' asked Birkett.

'I was not, sir.'

'Did you ever use the hammer, which is an exhibit, in any way at all, let alone hit a woman?'

'I have never seen it.'

'Had you anything to do in any way whatever with the death of the woman you lived with?'

'No, sir.'

Birkett sat down.

Under cross-examination by Cassels, Mancini did not deviate in a single detail from the narrative he had already given. He said that he believed his mistress had been murdered by one of her clients. He described two particular visitors, and told how, after they had called on her on one occasion, she had told Mancini that they must move to other lodgings. They did move, but the same two men arrived there shortly after. One day on Brighton sea front, while Mancini was walking with Kaye, a young man had appeared and slashed Mancini's face with a razor. He had then tried to do the same to Kaye. Mancini had knocked him down, and the man had got up and run away.

Referring to Mancini's not having reported Violette Kaye's death to the police, Cassels asked him, 'Were you anxious to avoid the police for a reason?'

'No,' said Mancini.

'Were you not destroying useful evidence in disturbing the body and clearing up traces?'

'I did not think of that.'

'You were determined no eyes should ever see that body again if you could help it?'

'I knew one day it must come out.'

'You intended to disappear yourself?'

'No, I trusted in God, as I do now.'

When Mancini had left the witness box, Birkett called several witnesses who showed that Violette Kaye had regularly been under the influence of drugs. At the end of the defence case, Birkett turned to the jury for his summing up. The Crown case, he told them, was that his client had murdered Violette Kaye with a hammer.

'I waited to hear some suggestion when Mancini was in the witness box as to why he had done it. There has not been one word upon this vital question. I submit that this omission in the case for the Crown destroys it. All the evidence before the death of Violette Kaye is that they were friendly, affectionate, had no quarrels or rows, no anger, no words of bitterness, no malice – none of those things which are concomitant with cruelty or injury.'

On the drugs question as well as that of motive, said Birkett, the jury could not have been satisfied beyond reasonable doubt.

'Is it not a most astounding thing that there was morphine in the body, that it was more than a medicinal dose, that it may have been a fatal dose? Is it not astounding that when Mancini was in the box he was not asked a single question about it? What part does morphine play in the theory of the Crown? Is he responsible for it? If it is to be suggested that he was, he should have been asked about it.'

Birkett suggested that the hammer might have been scooped up with some coal in the cellar, and been burned by being accidentally tipped on to the fire along with the coal, then removed later with the ashes. 'But supposing a man had done this terrible thing, struck a woman with a hammer to kill her, don't you think he would have got rid of the hammer? Of course he would. He could go to the end of the pier at Brighton or get a boat and row out and drop it into the depths of the sea where no human eye could ever see it again. Don't you think he would? Doesn't that put doubt in your mind?'

Spilsbury's evidence, too, had varied, said Birkett. In the committal proceedings he had said the larger end of the hammer had probably caused the fracture. Now he was saying it was most likely the smaller end. And as for Lynch's statement that the blood on Mancini's trousers looked as if it had spurted from an artery, it had been shown that the trousers had not come into his possession until several weeks after Kaye's death.

'I am not attacking the good faith of either Sir Bernard Spilsbury or Dr Roche Lynch,' said Birkett. 'Men may have names and reputations, degrees, distinctions. But high and low, famous and obscure, known and unknown, men are all human and fallible. We have the firm fact clearly proved that those garments upon which the greatest stress was laid about blood being deposited from a distance were neither worn by the prisoner nor in his possession until after the death of this woman. The case for the Crown is simply riddled with doubt.'

Violette Kaye might have died by several other means than that alleged by the prosecution, he reminded the jury. Birkett then turned and pointed at Mancini. 'This man lived on her earnings, and I have no word whatever to say in extenuation or justification. None.'

He paused, then: 'You are men of the world. Consider the associates of these people. We have been dealing with a class of men who pay eightpence for a shirt and women who pay one shilling and sixpence or less for a place in which to sleep. It is an underworld that makes the mind reel. It is imperative that you should have it well in mind that this is the background out of which these events have sprung.'

He referred to the state of fear in which Mancini had said Kaye lived, and of the razor attack. 'Is it too much to say that you ought to consider gravely that the reasonable probability about it all was that in that unhappy woman's life, a dreadful and unspeakable life, blackmail may have formed a considerable part?'

'. . . now that the whole of the matter is before you,' said Birkett, rounding off his hour-long speech, 'I think I am entitled to claim for this man a verdict of Not Guilty. And, members of the jury, in returning this verdict, you will vindicate a principle of law, that people are not tried by newspapers, not tried by rumour, but tried by juries called to do justice and to decide upon the evidence. I ask you for, I appeal to you for, and I claim from you, a verdict of Not Guilty.' He came to a halt, everyone thinking he had finished. But then, his gaze sweeping the jury box, his voice rang out again: 'Stand firm.'

Cassels' summing up was short, which further underlined the fragile nature of the Crown case. It amounted to suspicion arising from Mancini's concealment of the body, but that had been more than adequately explained already.

Mr Justice Branson then summed up the evidence, during which he said: 'I shall say one word of warning. This is not a court of morals but a court of law, and you must not allow the natural revulsion which one must feel against a man who so supports life to affect your judgement against this man. Do not feel any kind of resentment against him which would lead you to draw an inference against him which you would not draw against a man who had not spent his days in that kind of life.'

Nearly two and a half hours after retiring, the jury returned with their verdict that Mancini was innocent. At the announcement: 'Not guilty,' Mancini appeared as if in a daze, unable to take it in. As if he could not accept that it was all over, that he had been found innocent and was a free man, he just kept repeating to Birkett, 'Not guilty, Mr Birkett? Not guilty, Mr Birkett?'

Birkett replied, 'Now go home and look after your mother. She has stood by you and been a brick.'

In spite of the praise heaped upon Birkett for his great

work that day, he later admitted that the victory had given him 'very little pleasure', adding, 'But the acquittal seems to have impressed the popular imagination.'

Birkett's low opinion of Tony Mancini probably mattered little to Mancini himself. He had made a miraculous escape from the very shadow of the gallows. Whatever worth to others his life was deemed to be, it had been saved. And it was more than he had dared to hope for.

Meanwhile, with Tony Mancini's acquittal, the murder of Violette Kaye became officially regarded as an unsolved murder.

Mancini's Confession

Edited and with additional material by Bernard Taylor

The account of the crime, Tony Mancini's trial and acquittal, do not end the story.

For many years following his acquittal Mancini seems to have led a nomadic life, first working in a travelling fair, and afterwards as a merchant seaman. Then, in the 1970s, whilst living in Liverpool with his second wife, he gave an interview to the journalist Alan Hart of the *News of the World*, in the course of which he related details of his past life. At one time, he said, whilst working for his gangster boss, Sabini, he was ordered to 'mark for life' a certain man who had informed on one of Sabini's relatives. Mancini proceeded to tell Hart that he went into a pub where the man was leaning on the bar, drinking. Taking an axe out of his pocket, said Mancini, he lopped off the man's left hand and, leaving the axe embedded in the bar's surface, turned and, unhindered, walked out to a getaway car. 'Everybody knew I was responsible,' Mancini said, 'including the police. But I had a cast-iron alibi and the witnesses were afraid to talk, so I was never charged.'

Mancini then went on to tell Hart that on another occasion he had turned the handle of a meat mincer while another gangster's hand was held inside it.

These sordid and gruesome reminiscences were not the purpose of the interview, however. In the *News of the World* of 28 November 1976, in an article headed *I've Got Away With Murder*, Mancini also confessed to the murder of Violette Kaye. He could not now be legally harmed by such a confession; he could not of course be tried again for a crime of which he had been acquitted, and having passed the age of seventy he was secure from prosecution on any charge of perjury.

Shortly afterwards Mancini met Stephen Knight and began a correspondence with him, as a result of which, in May 1978, he travelled to London and submitted himself to three days of interrogation, in the course of which he once again confessed to the murder of Violette Kaye and told what he swore to be the *true* story of the events of that 10 May 1934.

Following the interview he swore an affidavit before a solicitor that all he had said was the truth.

Mancini began the interview by telling how he had gone to live with Violette Kaye. In the early 1930s he had known her for some little while but there had been no serious commitment of any kind in their relationship. She had once been a soubrette (adopting the professional name of Kaye), but drink and drugs had put an end to her work on the stage and she had turned to prostitution for a living. The relationship between them began when Mancini, while working as a bouncer at the Silver Slipper, a club in London's Wardour Street, was hospitalized after being badly injured in a fight with some of the club's visitors who had come from the East End. Violette Kaye visited him in the hospital where she told him that she had just returned from Brighton and on going to the club had been told about the fight. Said Mancini: 'She burst out crying and then she said, "Give it all up because they're gonna kill you. They've vowed to kill you."' She then told him that she loved him and ended up by asking him to go to Brighton with her.

Mancini to Knight: So I said, 'Well, I'll think about it. How would I live down in Brighton?' She said, 'Oh, you've no need to worry. I can get a nice little flat down there and we'll manage.' I said, 'Oh, no. I've never been a ponce in my life. I'm not going to start now.'

Knight: She was a prostitute then, was she?

Mancini: Oh, she was a well-known prostitute. She had her own particular clients. I don't know who they were 'cause she never used to tell me . . . Well, not well-known people, but they had plenty of money. They were rich people.

Knight: So she was a 'high class' prostitute?

Mancini: Oh, she wasn't a low class prostitute, no, no. She was a high class one. More of a call girl.

Mancini then related how, after being discharged from the hospital, he returned to the Silver Slipper where he was given a month's wages by his employer, and told, 'You know if they come down again my club's gonna suffer. You'll have to find another job.' Mancini went on:

'So she was standing at the bar at the time. She said, "He's no need to. He's coming with me to Brighton." I went back to my flat – it was a furnished flat. I didn't even give notice. I just packed my gear and we caught the train from Victoria to Brighton. And she'd already took this flat at 44, Park Crescent. And I began looking around for a job . . . I couldn't find a job nowhere and of course what few pound I had had run out. I was going to Sherry's and cocktail bars looking for jobs and trying to get in with the mob there, but they were very closely knit and they wouldn't let no outsiders in. So of course my money ran out and I said, "I'm sorry, I have to go back to London. I've got no money." She said, "Oh, no, you won't," and she locked the wardrobe and hid my clothes and I said, "Oh, what the hell? It's a lovely summer. I'll stay here." So I used to lie on the beach.'

Mancini's account goes on to tell that he was later told by a member of the Brighton police to go back to London – 'We've got enough trouble without you coming round here . . .' – and warned that if he did not, then they would 'get' him – 'one way or the other'.

Continuing his story, Mancini said that one evening he said to Violette that he would take her out. 'I'd been to the casino and I'd hit lucky, and I'd won thirty quid, so I said, "Come on, I'll take you out tonight. We'll have a nice meal with a bottle of wine and we'll go dancing." She used to love dancing, you see. She said, "No, I'm sorry, I've got a client to see – he's taking me out tonight and I don't want you to come back till three o'clock in the morning." Then I suddenly realized it wasn't my home at all, that it was just where I slept, you know, and I said, "Oh, to hell with you and your clients," so I went out and I went to Sherry's and I got a little drunk, you know, and picked up a girl there and went back to her place and stopped the night, you see. Got home about eight o'clock, half-past eight in the morning and she was in bed. So she said, "Where was you last night?" I said, "Where was you?" I said, "What's good for you is good for me. Anyhow, today I'm getting a job. That's it. I don't care what it is. I'm getting a job."'

Mancini went on to relate how, in his search for a job, he 'got friendly' with a girl called May Woods who worked on the rifle range at the fun fair. 'She was a nice little thing – come from London – Balham she came from. Father used to drive an undertaker's hearse.' Mancini told her that he was looking for a job and asked her whether she knew of any. In reply she told him: 'Well, they had some trouble in the Skylark yesterday and my boss knows the boss of the Skylark and he said to my boss, "If only I could find a feller that could take care of the troubles." Hang on – I'll shut up and I'll take you down there.'

Mancini continued: 'So she put the shutters up and she took me down there and she had a word with him, and I'm outside and she called me in. She said, "This is Tony." So he said, "So you reckon you could take care o' the trouble?" I said, "Yeah, I think so." "Who did you work for in London?" I said, "Jack Spot." He said, "You *can* take care of yourself. Well, you'll have to wait on table, like, just as an excuse to have you here, like I'll give you extra money if there's trouble. Can you handle it?" I said, "Oh, yeah." I forget the wages now. It was very poor, but it was enough to live on in those days. I could have paid my rent and kept myself in food and still had a few quid over. I said, "I'll take it." Never waited on table in my life, you know. Anyway, I used to carry two plates of fish and chips, one in each hand. I couldn't carry more . . . So I got up about nine o'clock the next morning, bathed and washed and shaved [to go] to work, you see. He opened at ten. So she woke up. She said, "Where're you going?" I said, "I'm going to work. Never mind where I'm gonna work," I said, "I've got a job. So you'd better start looking for somebody else to look after you because I've had enough of this nonsense."'

Knight: There had obviously been a change in your feelings towards her.

Mancini: Yes.

Knight: At your fondest for her, how had you felt? Did you ever love her?

Mancini: At first, yes. Because she was very gentle and very feminine and – she cared for me very much. But then when she used to get drunk her personality changed completely. She became from a sweet, feminine woman into a brawling slut. Have you ever seen a drunken woman? Not a very pleasant sight. She used to curse and swear and use all kinds of four-letter words. She used to fall over and – er – pee herself and all this, you know. She was *disgusting* when she was drunk. Absolutely *disgusting*. I only saw her drunk once and I felt so disgusted with myself – being with her, you know. Anyway, I got the job, and I wouldn't tell her where I worked, you see, so she was determined to find out. She must have had me followed, 'cause she never got up that time in the morning, you see. Must have had me followed, you see, 'cause one day she walked in there [the Skylark Café], drunk – or under the influence of drugs. I don't know which she was but she wasn't herself. She was very unsteady and she had this wild look in her eyes, and she hadn't even combed her hair, which was very unusual. She said, 'So here you are.' I said, 'Get out of here. Get out. Don't start no trouble here. I'm very happy here.' I *was happy* there, you know.

Knight: This was 1934?

Mancini: Yes.

Knight: How long had you been there at this time?

Mancini: About three or four months. And I was earning good money – tips from the customers and a couple o' bits o' trouble 'e gave me a fiver for because I just threw them out – with no trouble at all. And they used to steer clear of it because they knew if they went there they'd get more trouble than what they bargained for, you see. So the word got round and 'e said, 'Thank

God,' he said, 'they're leaving me alone for a change,' he said, 'thanks to you, Tony. Thank you very much.' And he used to give me a fiver now and again, like, you know, which was – in those days a fiver was a lot of money. So, anyway, she had a cup of tea and she said, 'So my money wasn't good enough for you?' And it was packed with people, you know. The boss looked at me and said, 'Do you know this lady?' I said, 'Unfortunately, yes.' He said, 'She's causing a disturbance. Get her out.' [She said] 'Don't touch me, you ponce!' I just picked her up and turned her round and got her outside and she sat on a bench outside on the beach. She sat there about an hour, kept on looking in but she didn't come in no more. Then she disappeared. So, I got home about seven o'clock that night and, er, she was lying on the bed and, er, she woke up and she said, 'So you're back.' I said, 'Yes.' She staggered up off the bed and she started to spit at me and curse at me and swear at me. 'You're not getting away. I'm not letting you get away. I know what you want to do. You're sick of me . . .' and all this carry on, you know. 'You're tired of me because I get drunk. I can't help it; I'm so unhappy,' and all this. All of a sudden she said, 'You're a bastard!' and she came at me with her hands and scratched my face, so I pushed her away with my hand. She fell down, then she got up again. She came up to me and she spit in my face, got hold of me like this and ripped my shirt and tried to strangle me and so . . . I was slowly losing my temper, like, you know. She kept on, and she said, 'I'll mark you so nobody else wants you,' and she turned away and she picked up this hammer. She came running at me with it. It was in the fireplace. She made a wild swing at me. So I hit her.

Knight: With?

Mancini: My hand.

Knight: Fist?

Mancini: Yes. And she shot across the room. We had a fireplace like this. It had a brass fender round. Big brass knobs on each end. Have you seen the sort?

Knight: Yes.

Mancini: And a great big brass knob in the middle. Well, she must have wet herself as she fell down on the floor, 'cause as I hit her she staggered back and slipped on this wet. She keeled over and hit her head on there, you see, [bangs the knob of the fender] on the knob. I think it was the right-hand side – left-hand side it was.

Knight: Of the fireplace?

Mancini: On her head.

Knight: Where had your blow struck her?

Mancini: On the chin.

Knight: And you'd been a boxer.

Mancini: Yeah. So she – as I went to pick her up – I suddenly felt upset that – you know – 'cause I'd never hit her before, you see. Never. I don't hit women, you see. I never have done. I mean, they can hit me and I never hit them back because it was the way I was brought up. You just don't hit women. And I said, 'I'm sorry, love,' I said, 'I didn't mean it.' And she just spit in my face like that – *sttt*! And I don't remember – I just got hold of her, of her shoulders and was banging her head on the floor, like that. I said, 'Don't you spit at me!' And I don't know how long I was like that. And when I came to out of my rage she was lying like that . . . quite still, you see.

Knight: You were banging her head on . . .

Mancini: On this fender.

Knight: On the *fender*. In rage?

Mancini: I didn't know I was . . .

Knight: So . . .

Mancini: That's what I must have done.

Knight: So what killed her was not the accidental fall

and the blow on the head as she fell. It was you banging her head on the fender.

Mancini: Yes . . . I don't remember really, but that's what I must have done, as far as I can recollect. I remember picking her up and banging her like that, and then it all went a red haze.

Knight: You mentioned this 'haze' when we were speaking before. It's this period of blankness that I'd like to examine more closely if we can.

Mancini: Well, nobody yet can ever say how long they don't know what they're doing, because you don't look at your watch before you go into a blank and you don't look at your watch when you come out.

Knight: What exactly is 'going into a blank'?

Mancini: Well, I'll tell you. It's a blind rage, a pent-up blind rage that suddenly bursts like a storm inside your brain. And it blanks out all reasonable thought, all sensible thought.

Knight: But during that time you know what you're doing?

Mancini: No! You don't know. When I read about people committing a murder and they say they don't remember, I believe them. Because these things happen.

Knight: Do you think that when people are in this condition they are not responsible for –

Mancini: They are definitely not responsible for what they do. A psychiatrist in another court case said it's quite possible – it is within the realms of possibility that this man had a mental blackout caused by anxiety, rage, mental hurt . . .

When she was dead and I put her in the cupboard, I had a wash, drunk half a bottle of whisky and went out for a walk. Trying to think what to do. I knew she was dead of course. And I knew that I was as good as dead myself. With my record and her record and the hatred of the local police and the hatred of Scotland Yard together combined, for me, I stood no chance. I was as good as dead, you see. I'm not a coward. I don't mind dying, but I had a horror of hanging. Well, all men do, don't they?

Knight: Most, I should think.

Mancini: Obviously. If you can fight and have a go defending yourself – well, if you get killed that's too bad. But to have your arms pinioned and your legs pinioned and you've got no way to fight back, that's a dreadful thing to think about, isn't it? However, I found myself at Sherry's. And I found that I could lower the safety curtain in my mind.

Knight: Quite soon after?

Mancini: The same night. I could lower this safety curtain and it would blank it out completely. What had happened was blanked out as though I'd drawn fire curtains across my mind for that period and I couldn't see. The only time I thought about it was when I got back to the flat. Then I realized of course that I had to move, that I couldn't leave the body there. So I got this room in Kemp Street, down in the basement. Next problem was, how could I move the body?

Knight: How soon after Violette's death did you get the room in Kemp Street?

Mancini: About a week.

Knight: So you lived with it in that room in Park Crescent for a week to start with?

Mancini: To start with. Now how could I move the body? And how long could I keep it there? I never thought – it was summer time. It was hot. I must have been out of my mind. I must have been insane to think that I could keep a dead body in a small room about this size, in a basement in a hot summer without being found out. I never thought about these things. It was momentarily self-preservation, do you understand me? So I went to the market and I got myself a sea trunk. The straps were broken. I took it back to the flat. Then I had to open this cupboard door, and that took a lot of doing.

Knight: You hadn't opened it for a week?

Mancini: (shaking his head) That took an awful lot of doing.

Knight: Had it begun to smell in that time?

Mancini: Yes. Well, not too much, but it began to – you know. Anyway, I had some whisky there and I had a good shot of whisky – and as I opened the door this arm fell out like that [illustrates with a gesture]. And she was stiff. Hunched up stiff like that [again illustrates]. *Rigor mortis* had set in, you see.

Knight: But the arm was still limp.

Mancini: Yes, still fell out like that. So – I picked her up and put her in, and then put some old clothes over her.

Knight: Where had you obtained the trunk?

Mancini: From the old open market in Brighton.

Knight: How much did you pay for it?

Mancini: Half a crown. It was half a crown or seven-and-six. It was half a crown, I think.

Knight: It was an old one, then, obviously?

Mancini: Oh, yes. Then I had to buy some rope; and I tied the rope round. Then I had to get a hand cart and couldn't get it [the trunk containing the body] up the stairs to the street. So I went to the top of the basement steps in Park Crescent and I stood there and a couple of young boys came along. I said, 'Would you give me a hand, lads?' 'Sure, sir.' And they helped me out with the trunk and put it on the wheelbarrow, you see.

Knight: How old were they?

Mancini: Ten or eleven, twelve, thirteen. I'm not sure. So we're walking to Kemp Street and they're helping me to push it. I said I'd give them a couple of bob. And we

pass this café. 'Couldn't 'alf do with a cup o' tea, mister.'
'Oh, thirsty work, sir.' I left the handcart with the trunk
on it tied down outside the café while we had a cup of tea
and a bacon sandwich. Then we went to Kemp Street and
I saw the landlady. 'Oh, yes,' I said, 'this is all my stuff.
There are a lot of books and that, and I've got some
cleaning fluid. It gives off a bit of a strong smell,' I said,
'but there's nothing wrong.' 'Oh, all right, mister.' So
down we went. Put it here. And there was my bed here
and there was the trunk there [right alongside it]. And I
slept with that for six weeks like that, until of course it
became unbearable.

Knight: What did you do? Could you do anything to
stop the smell?

Mancini: I opened the trunk and just poured disinfectant over it and . . .

Knight: Did that help?

Mancini: No. It did at first, but it wore off.

Knight: She must have been looking pretty horrible by
this time.

Mancini: I never looked at it. I couldn't look. My friend
John Hill, the criminologist, has a photograph of the
decomposed body and he said to me, 'Do you want to
look at it?' I said, 'Not if you paid me ten million pounds
would I look at that picture.' And I still haven't looked at
it. I couldn't. I couldn't.

Knight: You didn't look at the body at all while you
had it?

Mancini: I couldn't.

Knight: The flies must have been a problem in the
summer too.

Mancini: There was no flies. That's the – could be – it
was shut tight, you see, and roped, in knots. But it began
to ooze from the bottom of the trunk.

Knight: The disinfectant, you mean?

Mancini: And the decomposing parts of the body. The fluids, you see, from the body. I was forever wiping it up and putting disinfectant down. Anyway, it was driving me out of my mind. Then I opened the paper one morning and there it was: *Dismembered Trunk Found in Brighton Station and Another One in Victoria Station* – or was it Waterloo Station? Victoria – *Massive* house to house search. The next morning I read – they used to give lists of names of the streets where they were going to search, you see, so that the people who lived in the houses would be in: 'Please be in between so-and-so times as your house will have to be searched.' Kemp Street was on the list. Well, that time I didn't go home. I just went to Sherry's, then went to an all-night café and then I caught the early morning train, the five o'clock train, to London. And I was so tired I stretched out along the long back seat of the carriage. I fell asleep and I must've got to Victoria and got half way back to Brighton before I woke up. I forget where it was, some little place. I woke up. 'My God!' I jumped out, crossed over the railway line and went back to London. And that's when the chase began.

After the main interview Stephen Knight questioned Mancini more closely on the killing itself:

Knight: You had tried unsuccessfully twice before, while in London, to go straight. I have the impression you thought of your job at the Skylark as your last chance.

Mancini: This was my last chance.

Knight: So here you were, with your last chance, as you saw it, to go straight, striving to go straight. You were living with this woman whom you started off loving, but whom gradually, for a combination of reasons, you had come to dislike – and even, in the end, you said she *disgusted* you.

Mancini: Yes.

Knight: She was the one real obstacle to your making a

reasonable life for yourself. You had a *motive* for killing her.

Mancini: Don't tell me! Everybody else thinks so, but that wasn't so.

Knight: You don't think you had a motive?

Mancini: I had . . . I suppose to the outside world I had a motive. But murder never crossed my mind.

Knight: You are going to say 'No' straightaway to my next question. Can I just ask you –

Mancini: Yes, of course you can.

Knight: – to think for a few moments before answering the question. Had you at any time during your relationship with her, in its very worst moments, in your greatest disgust with her, considered the possibility of killing her?

Mancini: I don't have to think. All I had to do was to leave her, just pack up my few belongings and catch the train back to London. We weren't married.

Knight: Wouldn't that have meant not going straight any more?

Mancini: I'd have found a job somewhere. I'd no doubt have gone back to crime again, which would have been better for me, I suppose, in a way. But what happened? You see? Murder hadn't ever crossed my mind. I wasn't a *killer*. I was a fighter but I wasn't a killer. I never had been a killer. You know . . .

Knight: You've spoken for the first time today of a hammer. There was a hammer in the room.

Mancini: Yes, there was, which she threw at me.

Knight: Of course the hammer has played a part in the story ever since the beginning, hasn't it? It was alleged by the prosecution at your trial that *you* hit *her* with the hammer.

Mancini: This is not true.

Knight: So what was the hammer doing in the room, first of all?

Mancini: Well, she used to always lay a fire because she used to have these shivering fits which of course now I know was the after-effects of drugs. So she used to break the coal up downstairs and fill the coal scuttle, and throw the hammer on top of the coal, bring the coal scuttle upstairs from the cellar and build a fire – and when she came home if she felt shivery she'd light the fire. And she used to always throw the hammer into the er . . . fender. Just by the fender there. It was a little short one, with a sawn-off handle and two heads. You know, only little.

Knight: By two heads, you mean one double-sided head, not a claw hammer?

Mancini: That's right.

Knight: Is that the hammer that the police found in the cellar?

Mancini: Yes.

Knight: How did it get from that room down into the cellar?

Mancini: Because when I lit the fire – right? – I suddenly became icy cold, and I was going to stop up all night. I lit the fire.

Knight: After she was dead?

Mancini: Yes. And I kept the fire roaring all night because I was shivering like that. It must have been the shock or the ague . . .

Unfortunately the last page of Stephen Knight's verbatim account of his interview with Tony Mancini has been lost.

One can perhaps imagine, however, that he would have continued to question Mancini about the hammer found in the cellar at Park Crescent. How did it come to be charred? Was the burning of it done intentionally, in an attempt to destroy it? If these questions were asked – and they probably were – then one can now only guess at Mancini's answers. If Tony Mancini's sworn account, above, is true, and the hammer had no part in Violette Kaye's death, then there was no need to destroy it. In which case perhaps Mancini attempted to destroy it in the fear that it would be *thought* to be the murder weapon. Or perhaps the burning of it was the result of pure accident; perhaps when keeping the fire going during the night following the murder he tipped the hammer, unnoticed, on to the fire along with the coal.

However, in certain respects Mancini's sworn confession to Stephen Knight differs slightly from the account he had given earlier to the journalist Alan Hart. To Knight he said that when Violette Kaye came for him, swinging at him with the hammer, he took it from her and then hit her with his fist. Under the blow, he said, she staggered back and slipped in her own urine, falling and hitting her head on the knob of the fender. Mancini then said that he felt upset at the fact that he had hit her – 'I don't hit women, you see. I never have done' – and went to her, saying, 'I'm sorry, love, I didn't mean it.' She, however, spat at him, following which he beat her head against the fender knob until she was dead.

To Alan Hart, though, he said that after he had taken the hammer from her she had shouted at him, 'Give me that hammer,' and that he had replied, 'I'll give you the hammer all right.'

Mancini's words, as quoted by Alan Hart, continue:

'Then I threw it across the room at her with all my strength. It caught her on the left temple and she spun round twice like something on a fairground. Her eyes were bulging out of her head. Then she fell like a ton of bricks on the brass fireplace surround. I ran over to her and shouted, "You stupid bitch. Look what you've made me do." As I was shouting I was holding her by the shoulders and banging her head up and down . . .'

Whatever is the true explanation, Tony Mancini has

admitted that he did indeed kill Violette Kaye. Whether he told either of the two writers, Hart or Knight, the whole truth and nothing but the truth, however, must remain another question.

The Witchcraft Murder

The Mysterious Death of Charles Walton

BY STEPHEN KNIGHT

The Devil, it is said, presents his neophytes with three familiars, or animal servants – a bird, a cat or a dog – in exchange for their souls. A hellish black dog plays a prominent role in the savage, unsolved murder of Charles Walton at the Warwickshire village of Lower Quinton in the closing months of World War Two.

Lower Quinton lies about eight miles from Stratford-upon-Avon, a mile or so from the main A34 between Stratford and Chipping Norton.

The village is at the heart of an area where witchcraft and black magic have flourished for centuries, possibly even for thousands of years. Some authorities have stated that it was in places like Lower Quinton that the youthful Shakespeare gained the knowledge of sorcery that he used to such devastating effect in *Macbeth*. Even today, black Sabbaths are said to be held within the circle of ancient stones that dot the hilltops of that part of the Cotswolds.

Almost every village in Warwickshire has its own legend associated with the witches. At Long Compton it is the familiar stagecoach drawn by headless horses. Alscot is supposed to be haunted by a ghost that is half man, half calf. And Ragley Park claims a Lady in White. But at Lower Quinton, the most deeply-rooted fear is of a spectral black dog.

The Dog, bigger than a natural hound, is said to appear without warning and to disappear no one knows where. Years, or even decades, might elapse before it returns again. He who once beholds the Dog is doomed, says the legend, and sudden death will inevitably follow.

In 1945, one of the oldest inhabitants of Lower Quinton was seventy-four-year-old field labourer Charles Walton. There was something about Walton that set him apart. He had lived the life of a hermit in a tiny thatched cottage and now, partly crippled with rheumatism, lived with his niece, Miss Edith Isabel Walton. All his life Walton had been a loner. He shunned the company of people and gravitated instead to the birds and animals that lived in the surrounding fields. He used to say that he was able to understand the birds and to communicate with them in their own languages. He walked everywhere but seldom went more than a mile or so from his home. He had the reputation of being a miser, and some said he was a wizard. He earned only 1s 9d an hour cutting hedges for a local farmer, Potter, yet he had a bank account, a rare thing for a man of his station in those days. Where did he get his money? The villagers were in no doubt; he had a secret store of cash obtained from people who paid him to work spells for them. Walton never joined the other villagers in either of Lower Quinton's two pubs, although he spent more than most of them on drink. He would buy barrels of cider, up to twelve gallons at once, and cart it home on his wheelbarrow to consume in the isolation he loved.

On Wednesday, 14 February 1945, a fine, sunny St Valentine's morning, while the world outside was intent upon the outcome of the Yalta conference between Churchill, Roosevelt and Stalin, Charles Walton left home at 9 A.M. Before stepping out into the lane he had told Edith he would be home for his tea at his usual time, four o'clock. Edith had a war job at a nearby factory and would not be home before six, but she knew her uncle returned always at the same hour, prepared his own tea, and rested. Uncle and niece bade each other farewell and the old man made his halting, rheumaticky way along the lane and into the meadows that led up to Meon Hill, about a mile from home. He carried his walking stick, his double-pronged hay-fork and a sickle-shaped slash-hook. Edith never again saw him alive.

Walton did not return home at four o'clock. When Edith got back at six o'clock and saw from the untouched state of the food in her kitchen that her uncle had not been home, she grew alarmed. Her immediate thought was that his old legs had finally given way and that he might be lying up in the fields unable to make himself heard. Going to the cottage of her neighbour, Mr Harry Beasley, she told him of Walton's absence. Together they made their way to The Firs, the farmhouse of Mr Albert Potter, for whom Walton worked.

Farmer Potter seemed surprised. Charlie had been up on Meon Hill just after midday, he said. He had seen him. 'Leastways, I *think* it was Charlie,' said the farmer; he had certainly seen *someone* trimming the hedges about five hundred yards off when he had been in the fields at noon inspecting his cattle and sheep. And who else could it have been but Charlie?

Potter grabbed a torch and accompanied Edith and Beasley into the fields. It was now completely dark and there was a chill in the air. Following the jogging light of Potter's torch, they climbed slowly up Meon Hill, looking all about them for signs of Walton, occasionally calling his name, and listening intently for calls of help. Suddenly Potter stopped by an old willow tree. The light flashed across the ground so quickly that neither Edith nor Beasley could make out what it was that had stopped the farmer in his tracks.

Then, shining the torch full in Edith's face so that she could see nothing but the blinding light, Potter cried out, 'Stay there! Don't come any nearer! You mustn't look at this!'

The two men went forward to the dark shape stretched out on the earth.

'His injuries were hideous,' recalled Detective Superintendent Robert Fabian of Scotland Yard. 'The sickle blade of a trouncing hook had ripped his throat away and was stuck, still gleaming, in the wounds. His thin old arms were cut where he had tried to defend himself, his face was twisted wildly with fright and his body was pinned deliberately to the earth by the prongs of a hay-fork. It looked like the kind of killing the Druids might have done in ghastly ceremony at full moon.'

In addition, the sign of the Cross had been roughly hacked into the old man's neck and chest with the slash-hook. The hay-fork that pinned him to the ground had not only been driven through his neck, but penetrated six inches into the ground. It took two policemen to wrench the fearful weapon from the blood-soaked soil. Walton's walking stick, stained with blood, lay nearby.

Fabian, Scotland Yard's most famous sleuth, had been called in to lead the murder investigation by the Warwickshire Police. He was taken to the scene of the crime early on the morning following the murder by Superintendent Alec Spooner of Warwick.

'What motive?' asked Fabian. 'Robbery? Revenge? A quarrel?'

His assistant, Sergeant Albert Webb, looked at the bloody hay-fork. 'The work of a maniac?' he suggested.

Spooner took the London policemen aside. He looked at them a moment with what Fabian later described as 'a queer smile'.

'Well,' he said, 'perhaps you had better look at this.' He handed Fabian a book called *Folk Lore, Old Customs and Superstitions in Shakespeare-land*. The book, published fifteen years earlier, was by a Warwickshire parson called James Harvey Bloom. Spooner had marked a passage at the foot of page ninety-six:

In 1875 a weak-minded young man killed an old woman named Ann Turner with a hay-fork because he believed she had bewitched him.

Fabian blinked. Before he could comment, however, Spooner handed him another book. This one, by Clive Holland, was about forty years old and was called, simply, *Warwickshire*. Fabian read:

And even as late as 1875 the effect of ancient superstitions concerning witches and the 'Evil Eye' was seen in the crime of a man named John Haywood, who stabbed to death with a pitch fork an old woman eighty years of age, exclaiming whilst he did so that he would kill all the witches in Long Compton, and that there were sixteen of them.

At his trial for murder, during the course of his defence, he said, 'If you had known the number of people who lie in our churchyard, who, if it had not been for them [the witches] would have been alive now, you would be surprised. Her [the deceased] was a proper witch.'

It came out in evidence that this man for years had honestly believed that when cattle or other animals died, or any evil fortune befell his fellow villagers, such things were the direct result of the 'Evil Eye' of some unfortunate old women he asserted were 'proper old witches'.

The last paragraph particularly caught Fabian's attention:

His mode of killing the unfortunate woman he attacked was evidently a survival of the ancient Anglo-Saxon custom of dealing with such persons by means of 'stacung', or sticking spikes into them, whilst at the same time wishing the portion of the body so wounded might mortify or wither away.

Sergeant Webb was sceptical. He laid a hand on Spooner's shoulder. 'The mad, hectic life of the country is proving too much for you, sir,' he joked.

Spooner was not laughing. 'You wait and see, my lad,' he said.

'By afternoon,' Fabian wrote later, 'we had brought the twentieth century to Lower Quinton like a cold shower-bath.'

The help of the Royal Air Force at Leamington Airfield was recruited and an Avro Anson plane swooped low over Meon Hill, taking detailed photographs of the entire area. An old watch was missing from Walton's body and Fabian set a battery of Royal engineers searching for it with mine detectors. There was just a chance, he reasoned, that the watch had been torn from the old man in his death struggle and that it might bear tell-tale marks of the killer.

The local police suggested that the murderer might be among 1,043 prisoners of war at Long Marston POW camp about two miles away. In line with most British camps, Long Marston did not operate rigorous security. It contained Germans, Italians, Slavs and Ukrainians. Fabian got on to the Yard and summoned Detective Sergeant David Saunders of the Special Branch who spoke the languages of all the prisoners fluently.

Saunders's interrogation of the men at the camp eventually turned up a suspect. An Italian serviceman had been seen by some fellow prisoners trying desperately to scrub some blood from his coat. And a baker's roundsman driving near the scene of the murder had actually seen him cowering in a roadside ditch and wiping fresh blood from his hands. But the Italian refused to talk. His coat was sent to the West Midlands Forensic Science Laboratory at Birmingham, where Walton's blood-saturated clothes had already been taken.

Fabian was convinced they were on to the murderer. After questioning John Messer, the baker's roundsman, he sent a group of the Royal Engineers to the ditch where the Italian had been seen. It did not take long for their mine detectors to start the high-pitched whine that indicated the discovery of buried metal.

'Is it the old tin watch?' asked Fabian, holding his breath.

'No, sir,' said a soldier after a tense moment. 'It's rabbit snares.'

Rabbits put paid to the Italian POW theory once and for all. A short time after the finding of the snares, a police motorcyclist arrived in Lower Quinton from Stratford. He had a message from the laboratory. Tests on the Italian's coat had been completed. The stains on it were definitely blood – but not Walton's. It was not even human blood, but from a rabbit. The snares, the blood on the coat – Fabian suddenly saw it all: the prisoner had refused to answer questions in case he was found to have been giving the camp guards the slip in order to go poaching.

A sinister wall of silence greeted Fabian and Webb when they tried to talk to the villagers about the murder. There were 493 inhabitants of Lower Quinton and its neighbouring villages, Admington and Upper Quinton. Not one seemed eager to assist the police.

'We made our investigations in the village from door to door,' said Fabian. 'There were lowered eyes, reluctance to speak except for talk of bad crops and a heifer that died in a ditch. But what had that to do with Charles Walton? Nobody would say.'

Bad crops and a heifer that died in a ditch.

The detective's mind reverted to the story of the nineteenth-century 'witch' murderer, Haywood. *It came out in evidence that this man for years had honestly believed that when cattle or other animals died, or any evil fortune befell his fellow villagers, such things were the direct result of the 'Evil Eye'. . .*

Then came the incident of the Black Dog. Realizing the futility of questioning the villagers, Fabian took to scouring the ground around the Meon Hill for some previously overlooked clue that might send him off on a new scent. One evening at dusk, after days of fruitless searching, a black dog appeared. It ran down Meon Hill, passed close by Fabian and disappeared into the gathering twilight. Soon afterwards a farm boy came walking over the hill.

'Looking for that dog, son?' asked Fabian.

'Dog, mister?' said the boy, turning pale.

'A black dog.'

Terrified, the boy ran off without another word.

When Fabian told Superintendent Spooner of the strange incident of the dog, Spooner told him for the first time of the Lower Quinton legend of a spectral Black Dog with blazing, devil's eyes, and how whenever it appeared somebody died. That afternoon a police car had run over a dog in the village. Fabian was beginning to feel uneasy.

When cattle or other animals died . . .

Word spread that Fabian had seen The Ghost. The inhabitants, chary before, were now openly hostile. When he and Webb called at the Gay Dog pub for a chat with some of the regulars later that night, everyone was silent. Before he knew what was happening, everyone had put down his glass, got up and left.

'Cottage doors were shut in our faces, and even the most innocent witnesses seemed unable to meet our eyes,' said Fabian. 'Some became ill after we spoke to them.'

The day after the sighting of the black dog another heifer was found dead in a ditch.

Such things . . .

Soon after that, the corpse of a black dog was found hanging from a bush near the spot where Walton had been murdered.

. . . were the direct result of the 'Evil Eye' . . .

It was then that Superintendent Spooner discovered that the witchcraft covens had been meeting in the Lower Quinton area for more than three hundred years, and that the stone circle of the Whispering Knights, not far from where Walton had been felled, was still used for witches' Sabbaths.

Fabian made further inquiries about the legend of the Black Dog. Eventually he found someone who agreed to speak to him. 'We don't talk much about it,' he was told. 'Nobody has spoken about it for years. Not since afore the war, anyway.'

But Fabian did manage to discover that locals believed the Dog had appeared within living memory. An actual sighting. It was not all woolly, intangible superstition, it seemed. Fabian was surprised to find himself wondering if there was some truth in what he was being told. In 1885, he learned, a fourteen-year-old ploughboy had seen the Dog no fewer than nine times on nine successive nights on his way home from the fields. On the last night he also saw a headless woman, who passed him with an unnerving rustling sound. It was the sign of death, the boy knew that. The next day the ploughboy's sister died suddenly.

Fabian realized he had to find out more about local witchcraft lore. He went back to the two books Spooner had handed him on his first night in Lower Quinton. In the first, on page 100, he found the story of the plough-boy. It was reported exactly as it had been told to him, with one vital addition. The name of the ploughboy was Charles Walton.

The further Fabian pursued his ominous inquiries, the

more he wondered if he was confronted with a ritual fertility killing. In ancient times, he discovered, February was a propitious month for blood-letting festivals in which the earth was soaked with blood – usually the blood of animals but sometimes human blood – to give back the life drawn out in cultivation. A woman in Birmingham who claimed to know the secret of Lower Quinton told a newspaper that Charles Walton had been the blood sacrifice in a fertility rite. She said:

'Three or four survivors of an ancient cult live in the locality, but the actual murderer was a woman who was brought by car from a different part of the country.' She refused to give further details.

'We persevered,' said Fabian, 'took 4,000 statements, traced tinkers and gypsies. We sent twenty-nine samples of clothing, hair, etc., of various suspects to Birmingham laboratories for analysis. I had tramps detained in Somerset, boot repairers questioned in Salisbury . . . but the murder remained unsolved.'

One night towards the end of his long, fruitless sojourn at Lower Quinton, Fabian called upon a man he had been waiting all day to question. The man answered Fabian's rap at his door.

'I'm inquiring about the late Charles Walton . . .' began the policeman.

'He's been dead and buried a month now!' interjected the man. 'What are you worrying about?' And he closed the door in Fabian's face.

'So,' wrote Fabian ruefully in his book *Fabian of the Yard*, 'we had to leave it.'

Detective Superintendent Robert Fabian, who died in 1978, never published his true beliefs with regard to the Lower Quinton murder. In his first book, published in 1950, he gave the impression that he had no idea about the truth of the matter. In *The Anatomy of Crime* twenty years later he admitted a little more. 'I *think* I know who did it,' he said.

The fact is, Fabian had known since February 1945 who killed Charlie Walton. But there was never enough evidence even to make an arrest. He couldn't say what he knew about the murderer when writing his books because the murderer was still alive – and had the laws of libel to protect him. So Fabian had to be content to let the public regard Lower Quinton as his greatest failure.

The murderer, however, has now been dead for some years, and lies in a grave only a few yards from his victim. His death occurred not very long before that of Fabian himself, and it is quite likely that had Fabian possessed the strength during the last moments of his life he might well have published his beliefs. Shortly before his death in 1978, however, and not long after the death of the one he believed to be guilty, Fabian *spoke* very freely of the matter. One to whom he revealed his convictions was the writer Richard Whittington-Egan who was looking into the case at the time.

When Whittington-Egan learned that I was planning to write on the Lower Quinton murder he related Fabian's story to me, following which I at once tried to contact Fabian with the aim of getting him to give me a signed statement as to the identity of Walton's murderer. Unfortunately, however, Fabian was already very ill and was unable to see me, lacking even the strength to sign any prepared document. I did, though, have his story as it was related to me by my friend Richard Whittington-Egan.

All along, it appeared, Fabian knew that Charlie Walton had been murdered by his employer, that it was in fact Farmer Albert Potter who had killed and mutilated his old farm hand – and for a reason far removed from the dark world of witchcraft.

Fabian's theory, supplemented by facts unearthed in my own investigations, is as follows:

Albert Potter – and Fabian was totally convinced of this – was the only man who could have committed the murder. On his own admission Potter was the last person to see Walton alive. But he kept changing his story about when he had seen him and the investigators were never satisfied with his evidence. At first he said he had seen 'just Walton's shirt sleeves' at a distance of five hundred yards. But Walton had no sleeves to his shirt, and anyway, it is just not possible to pick out something as small as a man's arm against a background of a hedge at a distance of over a quarter of a mile.

The murder took place on Potter's land in daylight, and anyone getting up there would have been seen – it was, after all, on the side of a hill that can be seen for miles around. If it had been anyone who was not supposed to be in the fields the word would have gone round the closely-knit village like wildfire. Potter himself said that nobody else but Walton and himself would have been in the fields.

A further point is that as soon as Potter was told that Walton was late in coming home he suggested that he had met with some accident. Why jump straight to that conclusion? When he went up the hill in the dark with Walton's niece and Harry Beasley, Potter went straight to the place where the body lay. Walton had been working all along those hedges, but Potter knew exactly where to go. He was anxious also to splash his own fingerprints all over the murder weapon by trying to pull it out of the victim's body. He knew he should not touch anything, but he needed a good reason for his prints to be on that hayfork.

The inhabitants of Lower Quinton were superstitious people, and there were many signs that witchcraft might be behind the killing. But despite the eeriness of the place and the tales that were told, killing by witchcraft never provided for Fabian a satisfactory motive, and it was the motive that was needed for the building of a case. Farmer Potter had a motive, but the investigators had no way of proving it. Charlie Walton had never earned much, but most of what he came by one way or another he had put away for a rainy day. After fifty-odd years his little nest-egg was quite sizeable. Potter was having a bad time. The war had done his business much harm and he was in financial trouble. Walton's niece knew that Potter had persuaded her uncle to lend him money – quite a lot of money. The time for repayment of the loans came and went. Potter did not know what to do. By the beginning of February Walton was starting to press Potter for the return of his money. He wanted it back, and there can be little doubt that he confronted Potter with his demands in the fields that day, perhaps even facing him with his IOUs – if they existed – and threatening him with court action.

Farmer Potter was an unpleasant, sullen sort of man. He was also abusive and violent when drunk, which was not infrequently. It is unlikely that he planned to kill Walton. What probably happened is that during a heated scene with the old man Potter's anger flared up and he suddenly realized that he had only to get rid of Walton and destroy any receipts that bore his signature and his troubles would be over. So he killed him. The idea of disguising the murder as a Black Magic killing must have occurred to him almost immediately afterwards.

Apart from Edith Walton's certainty that Potter was the killer, Fabian's own suspicions were strengthened by the manufactured 'witchcraft' clues that started to appear. The heifer that died in a ditch . . . the corpse of a dog – and all reported by Farmer Potter.

So, Potter beat Fabian and his fellow investigators.

They had no proof of his guilt, and without receipts for loans no jury in the country would have convicted him. Fabian knew of his guilt, though, and, he said afterwards – as did Richard Whittington-Egan who years later spoke to many of them – so did most of the villagers.

Death in Hodgemoor Wood

The Brutal Murder of Helen Davidson

BY BERNARD TAYLOR

Wednesday, 9 November 1966 began as a very ordinary day for the Bakers of North Road, Chesham Bois, in the small Buckinghamshire town of Amersham. Herbert Baker, seventy-four, had retired from his work in a bank some twelve years earlier and now kept up a part-time job in the locality 'just to keep busy'. His wife, Helen – who for professional reasons had kept her maiden name of Davidson – was a medical doctor, and had practised in the Amersham area for a number of years. She was fifty-four years of age. She was Herbert Baker's second wife; they had been married for five years, their marriage having taken place in Wimbledon, the home of Helen Davidson's parents. By all accounts the couple were happy together.

On the morning of that Wednesday Helen and Herbert Baker worked together on the garden of their home. Then, after lunch, Mr Baker prepared to leave for his part-time job. It was 1.35 when he said goodbye to his wife and drove away from the house. He was never to see her alive again.

When Herbert Baker returned home later that afternoon he found his wife absent from the house. Her car was gone as well; also missing was her pet dog, a twelve-year-old wire-haired terrier named Fancy. Baker was not concerned; he and Helen had arranged to meet friends that evening, and he was quite sure that wherever she had gone she would not be late back.

However, as the time went by and she did not return he began to worry, and eventually he contacted some friends who joined him in searching for her. Finally, Herbert Baker called in the police, and the search for the doctor was widened.

About two o'clock the following morning the doctor's blue Hillman was found in a lay-by close to Hodgemoor Wood, on the Amersham to Beaconsfield Road. The car was still locked, and inside it were her handbag and binoculars case. A brief attempt to search the woods was made, but the darkness frustrated the effort and the search was called off until the dawn. When the search was resumed around eight o'clock the next morning under the direction of Chief Superintendent Kenneth Lovegrove the body of police searchers was swelled by numerous Gurkha soldiers from the Army school at Beaconsfield and, in the afternoon, by a number of English soldiers from Beaconsfield's Wilton Park.

It was about 2.15 that afternoon that the body of Helen Davidson was found.

It was discovered some 1,100 yards from her car, and just inside an area of the wood that was adjacent to some fields. The body lay at the edge of a clearing in the centre of a part of Hodgemoor Wood known as Highfield Grove.

The discovery was made by a young English serviceman and a police cadet. They found her lying on her back, dead, her head battered beyond recognition. She was fully clothed, her light-toned coat still buttoned. The strap of her binoculars was still around her neck, the binoculars themselves having been partly trodden or beaten into the carpet of soil and dead leaves. She still wore her gloves. Her left arm lay at her side while her right arm was flung up and back. Her left leg was stretched out before her, while her right was bent at the knee, and resting on its side. In a triangle formed by the position of her legs her pet terrier, Fancy, had nestled for warmth during the night, and there had kept vigil for close on twenty-four hours.

The young men who found the body quickly called out to nearby police officers, after which the young soldier was violently sick.

A local newspaper photographer was on the scene very soon after the body's discovery and managed to photograph it before the long arm of officialdom stepped in to prevent him. The resulting extraordinary picture shows the scene exactly as it must have appeared to the two young men who made the gruesome discovery, even depicting, and so poignantly, Helen Davidson's devoted little dog. It shows, too, the dreadful injuries made to the face: in the words of the police report: '. . . face obliterated by severe damage in the region of the eyes and an excessive amount of blood over the face.'

Following the discovery of the body word was sent at once to Scotland Yard while a murder hunt was got under way, for it was clear to everyone who saw the body of the doctor that afternoon that her death must have come about as the result of a particularly violent physical attack.

A closer examination of Helen Davidson's body was to reveal that someone had taken up some weapon, and, probably standing to one side of her and using immense force, had struck her across the front of the skull, in the region of her eyes. Her skull had been fractured by the force of the powerful blow and she had died instantly. Not content with that, however, it appeared that her killer had continued to attack her.

Detective Sergeant Tony Dale of the Amersham police was one of the first two police officers on the scene and was subsequently deeply involved in all the ensuing investigations. Only very recently having retired from the police force, he told me:

'When I first saw her lying there it looked as if she had

hardly any head. She was lying face upwards, and her face was absolutely covered in blood – which was black by the time we all came on the scene. It looked to us as if once she was on the ground her killer had repeatedly stamped on her head, so that the back of her head had been driven into the soil.'

Tony Dale remembers also Helen Davidson's dog, Fancy. 'She just looked at us,' he said. 'She stayed without moving for an hour or two while we worked round about her. She just followed us with her eyes. Then eventually somebody took her away to the police station to feed her. She couldn't have had anything to eat or drink for twenty-four hours.'

A guard was kept over the body of the dead doctor for several hours. During this time it was identified by Detective Constable John Childerley, and photographed by the police photographer. Also, one very important discovery was made: the murder weapon. It was a charred branch of a poplar tree, nearly three feet in length and four inches in diameter. Found not very far from the body, both blood and hair from Dr Davidson were found upon its surface.

About nine o'clock that evening Detective Superintendent Jack Williams of Scotland Yard arrived on the scene to add his own wide experience and knowledge to that of the Amersham team. Following his examination of the body it was removed by Land Rover to the Amersham Hospital where, that evening, Dr David Bowen, a senior lecturer in forensic medicine at Charing Cross Hospital, carried out a *post mortem* examination. Later, at the inquest, Dr Bowen was to report that 'the only injuries were to the head', and that death had been instantaneous, and caused by a haemorrhage due to a fractured skull. There was also a slight bruise or scorch mark on her neck, but this was believed to have been caused by pressure from the strap of the binoculars when they were pressed into the ground. When discovered, Dr Bowen said, the victim had been dead about twenty-four hours.

The brutality of the death of Dr Helen Davidson shocked not only the public but also the most hardened and experienced of the police. And it is hardly surprising; a photograph taken of the dead doctor's head after it had been cleaned of the blood that had smothered it shows the most dreadful injuries. The photograph does not bear examination for long; one quickly has to look away again.

One who saw Dr Davidson's body soon after its discovery was the local Chief Constable, the late Brigadier John Cheney, who had been a friend of the doctor and her husband. He said to a local reporter:

'I only wish the Home Secretary could have seen how she was murdered by some devil. I think then he would have changed his mind about hanging. Devils like this must be punished.'

Before the killer could be punished, however, he first had to be caught, and towards this end the investigators quickly realized that they had very little to go on.

In an effort to find evidence upwards of forty police with dogs began to scour the woods, looking for any likely clue, while helicopters took aerial photographs of the area, and appeals were broadcast for anyone who was walking in the wood, or who regularly walked or parked their cars there, to come forward.

Following another line of inquiry, investigations were made in an attempt to trace the doctor's last hours. It was subsequently found that round about 2.30 in the afternoon she had visited two patients in Amersham, after which she stopped at the Express Dairy in Hill Avenue to buy a bottle of milk. She was later seen in Amersham at around 3.45, though what she did and where she was for the hour in the interim was not discovered, though it is quite possible that she spent it at her home in North Road. And if she did not? And was it important, that hour? Perhaps we shall never know. Whatever she did, however, at about 3.45 she was seen driving up Gore Hill. She must then have been driving to Hodgemoor Wood, taking her binoculars with her, evidently planning to do a spot of bird-watching, with her terrier for company.

This much the investigators discovered, and there, more or less, the discoveries ended. In spite of all efforts nothing seemed to bring any of the required answers, and the police were left with a major mystery on their hands.

On the Sunday following the murder, Mr Herbert Baker, the widower, went ahead with his plans to read the lesson at the church at Widmer End where he was a lay preacher and conducted a service once a month.

On Thursday, 17 November, Helen Davidson was buried. First of all, in the afternoon, a private funeral service was held at Hyde Heath, followed by a memorial service and the burial at Little Missenden. Despite the cold the village church was full, and a collection was taken for a fund inaugurated in the doctor's memory. Rather strangely, she was buried in the same grave as that of Herbert Baker's first wife, Ruby who, until her death, had been Dr Davidson's patient.

Investigations into Dr Davidson's life revealed it to be, as far as anyone could tell, quite blameless. Living quietly with her husband, she had enjoyed not only her gentle hobby of bird-watching, but also painting and cooking. Inquiries were also made of her husband and family and friends. Not that any of them were suspected of complicity, but as a matter of course they all had to be questioned in order to be dismissed from future inquiries.

Wider investigations in the town of Amersham and the surrounding areas where the doctor had practised for many years revealed her to have been a most well-liked and respected woman. She had had approximately 3,500 patients on her register and while the police began to interview some of them in their search for answers, the local newspapers asked a number for their impressions of their late GP.

'I've found her to be a wonderful doctor – in fact the best I've known,' one of her patients told a reporter for *The Buckinghamshire Advertiser*. 'Whoever did this terrible deed has robbed us of a very wonderful doctor, who was not only a doctor but a friend. We shall miss her very much.' Another described her as a 'very kind woman' and a 'wonderful doctor'. Such comments typified the general feelings of the local populace.

Ex-Detective Sergeant Tony Dale has his own personal memories of Dr Davidson, for in 1966 in the absence of his family's own GP she had called at his home on the Saturday before her death to see his six-year-old son, Michael, who had bumped his head in a fall. And, without being sent for, she had called again the following day. 'That's the kind of woman she was,' Tony Dale says. 'She was kind and thoughtful and considerate.' The next time she featured in his life after her visit to his injured son was the following Wednesday when she was reported as missing and the next morning when he, Dale, set out to join the search for her. And that afternoon, of course, she had been found, Detective Sergeant Dale being one of the first to see her brutally battered body.

The more the police pondered the question before them the more they became convinced that the killer was a local man – someone from Amersham or one of the neighbouring towns or villages. Indeed, it was quite possible, they believed, that the killer might have been one of her patients, and, moreover, that someone could well be shielding him.

Detective Inspector Ernest Lund, Head of Amersham's CID, remained convinced of this theory and later said, 'I continue to believe it is a local person. Everything points to someone who knew the woods well. If this is so, then someone knows his identity. He could not have killed like that and then gone home and acted normally.'

So also had thought Detective Superintendent Jack Williams of Scotland Yard. 'Somebody in the locality must have a good idea who this man is,' he said soon after the investigations began. 'I should think this is the type of man who may find it hard to keep it to himself. This is a dreadful thing for a man to have on his conscience. He may open up and tell somebody something in some pub or café.'

The superintendent then appealed for anyone who knew anything concerning the identity of the killer to come forward. However, in spite of assurances that any assistance would be treated in strict confidence, there was no helpful response.

One result of the investigators' request for anyone to come forward who had been in or near Hodgemoor Wood that day was that they managed to trace as many as seventy people who were in the woods during the fatal afternoon. But, recalls Tony Dale, 'No one saw anything significant, although some of those seventy people saw each other.'

The police were getting nowhere fast.

Apart from being baffled by the major question of *who*, the police had still found no shadow of an answer to the question of *why*. What could have been the motive for such a brutal killing?

The motive for the crime was to remain one of the most puzzling factors. Clearly it was not robbery, for when her body was discovered Dr Davidson was still wearing her jewellery. Neither had there been any attempt at sexual molestation; there were no signs that any struggle had taken place. In fact the only disturbance to the woman's clothing was to her skirt, which was caused by her dog who had slept in the angle of her thighs during the night in an attempt to keep warm.

Perhaps, it was considered, the motive was one of revenge; perhaps the murder followed a revengeful attack carried out by one of the doctor's patients who harboured bitterness as the result of some past event, real or imaginary. Once again, though, inquiries revealed nothing on which the investigators could base any sound theory.

One possibility considered by the police was that the murder might have been the result of Helen Davidson seeing something she was not meant to have seen. But if so, then *what*? Perhaps, thought Detective Superintendent Jack Williams of the Yard, she had seen a couple engaged in some illicit courtship. Appeals were made in the local papers for any information in this respect. Perhaps, it was suggested, a married man might have murdered the doctor in the belief that she was an investigator watching the couple.

'It could well be,' said Detective Superintendent Williams, 'that somebody thought she was watching them, maybe for divorce proceedings or something, because it would appear that someone wanted to put her eyes out of action – and they appear to us to have stamped on her binoculars. We would like to know – confidentially, of course – if anyone is aware of any couples going into the woods of an afternoon for illicit courtship. It may well be that somebody is responsible who possibly cannot afford to be exposed.' Supporting the detective's request for help in *The Buckinghamshire Advertiser* was a photograph

of him in the 'Murder Inquiry Room' at Amersham
Divisional Police Headquarters thrusting forward the telephone receiver.

Relating the 'illicit lovers' theory to the murder
weapon, the charred poplar branch, Williams said:

'It shows that whoever went up there didn't have a
weapon.'

The 'illicit lovers' theory is possibly the correct one, of
course, though it rather seems to be stretching one's
credulity. However, with no clues to any motive the
police were understandably desperate to find one and
were clutching at straws; they could not afford to ignore
any theory if it stood the remotest chance of leading to an
answer to the mystery.

In the endless considerations of possible motives, it was
supposed by many who had known Dr Davidson that
should she have found herself in a problematical situation
she could have talked her way out of it. After all, in her
work as a medical doctor – and by all accounts she was a
very successful one – she was well accustomed to dealing
with the occasional difficult patient. Tony Dale spoke to
me of this, recalling that he had once been sitting in the
waiting room of his family doctor's surgery when he had
heard a raised voice coming from Dr Davidson's consult-
ing room which was close by. 'Somebody was shouting,'
he said, ' – one of her patients – demanding this and that.
And then I could hear Dr Davidson – being very calm,
and very firm. It was obvious that she had the situation
completely under control.'

The story of the ensuing investigations into the murder is
a disappointing one. Detective Superintendent Jack Williams was recalled to Scotland Yard after a period of less
than three months, when – and perhaps somewhat surprisingly, after so short a time – all *active* investigation ceased,

and inquiries were wound up. From that time the case rested in the hands of Detective Inspector Lund of Amersham, with the assistance of Detective Sergeant Dale. From the ex-detective sergeant I learned that he and Detective Inspector Lund did what they could for a further year until, in January of 1968, Lund left the country. With his departure, and with no leads to go on, the case was more or less shelved. It was only the press, it appeared, that kept it alive, as, on various anniversaries, one or other of the local papers around Amersham would write a piece on the mystery.

And not only the parochial newspapers. In November, 1974 the *News of the World* published an article on the case as one of a series of murder mysteries in which £100,000 was offered as a reward for information leading to the arrest and conviction of each of the killers. As with all previous efforts to find Helen Davidson's murderer, however, it was unsuccessful.

With no further police activity it appeared as if the huge file on the murder would never be reopened and was destined only to gather dust until time had rendered any conviction an impossibility.

But then, in the nineteen-seventies, there were certain developments in the case. The matter was *not* finished; the case had *not* been forgotten.

It transpired that following certain of his actions an Englishman living in Australia had come to the attention of the police there, following which communication was made with the Amersham constabulary about him. The man's behaviour consequently evinced great interest from the Amersham police.

The man in question – who must remain anonymous – had emigrated to Australia from Amersham shortly after the death of Dr Davidson – though it should be stressed that his emigration could not have been as a result of the doctor's murder, for his plans and arrangements had been made before the murder occurred. The man – whom I shall refer to as *Mr X* – had been a patient of Dr Davidson's and it is possible – by his own admission – that he might have gone to her for a necessary reference to support his immigration application.

From their communications with the Australian police authorities, the Amersham police learned that Mr X had an extremely violent side to his nature, one illustration of which was that whilst living in Australia he is said to have beaten to death two dogs belonging to his wife.

He became known to certain members of the local Australian populace, however, for reasons other than those connected with violence. In 1977, at the age of thirty-four, he advertised in a certain Australian newspaper for an 'intergalactic flying saucer – ten persons accommodation minimum'.

Interviewed and photographed by a local reporter following publication of the advertisement he said, 'I am looking for a better way of life,' and added that he and several other people – whom he would not name – would like to settle on another planet. 'Scientists believe there are more advanced beings in the universe than us,' he said. 'I would like to live with such a civilization and learn.' Anyone owning a flying saucer should contact him, he said, at the telephone number he had given in his advertisement. Asked by the journalist whether anyone had replied to his advertisement he said that he had already received several responses. 'Some were from cranks,' he said, 'asking what colour saucer I would like, but others were genuine.'

It was not long afterwards that Mr X, leaving three broken marriages behind him, returned to England, settling in Amersham again. And then, in the spring of 1979, he once again came to the attention of the local police.

There were two incidents that brought his presence so strongly back into focus. One of them was when he was stopped by local police for an alleged motoring offence. He is said to have responded to the apprehension by saying that they, the police, should stop persecuting him and concentrate instead on trying to find the killer of Dr Davidson. As the murder had occurred almost thirteen years earlier the police naturally found his remarks of great interest.

The other incident concerned a happening of a very violent nature. An old man was attacked, being beaten over the head with an iron bar, and as he was rushed to hospital he kept muttering the name of the murdered Dr Davidson. Very shortly afterwards Mr X was arrested and charged with the assault on the injured man, the latter, however, subsequently dropping the charge in favour of a less grave one.

Then, almost a year and a half later, in November 1980, Mr X was taken into custody by police investigators – under the direction of Detective Chief Inspector Norman Robson – for questioning with regard to the murder of Dr Helen Davidson.

Some forty-eight hours later – during which time he was questioned both at the station and in Hodgemoor Wood – Mr X was released without any charge being made.

Following Mr X's release he told *News of the World* journalist Peter Game, who traced him to his home, that he had a 'poor memory' of the time that Dr Davidson was murdered. 'I can't recall the time she died,' he said. 'It's a bit of a blank period.'

He went on to add, 'I am a medium, and fate will have its way. I denied killing the woman, but they might want to see me again.'

He then stated that he had been one of Dr Davidson's

patients. 'She was a wonderful woman,' he said. 'Everyone loved her. I probably went to her for references before emigrating. She was very good to me. And I am the man who was stopped for an alleged driving offence and told detectives to find the killer.'

With regard to the latter and the attack on the pensioner, he said: 'All that points to me. But the facts which pinpoint me could relate to lots of other people. I'm in contact with spirits on another plane. I know when things are going to happen. I knew some time ago I was going to be arrested, but even so it came as a bit of a surprise. I told the police I didn't know who the killer was. I have arranged to communicate with them again. Detectives might want to talk to me again and I'm willing to help them through my special powers.' He added, 'I know that somewhere in Amersham the killer is on the loose. But I can't commit myself to saying any more than that. I spent two days inside, but now I'm free. No one knows how long that might be for.'

Following Mr X's detention and release Detective Chief Inspector Robson was interviewed by a reporter from the *Amersham and Chesham Times*. The detective remarked, 'If anyone thinks I'm giving up now they've got another think coming. I feel we are nearer to the person who did this now than at any stage in the past fourteen years. I have had a hand-picked team of officers working on this. They are very keen. No way is this finished. It's always a professional challenge to solve any major crime – especially one as old as this. The next thing I hope to tell the press is that we have charged the killer.'

Ex-Detective Sergeant Tony Dale, questioned about the arrest and questioning of Mr X, says: 'I can't say that the man was cleared. We didn't have enough evidence to make a charge.' Asked whether the man had been interviewed originally by the police years before, at the time of the doctor's murder, Dale said that he had not.

Again recalling the three-times-married Mr X being held in custody, Tony Dale said that around that time they interviewed one of the man's ex-wives, in the course of which she told Inspector Robson that her ex-husband had had a fixation about dogs and an uncanny way with them. Even the least timid, unapproachable dog, she said, would cower in his presence.

Robson, like many of the other officers involved in the investigations, has since died. Now, thinking back to Robson's eagerness to put an end to the mystery, Tony Dale says, 'How he wanted to make an arrest – to make a successful charge. It would have meant so much to him – to have been able to wind this thing up.'

Unfortunately it didn't happen, and Robson died with the mystery still unsolved.

There have been no developments since the brief detention and subsequent release of Mr X in 1980, except that Mr X was once again interviewed by journalists.

In February 1986, an excellent piece on the crime written by Anne Edwards appeared in the *Bucks Free Press*. In her article she relates how she and a colleague tracked down Mr X to a flat in Amersham-on-the-Hill. There the man told Anne Edwards: 'I have not pleaded innocent yet. I have not pleaded guilty yet. Time will tell. Destiny will tell. I have said to the coppers that I could have had a bloody blackout and I could have done it.' Before Anne Edwards and her colleague left Mr X's flat he threatened them with dire consequences if they revealed his name.

Discussing the case with Mr Tony Dale, I asked him whether Mr X had indeed admitted that he 'could have done it' without being aware of it. The ex-detective sergeant said he could not deny that Mr X had said such a thing. And then Tony Dale revealed to me that Mr X had not been the only suspect.

It was then I learned that there had been another man who had been the subject of police investigations. However, little can be said about the other suspect as, like Mr X, he must not be identified. One can only reveal that he is now dead but that he was being investigated at the time of his death. It should also be added that there was no direct evidence against him, but, as again in the case of Mr X, certain circumstances connected with him had brought him to the attention of the investigators.

Apart from discussing the case at length with ex-Detective Sergeant Tony Dale, I also discussed it with Chief Superintendent Jim Dewhurst of the Thames Valley force, which, since the amalgamation of the various police bodies in 1968, has Amersham under its jurisdiction.

In my meeting with the chief superintendent the subject of part of our conversation was – as it inevitably must be in any discussion of the case – the possible motive for the crime – that motive which appears to be as elusive now as it ever was.

As we talked I put it to Chief Superintendent Dewhurst that possibly the doctor had come upon a 'flasher' on her walk. Perhaps, I said, she was walking through the woods, her terrier running beside her, when she was confronted by some man from the locality who, having seen her approach from a distance, had concealed himself and, perhaps only partly dressed, now leaped out in front of her, exposing himself. A moment later he realized that the woman was known to him, that she was, in fact, his GP. Then, in a blind panic as to what could be the result of his action, he struck her down.

It was, said Mr Dewhurst, a feasible possibility, but can, at the moment, be seen as nothing more than that.

On the subject of the motive, if one eschews every

possible considered motive such as the illicit lovers theory, an appointment in the woods, or the shame-stricken flasher, one is left with an almost motiveless crime. And perhaps that is the answer. Perhaps Helen Davidson's brutal death resulted not from any recognizable motive but from an almost spontaneous, and uncontrollable, desire to kill. There seems to have been an insane rage behind the power of that blow or blows that obliterated her upper face, and in the following actions when her head and her binoculars were trodden into the ground.

We do not know.

And perhaps we shall never know.

Twenty years have now gone by since the murder in Hodgemoor Wood. And the wood itself has changed in small, though noticeable ways in the interim. Now as Tony Dale tramps along beneath the trees, leading the way – 'There's always been an unpleasant feeling about this wood; it's an unfriendly place' – he has some difficulty in locating the exact spot where Helen Davidson's body was found. New paths have been made, he remarks; small saplings have become trees; older trees have been felled . . .

Eventually he stops, looking around him. Yes, he says, he believes this is it. But he is a little less than sure. One part of that area of the wood looks very much like another. And if Tony Dale is not certain of the precise spot then no one else can be, ever. But anyway, does it really matter? So much surrounding Helen Davidson's death is shrouded in mystery, so perhaps it is fitting that the spot where it took place should become a part of that mystery.

There is some irony in the thought, though, that while the spot where Helen Davidson's body was found is already becoming forgotten, her killer might still be a part of Amersham's daily life, still there, enjoying his freedom.

Bibliography

Books

ADAM, H. L.: *Murder by Persons Unknown*. William Collins Sons & Co. Ltd, 1931

BLOOM, JAMES H.: *Folk Lore, Old Customs and Superstitions in Shakespeare-land*. Mitchell, Hughes & Clarke, 1930

BRESLER, FENTON: *Sales of Justice*. Weidenfeld & Nicolson, 1973

BROWNE, DOUGLAS G. and TULLETT, E. V.: *Bernard Spilsbury, His Life and Cases*. George G. Harrap & Co. Ltd, 1951

FABIAN, ROBERT: *The Anatomy of Crime*. Pelham Books, 1970

FABIAN, ROBERT: *Fabian of the Yard*. The World's Work (1913) Ltd, 1950

GAUTE, J. H. H. and ODELL, ROBIN: *The Murderers' Who's Who*. George Harrap & Co. Ltd, 1979

GODWIN, JOHN: *Killers Unknown*. Herbert Jenkins Ltd, 1960

GOODMAN, JONATHAN: *Acts of Murder*. Harrap Ltd, 1986

HAMILTON, S. O. ROWAN: *The Trial of J. A. Dickman*. Notable British Trials (2nd Edition), 1926

HOLLAND, CLIVE: *Warwickshire*. Adam & Charles Black, 1906

HYDE, H. MONTGOMERY: *Norman Birkett*. Hamish Hamilton, 1964

JEPSON, EDGAR, *et al*: *Famous Crimes of Recent Times*. George Newnes Ltd

JEPSON, EDGAR, *et al; Great Stories of Real Life*. George Newnes Ltd

KNIGHT, STEPHEN: *Jack the Ripper: The Final Solution*. George Harrap & Co. Ltd, 1976

McCORMICK, DONALD: *Murder by Witchcraft*. Long, 1968

NORMAN, C. H.: *Essays and Letters on Public Affairs*. Frank Palmer, 1913

PARRISH, J. M. and CROSSLAND, JOHN R.: *The Fifty Most Amazing Crimes of the Last 100 Years*. Odhams Press Ltd, 1936

SAYERS, DOROTHY, *et al: Great Unsolved Crimes*. Hutchinson & Co., 1938

SPARROW, GERALD: *Vintage Edwardian Murder*. Arthur Barker Ltd, 1971

SYMONS, JULIAN: *A Reasonable Doubt*. The Cresset Press, 1960

TAYLOR, BERNARD: *Cruelly Murdered: Constance Kent and the Killing at Road Hill House*. Souvenir Press, 1979

WILSON, COLIN and PITMAN, PAT: *Encyclopaedia of Murder*. Arthur Barker, 1961

Journals

Amersham and Chesham Advertiser
Amersham and Chesham Times
Buckinghamshire Advertiser, The
Bucks Advertiser, The
Bucks Examiner, The
Bucks Free Press
Chiltern Newspaper
Courier, The
Daily Chronicle, The
Daily Graphic, The

Daily Telegraph, The
Free Press, The
Illustrated London News, The
Illustrated Police News, The
Kent and Sussex Courier
Kent Messenger, The
Morning Post, The
News of the World
Penny Illustrated Paper, The
People, The
Sevenoaks Chronicle and Courier, The
Sevenoaks Chronicle and Kentish Advertiser
South Bucks Weekly Post
South London Press
Standard, The
Sun, The
Sunday Express, The
Sydenham, Forest Hill and Penge Gazette
Times, The
Tonbridge and Sevenoaks Standard, The

Documents

Scotland Yard file MEPO3/127 (the William Saunders case)

Index